Reconciling Theology

Reconciling Theology

Paul Avis

scm press

Published in 2022 by SCM Press
Editorial office
3rd Floor, Invicta House,
108–114 Golden Lane,
London EC1Y 0TG, UK

www.scmpress.co.uk

SCM Press is an imprint of Hymns Ancient & Modern Ltd
(a registered charity)

British Library Cataloguing in Publication data
A catalogue record for this book is available
from the British Library

978-0-334-06138-0

Typeset by Regent Typesetting
Printed and bound by
CPI Group (UK) Ltd

Contents

Preface

As I 'laid down my pen', so to speak, on completing the manuscript of this book, my mind went back to one afternoon 50 years ago, which with hindsight I see as a key moment of my induction into the challenging world of 'reconciling theology'. Retrieving this memory may be the first step in answering the question that I put to myself: 'How did I actually get into all this?' Sometime in 1972 I walked into a Christian charity emporium (the 'Missionary Mart') in south London and immediately a pair of secondhand books in striking yellow and black dust covers caught my eye. On closer examination, they turned out to be by an author of whom, at that stage, I knew virtually nothing. The author was a certain T. F. Torrance and the books were the twin volumes of his *Conflict and Agreement in the Church*, published in 1958 and 1960 respectively. The unifying theme of volume 1 was 'Order and Disorder' and of volume 2 'The Ministry and the Sacraments of the Gospel'. These topics were almost unknown to me then. Reading *Conflict and Agreement* helped to launch me on an intellectual, spiritual and ecumenical journey, in which the extensive writings and the personal encouragement of Thomas F. Torrance would play a significant part.

Since then, I have spent a good deal of time and energy in grappling with the classic Faith and Order agenda to which Torrance's two volumes first introduced me. The specific topics of the ministry and the sacraments – and perhaps even more the first intimations of the dynamics of 'Conflict and Agreement' in the Christian church – seized my imagination.[1] At the time,

1 Torrance, Thomas F., 1958, 1960, *Conflict and Agreement in the*

I was beginning work on my doctoral thesis on Bishop Charles Gore (1853–1932), the most powerful theological voice in the Church of England in his day, and the conflicts and struggles into which his theological convictions led him.[2] So several avenues of theological investigation were converging in my thinking at that time and the ideas of conflict and convergence were never far away. The idea of 'reconciling theology' entered through an open door into my thinking at a tender age.

In the late 1980s and the early 1990s I was drawn into doctrinal and Faith and Order work for the Church of England (the Doctrine Commission and the Faith and Order Advisory Group, later redesigned as the Faith and Order Commission), including theological dialogue with partner churches, both in the UK and elsewhere in Europe. In 1998 I was invited to become the General Secretary of the Council for Christian Unity and so to have overall responsibility, from a staff point of view, for much of the ecumenical relations, conversations and ecumenical theology of the Church of England, working with the two archbishops, the many other bishops with ecumenical portfolios, the Archbishops' Council and the General Synod. In this capacity I succeeded Dr (now also Dame) Mary Tanner whose life has been devoted wholeheartedly to the task of reconciliation between the Christian churches and remains an inspiration and an example. Working with Mary, and also with Bishops John Hind and Christopher Hill, among several other notable bishops dedicated to a reconciling ecumenism, hugely strengthened both my motivation and my grasp of the Faith and Order enterprise.

So since those early days in the 1970s, I have longed to see the reconciliation of Christians, churches and theologies. The life and thought of Frederick Denison Maurice (1805–72) and

---

Church, 2 vols, London: Lutterworth Press: vol. 1, 'Order and Disorder', vol. 2, 'The Ministry and the Sacraments of the Gospel'.

2 Avis, Paul, 1988, *Gore: Construction and Conflict*, Worthing: Churchman Publishing. The title resonates with another Torrance work that made a marked impression on me: Torrance, Thomas F., 1965, *Theology in Reconstruction*, London: SCM Press.

of William Temple (1881–1944) have particularly guided this sense of direction. I aspire to be a mediating theologian, not so much in the sense of the German Protestant theologians of the nineteenth century (pre-eminently perhaps Ernst Troeltsch), for whom 'mediating theology' meant finding a meeting point between the Christian theological tradition and modern culture and science (though I am committed to that also), but rather in the sense of mediation between disputing parties who have become alienated from one another and are both experiencing the destructive consequences. As reconciling theologians, we look for deepening mutual understanding – a hermeneutic of unity – and a meeting point in belief and practice; we engage in theological bridge-building. In this we are following in the wake of the Holy Spirit, the Spirit of reconciliation, who is at work wherever God's children, whether confessedly Christian or not, engage in building community on any scale, for that cannot be achieved without interpersonal and inter-group reconciliation.

It seems clear that the practical mediating or reconciling task requires the support of a reconciling theology. To sketch the outline of such an approach is this book's aim and scope. The double meaning of my title *Reconciling Theology* is of course intentional. If a theology that has the potential to reconcile Christians and churches is to be put to work, we first need to go some way towards reconciling theologies themselves, softening and healing – as far as possible – the entrenched theological clashes and conflicts in the areas of presuppositions, arguments and conclusions. In attempting to reconcile theologies, we are already making use of a reconciled theology to mediate between the two. Only a reconciled theology – one that intentionally reaches out to polarized positions and tries to draw them closer together – can help to draw the sting of the serious disagreements that exist between Christians and churches and create a basis for future steps to full visible communion. That this is emphatically not a pipe dream, nor merely a naive fantasy, is testified to by the highly impressive collective achievements of ecumenical theological dialogue and *rapprochement* over the past half-century and more, as the volumes of *Growth in Agreement*, published at intervals by the World Council of Churches and Eerdmans, attest.

To be realistic, the process of reconciliation is never complete, but is by its nature an unending quest and an ongoing challenge. The task of reconciliation, especially in theology and philosophy, seeks the elusive satisfaction of a final resolution, leading to a sense of metaphysical equilibrium, composure and rest. But in this world much will always remain unresolved, untidily open-ended and centrifugal in tendency. The crooked timber of humanity will see to that, as well as ever-present cultural and ideological forces. The pressures of plurality are intensifying today as the voices of, for example, black, feminist and post-colonialist theologians and their communities properly become more audible and insistent, alongside the widening gap between European and North American theological traditions on the one hand, and majority world perspectives on the other. Unresolved conflicts belong to the essence of the human condition and point to its tragic dimension.[3] But that is not a reason for giving up in despair, any more than the partial success, the fragility, of reconciling efforts between individuals in families or other relationships is a reason for not bothering with mediation.

But why do we need a reconciled and reconciling theology? I believe that we need such a theology because we have a Christian church that is not only highly diverse but fundamentally unreconciled. The church is unreconciled in three main ways. It is unreconciled to itself because it is in fragments and is morally compromised and has a bad conscience. It is unreconciled to the world because it is typically viewed askance with suspicion and distrust. And it is unreconciled to God because it lies under judgement for its reckless loss of unity and its culpable loss of moral integrity. What we have – and what many of us belong to – is a church that is fragmented

3 Williams, Rowan, 2016, *The Tragic Imagination*, Oxford: Oxford University Press.

into mutually exclusive pieces, and where some Christians blithely imagine that it is their duty to God to vilify and condemn other Christians, excluding them from the Eucharist and even questioning their eternal salvation.[4] Our Christian church is one that has recently lost what it could scarce afford to lose – its integrity, credibility and public standing – through sexual abuse scandals and the useless, incompetent or actually corrupt methods that have been employed to respond to them (often to cover them up). So the premises of all the chapters of this book are i) that the church itself is unreconciled to itself, to the world and to God, and is therefore barely even the church; ii) that we should do all we can, by the grace of God, in prayer, study, dialogue and reaching out in love, to heal the wounds of the church; and iii) that we must start by doing some reconciling work within theology itself, scrutinizing its antitheses or polarities, its stereotyping and caricaturing, and the ideological justifications that are regularly put forward to defend divisive actions.

But how would we recognize a reconciled and reconciling theology if we met one? What makes a reconciled and reconciling theology different to any other theology? What are its motives and its marks? The most fundamental governing motive impelling a reconciled and reconciling theology, as indeed all Christian endeavour, must be the greatest of the traditional 'theological virtues': love (*agapē*, *caritas*; 1 Cor. 13.13). If we love God in Jesus Christ, it is because God first loved us (1 John 4.19). And if we love God in Christ, we must love Christ's church, his body, just as he does (Eph. 5.25–33) and extend that love equally to all our sisters and brothers within it. And if we love his church we must seek to heal its wounds of sin. Among those wounds are the deep scars of historic disunity; so our love will express itself in working for the restoration of unity or communion (*koinonia*, *communio*, *sobornost*). The definition of love is that it actively seeks the

4 Inter-Anglican Standing Commission on Unity, Faith and Order, 2021, *God So Loved the World: Papers on Theological Anthropology and Salvation*, London: Anglican Consultative Council.

good, the well-being, of the Beloved above itself and does so with unwavering intentionality. To love Christ is to desire what he desires and to pray the same prayer that he prayed and still prays: 'that they may all be one' (John 17.11, 21–23).

If love is the motive that impels reconciling theology, what are its marks? The marks or signs of a reconciling theology are naturally infused with the spirit of reconciliation. Above all, a reconciling theology is one that is not adversarial and instinctively hostile to any different theology, as some sadly are, but is irenic and conciliatory in its posture. It does not set out to be combative by default and, with sinful glee, seek to put others in the wrong. It does not indulge, with wicked delight, in stereotyping, travesty and caricature or in the undermining by snide innuendo of a rival position. So a reconciling theology is not defensive, but open to receive from what is new or strange or expressed in a different theological language and register. It is not reactive, but stretches out the hand of understanding and friendship to what seems 'other'. Reconciling theology is infused with a spirit of receptivity, eagerly absorbing from elsewhere whatever can correct, redirect and enrich its tasks. So we may say that reconciling theology – far from being arrogant, smug or triumphalist – knows that it has need of the other; it seeks completion from engagement – an engagement that is not uncritical but nevertheless is profoundly empathetic and receptive – with what is different.

To that extent, reconciling theology teaches us to think differently about difference. It is characterized by at least three main dispositions. First, a fundamental sense of *belonging*: an overwhelming consciousness that we belong to one another in the body of Christ and that it is not for any one of us to say that anyone else does not belong to Christ and to his body. We exist as Christians *in solidum*. Second, *recognizing*: reconciling theology is strong on recognition in that it looks with a friendly eye for potential dialogue partners and for whatever can be recognized as a facet of Christian truth, wherever it is to be found; it scans the world for the pearl of great price. Finally, *receiving*: reconciling theology is intentionally receptive, especially 'ecumenically receptive'. It is oriented to both giving and receiving, knowing (as the Prayer of St Francis of Assisi puts it) that it is in giving that we receive. Luke (Acts 20.35) attributes to St Paul a saying of Jesus that it is more blessed to give than to receive; but Paul would have been the first to point out that we can give only what we have first received (1 Cor. 4.7).

It is my aspiration in this book to delineate the rudiments of a reconciling theology that is inspired and motivated by these three qualities – a theological framework that promotes the spiritual disposition and practical intention that is the fruit of the continual actions of belonging, recognizing and receiving. The exercise will take more than one book, so *Reconciling Theology* is intended as the first of probably two volumes. In this current work I have set out the daunting challenge presented by an unreconciled church, which is barely the church at all, and I have also tried to portray what a reconciled church would look like in accordance with Scripture and theological principles. The planned sequel will address more specifically and concretely the pathway – the methodology to be followed – that is designed to bring about a relationship of deeper communion between the churches. I have been working on this agenda for many years now and have tried out various approaches to this set of issues. Some chapters of this book include material – not usually verbatim but fully rethought and rewritten – that has previously appeared in public lectures and journal articles. But about half of the word count consists of fresh material that has not previously seen the light of day in print.

Thomas F. Torrance's Foreword to one of his later books, *Theology in Reconciliation* (1975), describes well the orientation of this current work and I am glad to be able to acknowledge with admiration and gratitude a pioneer and paragon of reconciling theology in the age of ecumenism. Torrance wrote:

> Any theology which is faithful to the Church of Jesus Christ within which it takes place cannot but be a theology of reconciliation, for reconciliation belongs to the essential nature

> and mission of the Church in the world. By taking its rise from God's mighty acts in reconciling the world to himself in Christ, the Church is constituted 'a community of the reconciled', and in being sent by Christ into the world to proclaim what God has done in him, the Church is constituted a reconciling as well as a reconciled community.[5]

In tune with these principles, my final (and longest) chapter is entitled 'Envisioning a Reconciled and Reconciling Community'.

I am most grateful to David Shervington and his close colleagues at SCM Press for their enthusiastic support of this project and for bringing this first volume to publication.

Paul Avis
The Birth of St John the Baptist
24 June 2021

5 Torrance, Thomas F., 1975, *Theology in Reconciliation: Essays Towards Evangelical and Catholic Unity in East and West*, London: Geoffrey Chapman, p. 7.

I

'Unreal Worlds Meeting'? Illusion and Reality in Ecumenical Dialogue

The picture that many people in the Christian church seem to have of theological dialogue between the churches is of a bunch of idealists fantasizing about something that is never going to happen.[1] For these observers – generally church people who have not experienced ecumenical dialogue at first-hand – ecumenists live in an unreal world, detached from the awkward realities of church life. They tend to suspect that when ecumenists get together to engage in theological dialogue the distinctive historical traditions that they are there to represent tend to be traded in, thrown into the melting pot, so that the agreed texts that are brewed up form a tasteless ecumenical soup. As G. K. Chesterton once quipped, with reference to the idea of 'undenominational religions', they claim to include what is most beautiful in all the creeds but seem to end up with all that is dull in them. When a child mixes up the colours in

1 This chapter is a much revised and extended version of a very short paper that I gave at the Assisi conference of the Ecclesiological Investigations Network in 2012. That presentation was revised for publication and appeared in Mannion, Gerard (ed.), 2016, *Where We Dwell in Common: The Quest for Dialogue in the Twenty-first Century*, Basingstoke: Palgrave Macmillan, pp. 145–59. A very short version of this chapter appeared in *Theology*, 115.6 (November–December 2012), pp. 420–6.

the paintbox, he or she expects it to produce a wonderfully vivid result; instead, what *does* result is 'a thing like mud'.[2]

The idea that theological dialogue between the major Christian traditions (and, we could add, within them) is basically a pointless exercise, imbued with self-delusion and intellectual dishonesty, contributes to the cooler climate of ecumenism at the present time. Pragmatists (self-styled 'realists') assume that the churches are never going to change and that, therefore, significant steps towards visible unity are not going to happen. Those who believe that – for all the current difficulties – there is still much to play for, are dismissed as hopelessly idealistic. In this chapter I begin to explore the dilemmas around illusion and reality, vision and pragmatism, in the enterprise of forging Christian unity through theological dialogue. I weigh the extent to which churches and Christians are already united, while being, in some cases, divided where it matters most – at the Lord's Table, at the celebration of the Eucharist, the sacrament of unity. I examine here the received 'Faith and Order' goal of 'full visible unity' as an imperative of the gospel, and briefly indicate how ecumenical dialogue can be pursued with both realism and integrity.

Ecumenism in trouble?

The broad position of those who pride themselves on being hard-headed realists about ecclesiastical politics is that, while the ecumenical movement may have improved the climate of inter-church relationships, especially between church leaders, and created various opportunities for practical forms of co-operation on the ground (all the better if it saves money, of course), theological dialogue is basically a lot of hot air and all talk of visible unity is cloud-cuckoo-land. If it means that churches will be expected to change not only their practices

2 Chesterton, G. K., 1958, *Essays and Poems*, ed. Wilfred Sheed, Harmondsworth: Penguin, p. 133.

but also their structures, under the beneficent influence of other traditions, then that is another reason for sidelining ecumenism in the minds of some. Change that goes much further than mutual courtesy is neither realistic nor desirable in their eyes. 'Receptive ecumenism' is to be avoided. Ecumenical endeavour is a case of *unreal worlds meeting*.

As I began to research my paper for the Assisi conference, I discovered that 'Unreal Worlds Meeting' was the title of a paper given by my former colleague on the English Anglican–Roman Catholic Committee (English ARC), Nicholas Peter Harvey, at the Second Receptive Ecumenism Conference, 2009.[3] Peter Harvey tells me that he acquired it from a passing remark that the late Dom Sebastian Moore, OSB, applied to ecumenical dialogue of the more idealistic sort. In this form of words, both Moore and Harvey put their finger on a neuralgic spot in the world of ecumenical endeavour.

The passion for unity that motivates genuine ecumenical activity and draws Christians together in many contexts is strongly present at the grassroots of the churches in many countries. Without that passion and vision at the base level, ecumenism today would probably be defunct. It is the fact that lay Christians experience shared faith, common prayer and joint witness that keeps ecumenism alive. Local initiatives are the *sine qua non* of the ecumenical movement. But it is only rigorous theological dialogue that gives ecumenism intellectual integrity and legitimizes any steps towards greater unity at any level above the local, and even there in fact. So disbelief in the integrity and value of theological dialogue between the major Christian traditions strikes at the heart of the ecumenical enterprise, which is strongest at the grassroots.

---

3 'Receptive Ecumenism and Ecclesial Learning: Learning to Be Church Together', Joint 2nd International Receptive Ecumenism Conference and 3rd Annual Gathering of the Ecclesiological Investigations Network, organized and hosted by the Centre for Catholic Studies, Department of Theology and Religion, Durham University, UK and St Cuthbert's Seminary, Ushaw College, Durham at Ushaw College, Durham, 11–15 January 2009.

Various voices, from diverse Christian traditions, detect a general malaise in the ecumenical movement. In *That They May All Be One*, Walter Cardinal Kasper, former President of the Pontifical Council for Promoting Christian Unity, acknowledges that ecumenism is 'facing a critical moment'. There is, Kasper believes, 'a widespread conviction that traditional differences are irrelevant for the majority of people today'. But he also detects 'the emergence of a new confessionalism'. Moreover, he acknowledges that the ecumenical movement is sometimes accused of promoting relativism and indifference concerning questions of faith (a deadly accusation in the eyes of the Roman Catholic magisterium, and indeed of all the major churches). Altogether, Kasper discerns 'a new atmosphere of mistrust, self-defence and withdrawal'.[4] It seems that he does not exclude his own church from this judgement.

From a different perspective, the veteran Reformed theologian and ecumenist Lukas Vischer took stock of the ecumenical movement shortly before his death in 2008. His verdict makes sad reading. The movement had stagnated, he observed. There was a new assertiveness about denominational identity and denominational profile (compare Kasper's identification of a 'new confessionalism'). The churches had withdrawn into their shells. Ecumenical discourse now seemed to have little credibility. Vischer and colleagues went on to say, however, that the New Testament shows how unity in the apostolic church – unity in a multiplicity of expressions – had to be struggled for: therefore, the same kind of unity needs the same kind of struggle today.[5]

---

4 Kasper, Walter, 2004, *That They May All Be One: The Call to Unity Today*, London and New York: Continuum, p. 1.

5 Vischer, Lukas, Ulrich Luz and Christian Link, 2010, *Unity of the Church in the New Testament and Today*, Grand Rapids, MI: Eerdmans, pp. 2, 14.

Ecumenical gains consolidated

The cynical stance of the 'unreal worlds' tendency in our churches has undoubtedly contributed to the chilly climate in some areas of ecumenical relations – what some have exaggeratedly termed an 'ecumenical winter'. But such corrosive scepticism involves a gross distortion of the facts, a massive underestimate of what ecumenism has achieved under God. The ecumenical movement has reduced the *affective and cognitive distance* between Christian traditions. It has largely replaced suspicion, incomprehension and competition with understanding, trust and friendship; this in itself is no mean achievement, serving to diminish the affective distance and emotional friction between churches and Christians. But in the form of theological dialogue the ecumenical movement has also significantly scaled down the extent of church-dividing doctrinal issues between Christian traditions. It has achieved this by clarifying concepts, dealing with misunderstandings and pinpointing unresolved issues that require further study. It has established that there is (as the Second Vatican Council put it) 'a certain, albeit imperfect, communion' between (in this case) the Roman Catholic Church (RCC) and churches or 'ecclesial communities' that are not yet in full visible communion with Rome: 'For men [sic] who believe in Christ and have been properly baptized are put in some, though imperfect, communion with the Catholic Church' (Latin: *Hi enim qui in Christum credunt et baptismum rite receperunt, in quadam cum Ecclesia catholica communione, etsi non perfecta, constituuntur*).[6] By securing genuine theological convergence, ecumenical dialogue has reduced the *cognitive distance* and theological friction between churches and Christians, drawing them closer together. In other words, ecumenical dialogue has

6 Vatican II, *UR* 3: Flannery, Austin, OP (ed.), 1975, *Vatican Council II: Vol. 1: The Conciliar and Post-Conciliar Documents*, Northport, NY: Costello; Dublin: Dominican Publications, p. 455. The Council documents are online at www.vatican.va/archive/hist_councils/ii_vatican_council/index.htm.

brought into focus the inherent unity of the body of Christ, even though our present experience of that unity falls seriously short of the full visible unity that has consistently been articulated as the goal of the Faith and Order movement.

The extraordinary paradox of ecumenism is that the churches are, at the same time, both united and divided – that is, near to one another and yet still so far apart. They are generally, though not universally, *united* in baptism (though it would be better to say 'in Christian initiation')[7] and in the profession of the trinitarian baptismal faith, and in the liturgical use of the ecumenical creeds. There is also extensive agreement – though this too cannot be universalized – on aspects of ecclesiology, including the ordained ministry and the sacraments.[8] Provided that we do not insist that other churches speak our own language – in other words, provided we allow for the fact that (as Pope John XXIII put it in his opening locution at the Second Vatican Council) the essence of the apostolic faith is one thing and the way that it is articulated is another[9] – we can recognize a remarkable commonality of belief about the church.

This commonality of belief and practice, though real, is not something that can be glibly assumed on the basis of mutual goodwill or taken for granted on the basis of fellow-feeling or empathy between Christians of different tribes. It can only

7 See Avis, Paul (ed.), 2011, *The Journey of Christian Initiation: Theological and Pastoral Perspectives*, London: Church House Publishing; and the reports of Anglican–Baptist dialogue: *Pushing at the Boundaries of Unity: Anglicans and Baptists in Conversation*, 2005, London: Church House Publishing; *Conversations Around the World 2000–2005: The Report of the International Conversations between the Anglican Communion and the Baptist World Alliance*, 2005, London: Anglican Communion Office.

8 Kasper, Walter, 2009, *Harvesting the Fruits: Basic Aspects of Christian Faith in Ecumenical Dialogue*, London and New York: Continuum; Kinnamon, Michael, 2012, 'What can the Churches Say Together about the Church?', *Ecclesiology* 8.3, pp. 289–301; Clements, Keith, 2013, *Ecumenical Dynamic: Living in More Than One Place at Once*, Geneva: World Council of Churches.

9 Abbott, Walter M., SJ (ed.), 1966, *The Documents of Vatican II*, London and Dublin: Geoffrey Chapman, p. 715.

be the result of an arduous process and journey of theological engagement over time. That process of theological engagement, interface and dialogue will be marked by five methodological qualities, not all of which have always been met before now: 1) It is scholarly and rigorous and digs deep, infused with empathy, into the bedrock of the traditions. Academic calibre is a qualification for most of those taking part and representing their churches and the churches' traditions – so no tokenistic passengers. 2) It avoids deliberately vague or ambiguous formulations that can later be subjected to diverse interpretations and even haggled over. A form of words that papers over a difficulty and that both 'sides' can accept is not necessarily true to either tradition and gives hostages to fortune. 3) It is truly representative of the spectrum of the traditions within the churches concerned, rather than a gathering of rather like-minded and amenable, but not fully representative, individuals. 4) It follows a cumulative method and trajectory that consolidates and builds on the progress that has already been made, before attempting to break fresh ground. It moves from what is securely known between us to the challenging unknown that also lies between. 5) It tests its emerging conclusions, and at the same time facilitates the process of formal reception that will eventually be needed, by consulting with the constituencies that it represents *in via* rather than, as often happens, presenting a *fait accompli* to the sponsoring churches, which leaves little room for second thoughts. A 'take it or leave it' stance with respect to the final document is highly inappropriate and shows little sense of the delicate and dynamic nature of doctrinal accord, of the words that express it, and of the open-ended nature of the process of reception.

If these five criteria are met, a dialogue will have manifest integrity, ecclesial, theological and moral. The criteria will enable it to show genuine theological convergence, while at the same time highlighting those issues that may continue to hold the churches apart. By recognizing that certain issues 'require further study' (so putting it constructively, as well as diplomatically), a dialogue can ensure that difficulties do not prompt one or more of the dialogue partners to call a halt. Furthermore, such an approach can help to hold the churches together in ongoing dialogue rather than pushing them apart.

A fragmented Eucharist: does it matter?

While ecumenical *rapprochement* between the historic churches has brought significant gains, the churches remain divided at precisely the point where it most matters – at the celebration of the Eucharist. If, as the historic traditions (Roman Catholic, Orthodox and Anglican, as well as some Lutheran and Methodist churches) agree, the Eucharist is the source and summit of the church's life;[10] and if, as the eucharistic ecclesiology of Orthodoxy, Roman Catholicism and Anglicanism suggests, the Eucharist makes the church,[11] then unity in the Eucharist must be the criterion and the litmus test of any approach to unity. As the Anglican divine Richard Hooker (d. 1600) says, 'God by the sacrament maketh the mysticall body of Christ'.[12] And the Lambeth Conference 1930 stated: '... the Church claims that the Eucharist is the climax of Christian Worship'.

10 *Sacrosanctum Concilium* (*SC*) 7, 10; *Lumen gentium* (*LG*) 11.

11 De Lubac, Henri, 1954, *Meditation sur l'Église*, 3rd edn, Paris: Aubier, pp. 123ff; Zizioulas, John, 1985, *Being as Communion*, New York: St Vladimir's Seminary Press; Zizioulas, 2001, *Eucharist, Bishop, Church: The Unity of the Church in the Divine Eucharist and the Bishop during the First Three Centuries*, 2nd edn, trans. E. Theokritoff, Brookline, MA: Holy Cross Orthodox Press; McPartlan, Paul, 1993, *The Eucharist Makes the Church: Henri de Lubac and John Zizioulas in Dialogue*, Edinburgh: T&T Clark; new edn, Fairfax, VA: Eastern Christian Publications, 2006. See also Avis, Paul, 2007, *The Identity of Anglicanism: Essentials of Anglican Ecclesiology*, London and New York: T&T Clark, chapter V: 'Anglicanism and Eucharistic Ecclesiology'.

12 Hooker, Richard, 1977–, *The Folger Library Edition of the Works of Richard Hooker*, Cambridge, MA: Belknap Press of Harvard University Press, vol. 4, p. 46. See *The Lambeth Conferences (1867–1930)*, 1948, London: SPCK, p. 194 (Committee Report on 'The Christian Doctrine of God'): 'The Eucharist is the climax of Christian Worship'.

In the celebration of the Eucharist by priest and people, the three key tasks of the church's mission come into focus: the ministry of the word, the celebration of the sacraments, and the exercise of *episkopē* (pastoral responsibility); or, as the Second Vatican Council puts it, the triple *munera* of teaching, sanctifying and governing.[13] The Eucharist is the touchstone of unity. Without reciprocal eucharistic hospitality and interchangeable eucharistic presidency, the churches remain divided where it is most important that they should be visibly one body. The body of Christ – the ecclesial body and the sacramental body – is torn asunder.

How can we come to terms with the idea that the body of Christ is cut into pieces? I must confess that I find that notion almost incomprehensible. With my theologically realist ecclesiology I struggle to get my head around the 'blasphemous' idea that Christ is torn apart in his church. A century ago the inaugurator and pioneer of the Faith and Order movement, Bishop Charles Brent (Canadian by birth but a bishop of the then Protestant Episcopal Church of the USA in the Philippines and then of Western New York), prophetically deplored the divisions of the church as 'sacrilege and blasphemy', 'a moral affront' to the mission of Jesus Christ and 'an essential denial of His Spirit of love and fellowship'.[14] The Apostle Paul also uses this language when he speaks into the situation of schisms in Corinth: 'Has Christ been divided?' (1 Cor. 1.13). This rhetorical question invites the answer, 'No, that's impossible!' But the question stands and should continue to haunt us. When later in the same letter Paul speaks of the body and its members, his punchline is, 'So it is with Christ' (12.12). This is ecclesiological realism *par excellence*. As John Calvin comments, 'Paul

13 Vatican II, *Christus Dominus* (*CD*) *11*; *LG* 21, 25. Avis, Paul, 2005, *A Ministry Shaped by Mission*, London and New York: T&T Clark, pp. 21–42.

14 Kates, Frederick W., 1948, *Charles Henry Brent: Ambassador of Christ*, London: SCM Press, p. 26.

calls the Church "Christ"'.[15] 'For just as the body is one and [yet] has many members, and all the members of the body, though many, are one body, so it is with Christ.' If 'body' is a philosophically realist metaphor, so also is 'members'. It is a doctrinal realist truth that Christians are ontologically united to the body of Christ in baptism. As Paul says in the very next verse, 'For in the one Spirit we were all baptized into one body ... and we were all made to drink of one Spirit' (1 Cor. 12.13). How can baptized Christians continue to exist in a state of separation? It's a theological, Christological and pneumatological realist impossibility. Indeed, what we are confronted with is precisely an 'impossible possibility': the body of Christ alienated from itself and persisting in an unreconciled state.[16]

We might be tempted to reply: 'That's all very well, but the church has always been divided. We see division even in the New Testament. There were splits as a result of the ecumenical councils that defined the creeds. East and West finally broke apart in 1054. The combination of the Reformation and the Counter-Reformation brought further division that has now been projected globally. New churches that do not recognize most other churches are being formed every day. It can't matter as much as we think surely, or it wouldn't be like this? Shouldn't we make a virtue of necessity and learn to think differently about the oneness of the one, holy, catholic and apostolic church – basically, let a thousand flowers bloom?' As one author (W. C. Ingle-Gillis) has argued, God has given the

---

15 Calvin, John, 1960, *The First Epistle of Paul to the Corinthians*, trans. John W. Fraser, *Calvin's Commentaries*, ed. David W. Torrance and Thomas F. Torrance, Edinburgh: The Saint Andrew Press, p. 264. See also Ramsey, Arthur Michael, 1936, *The Gospel and the Catholic Church*, London: Longmans, Green & Co., ch. 3, where Calvin's comment is invoked.

16 On the image of the body of Christ and other key New Testament ecclesial images, see Avis, Paul, 2020, *Jesus and the Church: The Foundation of the Church in the New Testament and Modern Theology*, London and New York: T&T Clark, especially pp. 53–8.

church all that it needs to be the church; it cannot be impaired by internal separation; its divisions are providential.[17]

We need to examine more closely the thesis that division does not impair the ecclesial reality of the churches. The bad conscience of the churches, that the one church exists in a state of brokenness, error and sin and that its divisions are a result of human pride, is (Ingle-Gillis argues) uncalled for. Ecumenism is surely barking up the wrong tree in assuming that God wants the church to be visibly one. There is no need for the churches to feel that they exist in 'a sub-standard state of ecclesial being' on the way to something bigger and better. They do not need to feel bad about themselves, as though they are suffering from 'an ecclesiastical disease'. Their sense of provisionality is misplaced. They are hamstrung by guilt and lack of confidence, with the result that their teaching is half-hearted and their pro realist clamation lacks conviction.[18] Ingle-Gillis therefore seeks to find theological significance in what has conventionally been seen as a state of mutual schism. He draws on the writings of Thomas F. Torrance, Colin Gunton and John Zizioulas to show that the church is essentially a communion with the Holy Trinity. It is the embodiment of Jesus Christ, through the power of the Spirit, by the will of the Father. Working with a highly – I would say, excessively – realist ecclesiology, he argues that the particular churches that make up the one church cannot be lacking in anything that is necessary for their ecclesial authenticity, wholeness or fullness. Their divisions do not show that they are failing; they simply prove that they are communities on the way to a comprehensive reconciliation, and as such they are doing precisely what they are meant to be doing – moving gradually into deeper communion. Ingle-Gillis seems to be saying to the churches: 'Stop agonizing about your divisions; reclaim the fullness of Christ within you and proclaim the gospel with boldness!' But is this what the Spirit is

17 Ingle-Gillis, W. C., 2007, *The Trinity and Ecumenical Church Thought*, Aldershot and Burlington, VT: Ashgate.

18 Ingle-Gillis, *The Trinity and Ecumenical Church Thought*, pp. 30, 29, 39.

saying to the churches and what the Spirit has been patiently teaching for 2,000 years?

Ingle-Gillis's book is an interesting addition to the chorus of voices calling for a reassessment of ecumenism. As I read it, the argument is not only that ecumenical dialogue is unreal because its premises are false, but that it is not important and hardly even necessary. The book celebrates plurality in the purposes of God and as 'an ontologically significant fact of Church life'.[19] The church is not unreconciled in its present state. I concede that the author is correct in claiming that diversity is not opposed to unity. The opposite of unity is division and the opposite of diversity is uniformity. Nevertheless, there are some major flaws in the argument, intellectually able though it is.

First, Ingle-Gillis is working with a distorted concept of church unity, a caricature that enables him to claim that the unity the churches dream of is still up in the clouds and unreal. Unity is reduced to meagre structural adjustments: 'the mere integration of a few decision-making bodies'; or 'rounding up all Christians into one institutional body'.[20] The classical portraits of unity in the Faith and Order tradition – especially those of the New Delhi (1961) and Canberra (1991) Assemblies of the World Council of Churches – are careful, nuanced descriptions of spiritual essentials, not blueprints for the merging of institutions, and never have been.

Second, the problem with most churches is not lack of confidence or loss of nerve, such that they have to huddle together for mutual support and protection, but the opposite. The RCC and the Eastern Orthodox Churches are not bemoaning their incompleteness or beating their breasts about their provisionality! The RCC claims fullness for itself and denies it to others.[21]

19 Ingle-Gillis, *The Trinity and Ecumenical Church Thought*, p. 171.

20 Ingle-Gillis, *The Trinity and Ecumenical Church Thought*, pp. 50, 185.

21 *LG* 8; *Unitatis redintegratio* (*UR*) 22: '... the ecclesial communities separated from us lack the fullness of unity with us which flows from baptism, and ... have not preserved the proper reality of the

Roman Catholic and Orthodox Christianity is not haunted by a sense of provisionality. The issue there is misplaced theological and institutional complacency, coupled with blindness towards the authentic ecclesial nature of at least some other churches.

Third, the argument that we have been considering contains a methodological fallacy. It collapses together two perspectives on the church. On the one hand, there is the one, holy, catholic and apostolic church of the Nicene-Constantinopolitan Creed – that is, the mystical body of Christ, of which alone fullness and wholeness should be predicated. On the other hand, we have the particular, historically contingent, plurality of churches that, notwithstanding their participation in, or membership of, the *una sancta*, are marked by serious imperfections, including sins and crimes. The relation, connection and tension between these two manifestations of the one church is the central crux of ecclesiology, but the gap between them is not so easily bridged. It is not good theology to take the attributes of the former, the *una sancta*, and transfer them by a process of *a priori* deduction to the latter, the plurality of existing churches, in order to claim that they lack nothing that is essential to the church in the first sense.

Finally, there are some major problems with the ecclesiological model that assumes that the church on earth – the church militant – reflects or mirrors, at all adequately, the trinitarian life of God. The worldly, human realities of finitude, fallenness and embodiment make for a powerful eschatological tension between the Trinity and the church. The church is not an unsullied Platonic reflection of the Holy Trinity, mirroring eternity in time. The church comes into being in history through the saving acts of God (salvation history, *Heilsgeschichte*), especially through the incarnation, the cross and the resurrection and glorification of Jesus Christ and the mission of the

---

eucharistic mystery in its fullness [Latin: *genuinam atque integram substantiam Mysterii eucharistici*], especially because of the absence of the sacrament of Orders': Flannery (ed.), *Vatican Council II: Volume 1: The Conciliar and Post-Conciliar Documents*, p. 469.

Holy Spirit. Moreover, the work of Christ is not yet fully consummated: his prayer for unity awaits a complete answer. The very being of the church is eschatological and subsists at an epistemic distance from the life of heaven.

The divisions between the churches that Ingle-Gillis smooths away with questionable theological arguments are not merely friendly rivalries, but touch the heart of the gospel: God's way of salvation in Jesus Christ. The churches are not simply going their own sweet way. The absence of visible unity, and especially of eucharistic communion, is a tangible denial of the body of Christ. The unbearable paradox of ecumenism is that the churches are divided precisely about what the church is and who is in it. That painful anomaly shows why it is important to say of the churches that they are all incomplete, all provisional, all wounded; and it is that truth validating the search for ecclesiological convergence that motivates and empowers ecumenism.

Unity as the cause of humanity

So is visible unity as important as all that? Is it worth praying, working and struggling for? That is the uncomfortable question that must have crossed the minds of many of us who work for Christian unity. But such doubts should be dispelled. The cause of unity is also the cause of justice, freedom and full humanity. The history of Christianity has been scarred not only by hate-filled, condemnatory speech, schism, mutual excommunication and hardened division, but also by persecution, torture and judicial executions. And we should not shift the blame for that on to the Emperor Constantine, 'establishment' and the state connection, which some project as the root of all our ills. The historian G. M. Trevelyan wrote that Augustine of Hippo was perhaps the first, not to persecute Christians, but to *persecute Christians* (the Donatists) *for a Christian motive* and so, as Trevelyan put it, to turn the God of Jesus into Moloch. 'It was through Augustine rather than through Constantine that the

Church drank poison.' It remains hard for us to accept that Christians have tortured Christians for Christian reasons; it is the 'mystery of iniquity', of which St Paul speaks (2 Thess. 2.7, KJV) and seems impervious to reason.[22]

Of course, we may – and do – say that God does not want the church to behave in this way, any more than God really wanted the Israelites to exterminate the indigenous inhabitants of the Promised Land, the Canaanites. They (and we) simply misunderstand God's will; but (the argument runs) God does not mind our divisions, provided that we are tolerant and friendly and goodwill prevails, just like the ideal modern liberal democracy that seems to be some people's idea of heaven. Then the church in all its diversity can be admired as a many-splendoured thing! But that is not how I read the Scriptures. The prayer of Jesus as he consecrated himself to go to the cross was that his disciples should be visibly one as he and the Father were one. He evoked a unity that was manifest to the world in such a way as to enable the world to believe in him (John 17.21–23).

When I gaze at the crucifix, I sometimes wonder whether Jesus would have gone all the way to the cross if he had known what his followers would do in his name, not least what they would do to one another and therefore to his church. If he had known all that was to follow, would he still have gone ahead? Perhaps he would have turned sadly away, his mission incomplete and unfulfilled. Stanley Hauerwas has remarked: 'How odd of God to save the world this way, that is, by making us his church.'[23] But that is the least of it and hardly touches the wound. Dorothy Day's saying is more adequate: 'The Church is the cross on which Christ is crucified.'[24] It is to this

22 Trevelyan, G. M., 1930, *Clio, A Muse, and Other Essays*, London, New York, Toronto: Longmans, Green and Co., p. 42.

23 Hauerwas, Stanley, 2011, *Learning to Speak Christian*, Eugene, OR: Cascade Books, p. 7.

24 Day used various versions of this saying, which she attributed to Romano Guardini.

theologically intolerable situation that I apply Pascal's saying, 'Jesus will be in agony until the end of the world'.[25]

When we consider the bloody record of persecution, torture, execution and extermination, all infused with passions of fear and hatred, that have been carried out by the church's agents with the church's sanction and blessing, it seems that this instrument of God's peace, the church, has sometimes turned into its opposite. Then, as Martin Luther used to say, Antichrist sits in the temple of God.[26] The unimaginably cruel treatment that Christians have meted out to non-Christians and even to their fellow Christians raises what I choose to call the question of *ecclesiological theodicy*, the issue of evil and injustice in the church. Add to that the recent appalling revelations of clerical sexual abuse of minors and the culpable mishandling of that by certain church authorities, and you have a deeply disturbing challenge to the integrity of the church. How can one, as John Milton put it in the opening lines of *Paradise Lost*, 'justify the ways of God to men [sic]'?[27] How can we make sense of God's plan and purpose and Christ's intention with regard to the church; how can we account for the Holy Spirit's guidance of such a church? Therein lies a massive moral and intellectual challenge for ecclesiology.

25 Pascal, Blaise, 1966, *Pensées*, trans. A. J. Krailsheimer, Harmondsworth: Penguin, p. 313. The *pensée* continues: 'There must be no sleeping during that time.' No, indeed, but rather ceaseless work for unity!

26 According to Martin Luther, echoing 2 Thessalonians 2.4, antichrist 'takes his seat not in a stable of fiends or in a pigsty or in a congregation of unbelievers, but in the highest and holiest place possible, namely in the temple of God': Luther, Martin, 1955–, *Luther's Works*, eds Jaroslav Pelikan and Helmut Lehman, St Louis, MO: Concordia; Philadelphia, PA: Fortress Press, vol. 24, pp. 24–5. Luther takes this thought to an extreme when he says: 'There is no greater sinner than the Christian Church' (Sermon for Easter Day 1531): Luther, Martin, 1883–, *D. Martin Luthers Werke*, Weimar: Weimarer Ausgabe, 34/I, 276.7f. Can we bring ourselves to say this?

27 Milton, John, 1913, *The English Poems of John Milton*, Oxford: Oxford University Press, p. 114: *Paradise Lost*, Book I, line 26.

It is disunity that is unreal

There is nothing 'unreal' about Christian conflict, the absence of reconciliation, and there should be nothing 'unreal' about attempts to resolve it, to reconcile and to unite churches and the Christians within them. I have to say that in my 14 years as a full-time, professional ecumenist, and in the years before that, when I took part in ecumenical dialogue alongside my parish and academic work, I never experienced theological dialogue between churches as unreal. If I had found it 'unreal', shot through with self-deception and lack of authenticity, I would have had no truck with it. But, as they say, there is no smoke without fire and I am aware that there is a good deal of well-meaning but rather aimless and unfocused ecumenical activity around, as well as disappointment and disillusionment about what the ecumenical process has delivered concretely. But ecumenical theology has recently been undergoing reshaping and reform in order to move the centre of gravity away from the top-heavy institutional agenda, which admittedly sometimes prevailed in the past, to the interpersonal, communal and missional heart of the unity imperative – without giving up on the goal of full visible communion grounded in doctrinal accord, but instead bringing out its true import.[28]

So we need to take the 'unreality' charge seriously. As Paul D. Murray says in his Preface to the published proceedings of the first Receptive Ecumenism conference, what is called for is not fantasizing about unity, but disciplined attention to its nature and critical scrutiny of success and failure. The poetic vision, the dreaming of dreams, comes first (there is no progression without a vision), but rigorous analysis and hard-headed pragmatics soon follow.[29] Pope John Paul II pointed to the

28 See further Avis, Paul, 2010, *Reshaping Ecumenical Theology*, London and New York: T&T Clark.

29 Murray, Paul D. (ed.), 2008, *Receptive Ecumenism and the Call to Catholic Learning*, Oxford: Oxford University Press, pp. xii–xv: 'Some dreams are not simply subjective fantasy … but given to us by an Other whose dreams they are, and given to us precisely in order to

dedicated, disciplined vocation of ecumenism, the *ascesis* that it entails, when he talked about the 'purification of memories' and the need for 'truthful vision'.[30] Margaret O'Gara develops this idea when she points out that:

> ecumenical dialogue is a form of asceticism. It invites Christian scholars to enter into a process which may achieve no tangible success or rewards during their lifetime ... ecumenists must follow various ascetical practices: they repeatedly fast from celebrations of the Eucharist when not in full communion with the presider; they spend their time and talents on lengthy study of positions they only gradually understand; they endure the embarrassment and frustration that flow from the sins of their own and their dialogue partner's communion; and frequently their efforts are feared or suspected by members of their own church.[31]

There is a qualitative difference between a vision of unity inspired by the Holy Spirit, which has integrity because it seeks to move towards the ultimate horizon of visible unity step by step, always matching practical initiatives to doctrinal agreement, on the one hand, and escapist fantasizing in order to evade the pain and scandal of division now, on the other. Head and heart must come together in ecumenical work. The need for realism need not mean that pragmatism becomes the order of the day. Ecumenism seen as 'the art of the possible' cannot dispense with the sustaining vision of the glorious body of Christ (Phil. 3.21).

The ecumenical movement was hailed by its pioneers (Archbishop of Canterbury William Temple, for example) as a *novum*, a fresh work of the Holy Spirit. Were they wrong? In the history of the church spiritual renewal has invariably been

---

be born into being' (p. xv). See further on this theme, Healy, Nicholas M., 2000, *Church, World and the Christian Life: Practical-Prophetic Ecclesiology*, Cambridge: Cambridge University Press.

30 John Paul II, 1995, *Ut Unum Sint*, 2, 15.

31 Murray, *Receptive Ecumenism*, p. 35.

accompanied by fresh divisions. The new wine could not be contained within the old wine skins (Mark 2.22; Matt. 9.17). Whenever the Holy Spirit was poured out you could bet your life that there was a split looming. Could that be changing? Is there a straw in the wind? For example, the charismatic movement of the twentieth century was a movement of spiritual renewal within the churches and across the churches, not between them. On the Day of Pentecost Peter quotes the prophecy of Joel: 'I will pour out my Spirit upon all flesh, and your sons and your daughters shall prophesy, and your young men shall see visions and your old men shall dream dreams' (Acts 2.17; cf. Joel 2.28). Where the Spirit of God moves on the chaotic face of the deep, we dream not of division, but of unity, not of putting asunder but of gathering together, not of discord but of harmony – and that is how we know that the vision is of the Holy Spirit. We can be inspired by the Spirit both to dream the dream of unity and to work tirelessly in realistic ways for its progressive realization, encouraged by the extent of accord that has already been revealed.

In one sense, nothing is ultimately more unreal and untrue in the sight of God than the fragmented, unreconciled church of Christ. It is disunity that is the 'really unreal'. Karl Barth made this point, first bending over backwards to see the point of the sceptics about unity and then acknowledging the unfathomable mystery of the fact that the church of Christ is divided:

> There may be good grounds for the rise of these divisions. There may be serious obstacles to their removal. There may be many things which can be said by way of interpretation and mitigation. But this does not alter the fact that every division as such is a deep riddle, a scandal ... For the matter itself ... demands always, and in all circumstances, *unam ecclesiam*. And if history contradicts this, then it speaks only of the actuality and not the truth ... The disunity of the Church is a scandal.[32]

---

32 Barth, Karl, 1975–, *Church Dogmatics*, eds Geoffrey Bromiley

We cannot make sense of the church without faith in the one who promised its indefectibility – that it will not be overcome and will not ultimately go wrong, which is a doctrine accepted by all major Christian traditions. The obscure dominical saying 'the gates of Hades will not prevail against it' (Matt. 16.18) probably means that 'even the full fury of the underworld's demonic forces will not overcome the church'.[33] All ecclesiology is an activity undertaken in faith and this is no less true of the sub-set of ecclesiology that we call ecumenical theology. We recall that the church is an article of faith in the creed, the first subheading, as it were, after belief in the Holy Spirit. Our faith and hope are in the Spirit of Christ. The ultimate truth about the church lies not in empirical phenomena, bewildering and discomforting as they are, but in the scriptural promises of God and their eschatological fulfilment through the power of the Spirit of Christ. At this point, and in conclusion, some apt words from a very different religious tradition offer themselves for our Christian prayer for the church: 'From the unreal lead me to the real.'[34]

---

and Thomas F. Torrance, Edinburgh/London and New York: T&T Clark, IV/1, pp. 675–7.

33 Davies, W. D. and D. C. Allison, 1991, *The Gospel According to St Matthew*, 3 vols, vol. 2, *Matthew 8–18*, International Critical Commentary, London and New York: T&T Clark, p. 633; see the discussion of a range of interpretations, pp. 630–4.

34 Zaehner, R. C., trans., 1938, *Hindu Scriptures*, London: Dent, p. 34: Brihadaranyaka Upanishad, 28.

2

Transcending Denominationalism

The fact that there are now tens of thousands of Christian denominations throughout the world, some huge, some minuscule, is one of the most striking features of modern Christianity. Denominationalism is the most visible form of Christian pluralism, and though passively taken for granted most of the time, it remains one of the most intractable. Theological and ethical differences that often underlay the more obvious differences of practice and attitude between denominations were more prominent in the past than they are now. The very ethical and theological differences that formerly gave denominations their *raison d'être* now cut right across the major Christian traditions and are common to many of them – especially in the personal views of their members. But in official teaching and policy these historical differences remain serious obstacles to deeper convergence between the more conservative traditions or churches and those that are more accommodating to modern culture. So the Christian church in late modernity is marked by both *inter*-denominational and *intra*-denominational pluralism. This chapter examines the 'external' pluralism of the Christian Church, its manifest denominational structure, and asks how far inherited denominational identity, with its concomitant divisions, can be overcome or transcended.

'Denomination' devalued

For many devout Christians in the recent past their denomination was a source of pride. They gloried in the belief that

God had raised up their form of the church to bear witness to important truths and perhaps also took some pride in what human organizational flair could achieve. But almost inevitably an understandable pride in the strength of their denomination mutated into an ugly triumphalism. Their autonomous existence was a reason to bolster their own denominational identity over against that of other denominations, for had not God called them to be separate and, by definition, to be morally better and doctrinally sounder than others? And if their denomination was not only better and sounder, but also bigger and stronger, was that not a mark of divine approval?

To many reflective Christians today, those with an ecumenical conscience, denominationalism seems a deplorable distortion of the one church of Jesus Christ. Historically, the tide of denominational complacency began to turn when H. Richard Niebuhr pilloried denominationalism nearly a century ago in *The Social Sources of Denominationalism* (1929).[1] Niebuhr held up denominationalism as an apostasy from the true vision of the church, a collusion with the oppressive contours of social division, an ecclesial 'caste system', and a betrayal of Christian unity. This was the first nail in the coffin of denominational smugness and inertia. From that point it began to be acknowledged that a denominational church is an unreconciled church.

It seems that today no self-respecting ecclesiologist would be happy to accept the label 'denomination' for their church.[2] Theologians have a bad conscience about denominationalism. It has no place among the building blocks of an ecclesiology that takes *missional unity* as the key. The word 'denomination' suggests a broken-off part of the whole, a fragment, something that has to be marked as different and separate. Who would

1 Niebuhr, H. Richard, 1954 (1929), *The Social Sources of Denominationalism*, Hamden, CT: The Shoestring Press.

2 See Collins, Paul M. and Barry Ensign-George (eds), 2011, *Denomination: Assessing an Ecclesiological Category*, London and New York: T&T Clark. My cross-bench Anglican perspective is partly reflected in the latter part of this chapter.

say that the Roman Catholic Church (RCC) or the Orthodox churches were 'denominations'? The term just does not fit. Notwithstanding the internal tensions and struggles, and the elements of dysfunctionality within these two great traditions, they are both characterized by a sense of historic identity and universality. In some respects, my own church, the Church of England, has intentionally bought into a denominational identity in recent decades, in spite of its continuing position in the nation as the established church. In various ways it has colluded with the process of denominationalization, just when denominations are becoming *passé*. Personally, I find any complacency with regard to denominationalism – any collusion with its tendency – not only deeply distasteful but also sinful. I see denominationalism as a retrograde development and as a major ecclesiological and ecumenical problem.

Denomination defined

Russell Richey, the American Methodist *doyen* of denomination studies, brings denominationalism into focus in several useful, thought-provoking ways, which I have glossed and expanded.[3]

3 Richey, Russell E., 2014, *Denominationalism Illustrated and Explained*, Eugene, OR: Cascade Books, page references in my main text. See also Mullin, Robert Bruce and Russell E. Richey (eds), 1994, *Reimagining Denominationalism: Interpretive Essays*, New York: Oxford University Press, especially Mullin's essay, 'Denominations as Bilingual Communities', pp. 162–76. An important source for the American scene is Roozen, David A., and James R. Nieman (eds), 2005, *Church, Identity and Change: Theology and Denominational Structures in Unsettled Times*, Grand Rapids, MI: Eerdmans. For each of eight denominations in the USA the book provides a historical introduction, a sociological case study, a theological interpretation and a concluding reflection. The theological essays are uneven in quality. Roozen observes that it is the liturgical and the Pentecostal traditions that have proved most adaptive and resilient in the face of modern cultural challenges (p. 614).

(a) A denomination can be identified as 'a voluntaristic ecclesial body' that requires a situation of *de facto* religious toleration or freedom in order to exist (p. 2). A fundamental feature of denominationalism is that *we choose our own church*. A denomination is a multiple-choice option for modern Christians.

(b) By virtue of recognizing itself as a denomination, such a body is conceding the authenticity of other denominations and their right to exist. It is acknowledging its limitations. 'It knows itself as denominated, as named, as recognized and recognizable, as having boundaries, as possessing adherents, as having a history' (p. 3). On the other hand, an ecclesial body that claims to be *the church* or the only *true* church or the only *complete* church cannot see itself at the same time as a denomination, though observers in other churches may see it as such.

(c) In seeing themselves as part of a larger whole, denominations implicitly acknowledge an imperative to work for Christian unity, sometimes even seeing themselves as stepping stones to unity. Thus, Winthrop Hudson rejected Sidney Mead's view that denominationalism was essentially sectarian (p. 184). Taking his cue from John Wesley, Richey therefore speaks of the 'catholic spirit' of American denominations in their earlier days, while recognizing that they later became ends in themselves (pp. 185–7).

(d) Denominationalism is the collective pattern created by a plurality of denominations, the larger organizational ecology within which individual denominations exist and perhaps flourish (pp. 3–4, 8). Denominationalism presupposes a distinct socioeconomic ecology; it is the ecclesial system that typifies Christianity under the conditions of modernity, with its religious free market. American denominations originated as expressions of the energy, self-reliance and enterprise of American culture; they manifested the frontier spirit. The denomination is a 'creature of modernity', like the political party, the free press and – one might add – trade unions. As such it is characterized by organizational complexity, centralized control and the bureaucracy that is needed to administer it. Denominations are a function of institutional differentiation and secularization in modern societies (p. 183).

(e) Richey admits that the glory days of denominations are past. Disenchantment with denominational separation has set in among their members. The historic denominations are in decline and, as centralized, historic, bureaucratic institutions, they are nowadays objects of distrust and suspicion. They have lost their first love, their originating purpose, whereby they understood themselves to be instruments of the kingdom of God and to Christianize the nation. They were once 'missionary structures', but not anymore (pp. 187, 197).

(f) The brute sociological fact of denominationalism raises serious ecclesiological questions, focused not least on the fencing of the Lord's Supper or Eucharist which is universally understood as the sacrament of unity. Denominationalism provokes the question: What then and after all is the church of Jesus Christ? (pp. 8–9). Is the existing plethora of rival denominations, some of whom do not accept or recognize others, what God intends for God's church?

Richey's analysis is a fertile one, though sometimes slightly rose-tinted. His critical assessment is muted and it is not clear how far he accepts Niebuhr's indictment of denominationalism. It raises the question of how he accounts for the blatant realities – stronger in the past than now, but still needing to be accounted for – of inter-denominational rivalry, competition and the poaching of members, for inter-denominational polemic and mutual condemnation? What of the various denominations' historical claims to each manifest the best form of Christianity and to possess the one and only biblically sanctioned polity or form of governance and ministry among the churches? How would Richey come to terms with what Niebuhr called the 'bickerings, rivalries, and misunderstandings of divided sects'?[4] There is a faint sense of wanting to make a virtue of necessity in Richey's portrayal.

Momentously, once denominations have ceased to battle one another and have given up their exclusive claims, they have lost their *raison d'être* and have no standing ground. They have become dinosaurs heading for extinction, beached whales out of their element. The denominations represent the dismembering of the body of Christ. In Niebuhr's words, they 'have parted the garment of Christianity among them, unable to clothe the single body of Christ in the seamless vesture of his spirit'.[5] How easy it is to break away; how hard it is to heal divisions! The essential vision of the ecumenical movement, that of a united community of missionary disciples, poses a potentially lethal challenge to denominationalism.

'Denominationalism' deconstructed and defended

The currency of Christian pluralism is the word 'denomination'. Why is the term 'denomination', which is endemic in talk about the churches, especially among Protestants in America and 'Free Churches' in Britain, so popular? How does it square with those churches' claims and aspirations to catholicity? How can a denomination, which by definition stands for a part, be catholic, 'according to the whole'? 'Denomination' is clearly not a biblical word or idea, nor is it obviously a theological or ecclesiological term. It does not come down to us from ancient Christian tradition and it has no specific theological content – indeed, little content of any kind, as writers on this topic constantly lament. The word 'denomination' does not tell us anything of theological significance about the nature and mission of the church of Christ and the place of the church in the purposes of God – except this one thing, that the church is divided.

4 Niebuhr, *The Social Sources of Denominationalism*, p. 11.
5 Niebuhr, *The Social Sources of Denominationalism*, p. 10.

Those considerations make me wary of the word 'denomination'! If I want to speak theologically about the church, I use theological language. If I want to speak about the church sociologically, I use sociological language. 'Denomination' has the ring of social science and therefore implies a sociological theory about the place of the churches in modern society. The fact that the phenomenon of denominationalism could be (and was) related systematically to social factors by H. Richard Niebuhr in his classic study *The Social Sources of Denominationalism*, and the fact that denominational identity tends to become less important as other markers of ecclesial identity – such as attitudes to race, gender and sexual orientation – become more pronounced and more urgent, suggest that 'denomination' is indeed a social science concept. Sociologists are not concerned with the theological aspects of division in the church – they can pass no value judgement on that – but only with describing the role of the churches in society. They do not operate with the theological concept of 'the church', but with the empirical concept of 'churches'. But, strangely enough, we find church leaders using the sociological term 'denomination' when they are purporting to speak in a theological or ecclesiological register, and to me that is a puzzling and inept usage in the mouths of church leaders. However, it may suggest that we lack a commonly recognized language for speaking about the church in its divided state.

A recent attempt to champion the concept of denomination has been made by Barry Ensign-George. In a stimulating essay introducing a symposium on the concept of denomination in the major Christian traditions, he asserts not only (and counterintuitively) that the term 'denomination' is ecclesiastical and theological in origin, but also (and paradoxically) that it is 'potentially one of God's good gifts to the church' because it provides scope for diversity of faith and practice and allows individuals to slip in and out of churches (the phenomenon of 'switching').[6] For Ensign-George, the denomination is a vital

6 Collins and Ensign-George, *Denomination*, ch. 1, at p. 17, n.1 and

intermediate structure, placed between 'congregation' and 'church' or, as it might be better to say, between the church local and the church universal. It is a way of recognizing that 'we', the denomination, are not the whole church and that we are committed to the path of unity.

Admirably, Ensign-George makes it clear that when denominations are regarded as an end in themselves, they become idolatrous; they need to acknowledge their finitude and fragmentariness. He concludes by observing that 'Denomination as a category embodies an affirmation that the church may be pluriform without undoing its unity'.[7] To me this statement goes beyond paradox to the verge of unintelligibility, because I cannot see how the idea of 'denomination' affirms the unity of the church, either as a present fact or as a future hope – in fact, quite the reverse. It is interesting that Ensign-George brackets out of his discussion the question of whether the RCC and the Orthodox churches should be seen as denominations. In these two churches two ideas are combined: a) They regard themselves as exclusively (or at least substantially) 'the church' and deem all other ecclesial bodies that equally purport to be churches as other than – or at least less than – 'the church'. b) The idea that they might be just one denomination among others is abhorrent to them. Thus Christian unity and persisting in a denominational mindset do not belong together but exist in antithesis. So I do not agree with the subtitle of the volume, that 'denomination' is an 'ecclesiological category'.

A major problem with the term 'denomination' is its vagueness or, to put it more kindly, its fluidity and plasticity. As Gesa Elsbeth Thiessen notes, 'denomination' is now widely used as equivalent to 'church'.[8] I think such usage is just bad language,

---

p. 3. Ensign-George cites Hudson, Winthrop S., 'Denominationalism as a Basis for Ecumenicity: A Seventeenth-Century Conception', *Church History* 24.1 (1955), pp. 32–50, reprinted in Russell E. Richey (ed.), 2010 (1977), *Denominationalism*, Eugene, OR: Wipf & Stock, pp. 21–42.

7 Collins and Ensign-George, *Denomination*, p. 16.

8 Thiessen, Gesa Elsbeth, 'The Lutheran Church: Church, Confes-

but the real problem arises when we ask, 'church at which level?' Do we mean a church in a nation or sovereign state and, in some cases, in more than one nation, but within the same sovereign state (as in the UK)? Or do we mean a global Christian family, a world communion, a major Christian tradition? In other words, does 'denomination' fit the national or the universal scene, or both? The usage is slippery.

'Denomination' is not a word that I care to use at either level. I do not refer to my own national church, the Church of England, as a denomination, nor do I describe the worldwide Anglican Communion as a denomination. But neither do I refer to other churches by that term, whether Anglican or other, whether national or global, even if they actually refer to themselves in those terms. I pay them a higher compliment by acknowledging their ecclesial character. So it is not that I think that Anglicanism is somehow divinely protected from the language of denomination: I treat all other churches in the same way. It is not that I think that other churches are of Paul or Cephas or Apollos, while Anglicans are of Christ (1 Cor. 1.12)! I refer to all self-styled churches as churches and to the major global expressions of Christianity as 'Christian traditions' or (as the World Council of Churches does) 'Christian world communions' – or perhaps as 'families of churches'. In using the language of 'church' and 'churches' of ecumenical partners I am trying to do justice to their view of themselves and pay them the courtesy of speaking of them as they would wish to be spoken of because that is how they understand themselves. Where other churches openly refer to themselves, in their official documents or on their website, as denominations, I think that is deplorable and that they have basically lost the ecclesiological plot at that point. Churches should describe themselves in God-language and church-language. They should employ language that reflects something of the mystery of the church considered (as the New Testament does)

---

sion, Congregation, Denomination', in Collins and Ensign-George, *Denomination*, ch. 4, at p. 52.

as the body, the bride, the temple of Christ. Those whose role is to speak for the church are bishops, priests, presidents or elected lay and ordained leaders, not sociologists, and they should each stick to their brief.

Denomination, pluralism and privatization

Nevertheless, the concept of a 'denomination' has its uses and may be unavoidable in certain contexts and kinds of discourse.[9] The term 'denomination' recognizes the unique position of the churches in modern civil society – a society that is characterized by the radical differentiation and pluralization of institutions.[10] I say 'differentiation' and 'pluralization' deliberately, though these are not very elegant terms, rather than 'difference' and 'plurality'; this is because the churches, like other institutions, are subject to a remorseless socioeconomic process that separates them out from one another and drives towards ever-increasing specialization and plurality. This process is an aspect of the progressive complexification of modern Western society as a system. The process of complexification militates against what is held in common: in the case of the churches, shared beliefs and common structures. Each becomes a little system – or perhaps a sub-system – in a social ecology that supports many such entities but at the same time seems to

---

9 For history and analysis, in addition to the works, already referenced, by Richey, Niebuhr, and Mullin and Richey, see Richey, Russell E., 2013, *Denominationalism Illustrated and Explained*, Eugene, OR: Wipf & Stock. See also two small gems: Richey, Russell E., 'Denominationalism', in Nicholas Lossky et al. (eds), 1991, *Dictionary of the Ecumenical Movement*, Geneva: World Council of Churches; London: Churches Together in Britain and Ireland; Grand Rapids, MI: Eerdmans, pp. 265–6; Mullin, Robert Bruce, 'Denomination', in H. J. Hillerbrand (ed.), 2004, *The Encyclopedia of Protestantism*, 4 vols, New York and London: Routledge, vol. 2, D–K, pp. 580–4.

10 See the discussion in Avis, Paul, 2003, *A Church Drawing Near: Spirituality and Mission in a Post-Christian Culture*, London and New York: T&T Clark, ch. 3.

hold them apart. Institutional religion shares the same fate as other institutions in a society characterized by a high degree of structural complexity: it too becomes differentiated out and institutionally distinctive.[11]

In the conditions of late- or post-modernity, the churches require an institutional infrastructure with a bureaucracy to service it and a managerial ideology to legitimate that bureaucracy. The churches are specialized institutions, catering for particular spiritual, emotional, social and ritual needs, and in turn reinforcing those needs by providing them with a conceptual framework of interpretation and a structural habitation. In that way, they create specific ecclesial identities that tend to define themselves ideologically and therefore polemically over against other ecclesial identities. Although there are social and cultural differences between churches that exist side by side within one country – as there are between the Church of England and the Methodist Church of Great Britain, which are bound together in a Covenant – these differences are generally not differences of fundamental Christian belief, but of self-consciousness, or perhaps we could say 'ethos'. These social and cultural differences may be reflected in ecclesial structure, polity and governance – differences with regard to where authority is located and how it is exercised, differences in the balance between elements of hierarchy and elements of democracy, between the centre and the circumference. It is these kinds of 'political' differences – over episcopacy, papacy, congregational autonomy, etc. – that tend to get played up and that perpetuate division. We know who we are because we are not the other.[12]

It is arguable that, in post-modernity, the accelerating pluralism that was characteristic of modern society is rapidly

11 See Luhmann, Niklaus, 1982, *The Differentiation of Society*, New York: Columbia University Press, especially pp. 230, 248; Luckmann, Thomas, 1983, *Life-World and Social Realities*, London: Heinemann Educational, especially p. 130.

12 See the discussion in Avis, *Reshaping Ecumenical Theology*, especially ch. 4: 'The Hermeneutics of Unity'.

degenerating into sheer fragmentation. This perception seems to be borne out by the galloping multiplication of Christian churches and the proliferation of competing denominations, especially in the developing world. Given that there are now more than 34,000 separate Christian churches, however small, in the world, denominationalism seems to be here to stay![13]

The concept of a denomination arises where a social taxonomy or categorization of churches is employed. How does one particular Christian tradition compare with and relate to others that seem to sit alongside it? The idea of a denomination implies plurality: it hardly arises when there is not much with which to compare a particular tradition. In an overwhelmingly Roman Catholic country such as Poland, or in an overwhelmingly Orthodox country such as Greece, or in an overwhelmingly Lutheran country such as Norway, it does not make sense to refer to the RCC in Poland or the Orthodox Church of Greece or the Lutheran Church of Norway as 'denominations'. They are not one among many, except when they are placed in a global perspective; they are, to most intents and purposes, 'the church' of the nation. A denomination is a church that exists among a plurality of competing churches, where none of them is numerically dominant or enjoys a markedly privileged position.

The pluralism of modern civil society may be regarded as a neutral phenomenon: no particular value judgement need attach to it. But since the plurality of churches only became possible when states legislated for religious toleration, value judgements soon began to impinge. To extend toleration is to relativize and to relativize is to privatize. Public doctrine cannot be relative without ceasing to be public doctrine: it is an ideological framework that is widely acknowledged, if not everywhere endorsed. Private opinion is necessarily relative because it is almost infinitely diverse. So the pluralism of

---

13 See Barrett, D. B., G. T. Kurian and T. M. Johnson (eds), 2001, *World Christian Encyclopedia*, 2nd edn, New York: Oxford University Press, pp. 3, 10.

religion and of religious institutions is made possible through laws of toleration, but toleration implies relativization and the resulting relativism is an ideological reality that corresponds to the private realm. Historically, states have legislated for toleration only when they have had to do so. On the part of the state, toleration is a compromise strategy for maintaining social cohesion or political unity as an overarching framework within which a broad latitude of opinion and of expression can be allowed. As Owen Chadwick puts it: 'From the moment that European opinion decided for toleration, it decided for an eventual free market in opinion.'[14]

The process of pluralization that was accelerated by toleration had the effect of relativizing religious belief – that is to say, of undermining the credibility of exclusive claims to provide salvation. The privatization of religious commitment means, as Hugh MacLeod has put it, that 'religious language, religiously based assumptions about the world and religiously legitimated moral principles have become the preserve of committed minorities, rather than being part of the taken-for-granted assumptions of society as such'.[15] The privatization of religious belief and practice devalues it and helps to trivialize it. It becomes a matter of personal preference, of private predilection, to be viewed with a mixture of bemused scepticism and nervous apprehension.

Wolfhart Pannenberg has pointed to a crucial implication of pluralism and the consequent privatization of religious belief and practice: the fate of the integration of meaning.[16] Where

---

14 Chadwick, Owen, 1975, *The Secularization of the European Mind in the Nineteenth Century*, Cambridge: Cambridge University Press, p. 21. See also Jordan, W. K., 1932, *The Development of Religious Toleration in England*, 2 vols, London: Allen and Unwin; Lecler, Joseph, 1960, *Toleration and the Reformation*, 2 vols, London: Longmans.

15 Hugh MacLeod in Young, Frances (ed.), 1995, *Dare We Speak of God in Public?*, London: Mowbray, p. 4.

16 Pannenberg, Wolfhart, 1989, *Christianity in a Secularized World*, New York: Crossroad, pp. 29ff.

the state actively sponsors pluralism through a policy of toleration (one contemporary form of this is multiculturalism), public doctrine is reduced to a bare minimum; it becomes a skeletal framework, holding the ring for competing versions of the good life. Public doctrine can no longer provide the key to the integration of meaning that human life craves. The state ceases to legitimate a worldview, a set of values, a faith of some sort. That role now devolves to the family: it is in the family unit and through family activities and mutual support within the family that an integration of meanings, and therefore of life, can be achieved, and nowhere else; it is the family or nothing. The valorization of the family unit is the silver lining behind privatization. But is the nuclear family robust enough to serve this function? What happens when family life cannot stand the strain? The many social and economic pressures on the modern family render it incapable of fulfilling this moral and spiritual function on its own. Today the family as an institution seems to be struggling.[17] What do we look for then? Is this the moment for the state to step in and to try to reclaim at least something of its previous role as the legitimator of social stability? For example, should marriage be supported through the taxation system? The implications for our concern here are simply but seriously that denominationalism is made possible by religious toleration, but toleration is only possible at the cost of relativizing the claims that the denominations make for their beliefs. In turn, relativism plays into and reinforces the radical privatization of religious belief and practice that typifies Western society today, for various reasons that we need not delve further into here. This is the sting in the tail of denominationalism. Should we 'go with it' or fight against it?

17 See Barton, Stephen (ed.), 1996, *The Family in Theological Perspective*, Edinburgh: T&T Clark.

Denominationalism and Christian unity

If denominationalism is an inevitable product of diversity and complexity in modern Christianity (and that is a neutral description, not a value judgement about ecclesial division), is there any point in attempting to overcome it, in seeking unity? What is the relationship between denominationalism and the ecumenical vocation? It seems to me that there are certain paradoxes in play here. Ecumenism presupposes that there is a denominational structure to the Christian landscape; it is premised on a plurality of distinctive churches that subsist in a state of separation and competition that ecumenical dialogue seeks to overcome in order to bring about convergence, consensus, cooperation and eventual communion. When ecumenical dialogue proves fruitful it brings to light and brings into prominence what the churches have in common, as well as clarifying the real remaining differences between them. Ecumenism feeds on denominationalism, even as it seeks to overcome it. Without denominations the scope for ecumenical endeavour would be much reduced.

A glance at modern church history suggests that the rise of denominationalism and the advent of the ecumenical movement went hand in hand and that there might be a causal link between them, even if after a short time lag. In Britain the heyday of unchecked denominationalism was probably the second half of the nineteenth century and the first half of the twentieth. Roman Catholics were a marginal minority (except of course in Ireland). The Church of England was at its zenith and the nonconformist churches of England and Wales were also at the peak of membership and influence. Religious voluntary societies cut across the churches, bringing Christians together to make common cause for the sake of the Bible, missions, sanitation, temperance and other aspects of social reform. New movements of religious consciousness, whether catholic (liturgical and sacramental) or evangelical (biblical, evangelistic), created ferment within many churches, wherever such movements happened to begin; they reflected intellectual and cultural currents that were both broad and deep. It was in such circumstances that the first stirrings of the desire for Christian unity were felt. Ecumenism came out of strength, not weakness, and was bound up with the missionary imperative.

The founding of the Evangelical Alliance in 1846 to 'associate and concentrate the strength of an enlightened Protestantism against the encroachments of Popery and Puseyism, and to promote the interests of a Scriptural Christianity' was a straw in the wind – a form of pan-evangelical ecumenism. The 1888 Lambeth Conference, taking its cue from the Protestant Episcopal Church of the USA (now The Episcopal Church), formulated the famous Lambeth Quadrilateral (Scripture, sacraments, creeds and a common ministry based on the historic episcopate) as a basis for unity. After the interruption of World War One, the 1920 Lambeth Conference issued its seminal *Appeal to All Christian People*, which generated an ecumenical momentum that continues to this day. Until the Second Vatican Council (1962–5) Roman Catholics were prohibited by the pope from participating in ecumenical activities. The claim to be the one and only instantiation of the church of Christ precluded the minimal level of recognition accorded to other churches that is needed for dialogue and for local fellowship and cooperation. In the encyclical *Mortalium animos* (1928) Pope Pius XI made precisely this connection: the RCC was 'the one true Church of Christ'. Therefore, the way to unity was for separated Christians ('dissidents') to return to the fold and to submit completely to the papacy. 'No one is in the Church of Christ, and no one remains in it, unless he acknowledges and accepts with obedience the authority and power of Peter and his legitimate successors.'[18] So it was no accident that Vatican II simultaneously weakened the exclusive claims of the RCC (in the notoriously disputed phrase *subsistit*

18 Neuner, J., SJ, and J. Dupuis, SJ (eds), 1983, *The Christian Faith in the Doctrinal Documents of the Catholic Church*, rev. edn, London: Collins, p. 260.

in: *Lumen gentium* 23)[19] and committed Roman Catholics to work for unity. The Roman Catholic document that is most ecumenically generous in recognizing the ecclesial authenticity of other churches is Pope John Paul II's *Ut Unum Sint* (1995) and this is the encyclical that humbly and charitably asks for help from separated brethren in reinterpreting the papal office for an ecumenical age.[20]

Sometimes it is when, for the first time, we see our own church as simply one church among others that we become troublingly conscious of the disunity of Christ's church. With the realization that the church has disintegrated, separation is rampant and schism is a sin comes the passion for unity. The fact of complacent denominationalism is a standing rebuke to all the churches. It is eloquent testimony to the fact that they have failed – failed to heed the prayer and command of Christ and of the apostles in the New Testament that the Church should be visibly one.[21] H. Richard Niebuhr castigated the churches in America: 'Denominationalism in the Christian Church is an acknowledged hypocrisy. It is a compromise made far too lightly, between Christianity and the world. It represents the accommodation of Christianity to the caste-system of human society.'[22]

The divisions within the Church – of which the culture of denominationalism is a blatant manifestation – raise the question whether the community that Christ intended actually exists on earth, or whether what we have instead is the *simulacrum* of a church. Only a miracle of grace can preserve the church on

19 Abbott, W. M., SJ (ed.), 1966, *The Documents of Vatican II*, London and Dublin: Geoffrey Chapman, p. 23.

20 For Anglican commentary on *Ut Unum Sint*, see House of Bishops of the Church of England, 1997, *May They All Be One*, London: Church House Publishing; Santer, Mark, 'Communion, Unity and Primacy: An Anglican Response to *Ut Unum Sint*', *Ecclesiology* 3.3 (2007), pp. 283–95.

21 See, further, Avis, Paul, 2010, *Reshaping Ecumenical Theology*, London and New York: T&T Clark, especially ch. 10: 'Forging Communion in the Face of Difference'.

22 Niebuhr, 1954, *The Social Sources of Denominationalism*, p. 6.

earth in the teeth of the human drive to assert difference and to mark separation. We cannot be complacent about denominations. To acquiesce in denominationalism is a confession of failure; to glory in it is a mortal sickness. Denominationalism can only justifiably be seen as something to move on from as swiftly as possible. When churches are able to enter into relationships of ecclesial communion or 'full communion' (in North American terms), denominationalism becomes blunted and that is probably why proposals for unity or communion are fiercely resisted by some in the participating 'denominations'. Churches discover a symbiotic relationship; they grow together and change together as they interact with one another. The more intense the interaction, not only in theological dialogue but also in local expressions of fellowship, worship, service and outreach, the weaker becomes the consciousness of alienation, otherness and 'over-againstness'. The fact that two churches are now in growing communion with each other alters their identity, their self-perception. A denominational mindset can be repudiated and progressively left behind.

The other side of the coin is the fact that the more that theological dialogue and local ecumenical cooperation reveal what the churches have in common, the more the exclusive or distinctive claims of each tradition are undermined. Denominations revel in being different; without difference they have no standing ground. Their rationale is that they offer something different, something better and – it used to be said – something unique: the only way of salvation. Why should we continue to champion the claims of our own tradition over against those of others once we have come to see that we are 90 per cent the same in all that matters? We hold a common faith, worship using very similar liturgical forms, and experience a high degree of convergence even in the traditionally divisive areas of ministry and sacraments. If we take this stance, then we are bound to lose the will to go to the stake for 'our' church. Denominational differences have been relativized and moved to the periphery; they are not that important anymore. So what stops us joining together? What remains genuinely church-dividing? What possible excuse can there be for not uniting forthwith?

By the same token, denominational differences are played down when common issues cut across all the churches. Do we not all currently struggle with issues of funding and resources? Are not many of us tearing ourselves apart over homosexuality in the church and ministry? Are we not equally struggling to make our mission and evangelization effective in the face of secularist opposition and consumerist apathy? It makes sense to join forces. We are all in the same boat; we must sink or swim together. Are genuine differences – perhaps about bishops or the pope – sufficiently important to stop us pulling together? Unity in mission is not only a visionary ideal, but also a practical necessity.

But it might seem that the interest goes out of ecumenism when it loses its sharp edges. Controversy is the lifeblood of theology, including ecumenical theology. Walter Kasper, the former President of the Pontifical Council for Promoting Christian Unity, believes that dialogue between the RCC and the other major Christian traditions has now moved beyond polemic: '[I]t can happily be stated', Kasper avows,

> that some of the classic disputes, which were at the root of our painful divisions, have today been basically resolved through a new consensus on fundamental points of doctrine. In other disputed questions there is at least convergence, which has helped the dialogues to move beyond previous polemical stances, and has created a more relaxed ecumenical atmosphere in which an '*exchange of gifts*' has been enriching for both sides.[23]

If only it were so! The timing of Kasper's hopeful report was unfortunate: it was published just as the storm broke over Pope Benedict XVI's overture to disaffected Anglicans in the

---

23 Kasper, Walter, 2009, *Harvesting the Fruits: Basic Aspects of Christian Faith in Ecumenical Dialogue*, London and New York: Continuum, pp. 197–8, italics original.

Apostolic Constitution *Anglicanorum coetibus* that provided for Ordinariates.[24] Although the pope's initiative was presented as a pastoral response to the pleas of alienated Anglican traditionalists, it was essentially an incitement to separation, an inducement to go out of communion with one's church, which is schism. Schism is a sin in the church's book and separation could only be seen in this case as not a sin, but a right action, if Anglican churches, including the Church of England, were judged not to be churches in the proper sense. But that line of thought, implying the unchurching of ecumenical partners, is the antithesis of all that the ecumenical movement has stood for and, on that basis, was deplored as such by many Roman Catholic ecumenists.[25] Official Anglican responses at the time were muted and polite, albeit spoken through gritted teeth. Subsequent Anglican reflection has been tinged with bitterness.[26] Ecumenism discovered that dialogue sometimes needs to be polemical after all.

Anglican denominationalism?

It would be rash to attempt to generalize about worldwide Anglicanism with regard to its denominational consciousness. What may be true of many of the churches of the Anglican Communion may not be true of the Church of England, the most ancient – together with the Church of Ireland – of Anglican churches and historically seen as the Mother Church of the

---

24 Benedict XVI, *Anglicanorum coetibus*, www.vatican.va/holy_father/benedict_xvi/apost_constitutions/documents/hf_ben-xvi_apc_20091104_anglicanorum-coetibus_en.html, accessed 2.11.2021.

25 For a public critique of *Anglicanorum coetibus* from a Roman Catholic point of view, see Mannion, Gerard, 'A (Strange) Sort of Homecoming?', in Martyn Percy and Robert Boak Slocum (eds), 2013, *A Point of Balance: The Weight and Measure of Anglicanism*, New York: Morehouse; Norwich: Canterbury Press, ch. 10.

26 See, for example, 'Anglicans and Catholics in Communion: Patrimony, Unity, Mission', *The Messenger of the Catholic League* 292 (April–August 2010).

Anglican Communion. The Church of England may turn out to be the exception that proves the rule with regard to denominational identity among Anglican churches. The Church of England is unique among Anglican churches in being an established national church. Other Anglican churches are certainly national churches, but the English church is the only one that is still fully established by law.

Russell E. Richey has suggested that 'To characterize a denomination as a body with identifiable boundaries and leadership is to insist that it can be mapped, its members counted, its headquarters marked, and its present leadership named.'[27] This is precisely what cannot be done with the Church of England. It does not have clear boundaries as to who is in and who is out; there is no membership roll as such (the Church Electoral Roll is for purposes of governance, not sacramental participation; the two are not equated in English Anglican polity). Leadership is divided in a church of 42 dioceses, diocesan bishops and diocesan synods, notwithstanding the existence of two archbishops and a General Synod (the archbishops do not have jurisdiction outside their province, though the Archbishop of Canterbury has latent visitatorial powers in the Province of York as well as Canterbury). The Church of England does not have a headquarters. As someone who used to work at Church House, Westminster, I am acutely aware that Church House is not the national HQ with executive powers, but simply an administrative centre that exists to serve the dioceses and parishes that make up the Church of England. The ecclesial centre of gravity of the Church of England is not at its administrative centre. The principle of subsidiarity shapes the polity of the Church of England.

A church that is strongly identified – even more strongly than the Church of England – with the nation or the state (of course, nation and state are not always coterminous) does not fit easily into the category of 'denomination'. In its context

27 Richey, Russell E., 'United Methodism: Its Identity as Denomination', in Collins and Ensign-George, *Denomination*, ch. 5, at p. 71.

and in popular perception, it is *the* church, not *a* church. It is the defining representation of Christianity in that context, not one of many competing claimants. The Church of England may be regarded as a 'national church' *par excellence*, with its parochial and diocesan ministry and cathedrals extending back into their remote beginnings in the Middle Ages, together with its recognition in law and in the (unwritten) constitution as the *established* church. The Church of England is the only Anglican Church that is still actually established, though since all churches in the world are subject to the law of the land, and the precise relationship of any church to the law of the land is a matter of degree, some Anglican churches still retain certain vestiges of establishment.[28]

To start close to home for me, there is the instructive case of 'The Church in Wales', disestablished in 1920, which retains some significant aspects of establishment, especially with regard to the occasional or pastoral offices (*rites de passage*). Its clergy are obliged by law to baptize, marry and bury all parishioners for whom these ministries are requested. The title 'The Church in Wales' is not indicative of a fully disestablished church, nor does it suggest that Welsh Anglicanism sees itself as one denomination among others. Its archbishop is called 'Archbishop of Wales' (not '*in* Wales'), a title that has strong overtones of territoriality and national identity. On these grounds alone, there is something to be said for the suggestion that the Church in Wales was 're-established' when it was 'disestablished'.

The Church of England may be the only fully established Anglican Church, but it is certainly not the only *national* Anglican church. Within the Anglican Communion many – though not all – churches (or provinces), especially those in the former dominions of the British Empire, see themselves as national churches, even when they are not the largest church and not

28 See, further, Doe, Norman, 1998, *Canon Law in the Anglican Communion*, Oxford: Clarendon Press; Avis, Paul, 2001, *Church, State and Establishment*, London: SPCK; Cox, Noel, 'Legal Aspects of Church-State Relations in New Zealand', *Journal of Anglican Studies* 8.1 (2010), pp. 9–33.

established churches. A classical definition of the Anglican Communion, formulated by the 1930 Lambeth Conference of Anglican bishops from around the world, described it as 'a fellowship, within the one, holy, catholic and apostolic Church, of those duly constituted dioceses, provinces, or regional Churches in communion with the See of Canterbury' that are characterized by their catholic faith and order and by the fact that they are 'particular or national churches ... bound together ... by mutual loyalty sustained by the common counsel of the bishops in conference'.[29] But are these national Anglican churches also denominations, even if they would not use that language about themselves? If we define a denomination as a church that exists among a plurality of competing churches, none of which is numerically dominant or enjoys unique legal privileges, we can ask whether a national church and even an established church can *also* be regarded as a denomination. First, let us apply this rough definition, with its criteria of numerical ascendancy and legal privileges to the established Church of England.

The Church of England is the largest Christian Church in England. It has baptized more than 20 million of the population of 60 million. Although the numbers worshipping week by week (though in many cases not every week) hovers below the 1 million mark (about the same number as the RCC in England), its actual pastoral constituency of people who have a meaningful contact with the Church of England – through its numerous church schools, through Sunday school, youth groups, the occasional offices of marriage and funeral services, and community events – is many times larger than this. It is the numerically dominant church in England, though not overwhelmingly so, and like all of the historic churches it is declining numerically and in other ways.[30]

---

29 1930 Lambeth Conference, Resolutions 48 and 49: Coleman, Roger (ed.), 1992, *Resolutions of the Twelve Lambeth Conferences 1967–1988*, Toronto: Anglican Book Centre, pp. 83ff.

30 See Avis, Paul (ed.), 2003, *Public Faith: The State of Religious Belief and Practice in Britain*, London: SPCK, especially ch. 7: David Voas, 'Is Britain a Christian Country?'

The Church of England's legal monopoly was undermined as long ago as 1689 by the Act of Toleration and then completely destroyed by the abolition of the Test and Corporation Acts and by the political and civic emancipation of Roman Catholics in 1829–31. However, the Church of England still retains a number of legal and institutional advantages: for example, in the areas of chaplaincy (prisons, hospitals, armed services, ancient schools and colleges), the General Synod's power to enact primary legislation so that church law is part of the law of the land, and the presence of 26 bishops *ex officio* in Parliament, in the House of Lords, and not least the role of the Sovereign as its Supreme Governor.

Given its numerical ascendancy and its legal privileges, should the Church of England be regarded as a denomination, as one denomination among others? One way of answering that question is to consult the Church of England's own understanding of its identity and mission. For evidence, we might look to the General Synod, and in particular to the House of Bishops within the Synod. As someone who was closely involved with the General Synod for more than 20 years, first as an elected member and subsequently in an executive staff capacity, I am convinced that the General Synod and the episcopate in particular does not see itself in denominational terms. The name 'The Church of England' is taken quite literally. There is little awareness of being simply one church seeking to take a role among a plurality of other churches. Rightly or wrongly, the Church of England in its national manifestation does not think of itself as one denomination among others. Seeing itself historically as going back through the Reformation to the beginnings of Christianity in England and so to the church of the apostles, it simply sees itself as 'the church'. As the established church, with a nationwide mission and ministry that is carried out at every level of national life, from the parochial, through the regional (diocesan) to the level of state (with reference to the Crown and Parliament), it still sees itself as the church of the English people. As a church that is both catholic and reformed, it sees itself not as a particular option among Christian churches, but as the authentic church of the land.

To push the case even further in a politically incorrect direction, many Anglicans in England really cannot see why the other churches are needed! Why can't other Christians simply go along to their local parish church? All are welcome there; no one is ever turned away. All baptized Christians in good standing are welcome to receive Holy Communion at Anglican celebrations of the Eucharist. No denominational peculiarities are rammed down people's throats. Surely there is nothing to offend Christians of goodwill here? There is nothing about the modern Church of England that should grate on the conscience of individuals, preventing them from joining in communion with it. Of course, there are various eccentricities, foibles and stupidities going on in parish life and sometimes at the diocesan or national level, but the Church of England is spacious enough for most of these irritants to be avoided. Other churches in England do not have to defend themselves against the established Church; they are not persecuted or even cold-shouldered. They do not need to be separate themselves in order to preserve certain cherished insights that are thought to be missing from Anglicanism, because the Church of England is a very broad church, where many varieties of belief and practice flourish unhindered. It would surely be a very exacting kind of Christian, one very difficult to please, who could not find a niche somewhere in the historic church of the land. I suspect that that is not far from how many Church of England people, rightly or wrongly, think about their church in relation to the alternatives. What they fail to realize is that, in many cases, other churches exist because of the historic failures and sins of the Church of England itself.

Now, if this characterization of the self-perception of the Church of England as *the* church in England is broadly on target, we need to ask whether that church is deceiving itself. Has it come to terms with the radical pluralism of the religious scene in England? Has it faced up to its long-term decline? Has it got its head buried in the sand with regard to the actual numbers attending its services? Denominationalism is a reality that affects all churches in the Western world. To be in denial about prevailing tendencies that push all churches towards denominational identity and denominational behaviour is an ecclesiastical delusion.

Although the Church of England may find it distasteful to be described as a denomination and may tend in self-defence to cling to some of the fading glory from its heyday in late Victorian and early Edwardian England, when nearly three times as many stipendiary clergy served a population of less than half the present size, the undeniable fact is that sometimes it does behave like a denomination. The creation of the Archbishops' Council in 1999 seemed to indicate a perceptible shift of the centre of gravity from the parishes and dioceses, where the church's ministry and worship were still deeply woven into the texture of English community life, especially in the countryside, to the national centre. The boards and councils of the General Synod became subsidiary operations of the Archbishops' Council and the Church of England centrally produced its own logo: it was turning itself into a market brand. For some time the telephone switchboard in Westminster answered calls with the words 'The Church of England; how may I help you?' That was regarded as outrageously presumptuous by many in the parishes and at diocesan level, who believed that they and those like them, with their weekly round of worship and community service centred on the parish churches, were the real Church of England. The constitutional aspects of the 'Renewal and Reform' programme that is currently preoccupying the archbishops, the bishops and the General Synod marks a further step towards the centralization and standardization of the Church of England.

On the other hand, there is much about the Church of England today that militates against a denominational self-understanding. Its Canons locate the centre of gravity in the diocese, seen as the community of word and sacrament that is gathered by the bishop and as the bishop's sphere of oversight, where he or she is the chief pastor (Canon C 18). When

Anglicans are being self-consciously ecclesiological, they talk of the diocese as the local church. There are about 13,000 constitutive parishes that comprise the Church of England on the ground; its many chaplaincies in schools and colleges are equally a grounded presence. Again, the Church of England is unlike a denomination in that it does not have a membership roll. The Church of England does not keep a list of signed-up members. It has a Church Electoral Roll, but this is an instrument of church governance whereby parishes are integrated into the synodical structure, not a comprehensive membership roll. The Church of England does not use the language of membership in a denominational sense. In its official documentation it refers to 'members' in various contexts, but no coherent meaning can be discerned here and the word would have been better avoided. The meaning of membership that is dominant in Church of England discourse is the Pauline idea of membership of the body of Christ through baptism (1 Cor. 12.13). The classic catechism informs the candidate for confirmation that in their baptism they were 'made a member of Christ, the child of God, and an inheritor of the kingdom of heaven'. Strictly speaking, all baptized parishioners who have not formally opted out could be regarded as being within the Church of England. If they have some involvement, however peripheral, with the life of the parish and if they occasionally attend their parish church, even if only for weddings and funerals, it would certainly make sense to see them as participating in the Church of England. But the Church of England is not interested in making members for itself. It aims to provide many different avenues and opportunities to maximize the participation of individuals and households in the life of grace in God's church and then to encourage them to become committed disciples of Jesus Christ as they follow the path of Christian initiation through baptism to confirmation and first communion.

To sum up, the centre of gravity of the Church of England is found in its daily and weekly liturgical worship, its long history, its nationwide mission and its parochial and diocesan make-up. These aspects are not conducive to a denominational identity. On the other hand, there are indicators of a shift to a more denominational consciousness within that church at the centre, rather than in the parishes. The Church of England may be balanced on the cusp of denominationalism, but it would be rash to predict which way it will fall, or whether it will continue to hover there for some time. The congregationalist tendency within many parishes may seem to point in a denominational direction, rather than towards a wider catholicity. Similarly, many 'fresh expressions of church', for whom denominational issues are very marginal, tend to put the emphasis on the local, the relational and the communal, and consequently sit light to parish boundaries and the wider church.[31]

The more historic churches of the Anglican Communion do not officially define themselves as denominations, but as 'provinces' or churches of the Anglican Communion and, above all, as belonging to the one, holy, catholic and apostolic Church of Jesus Christ. Unlike the Orthodox churches or even the RCC (notwithstanding Vatican II), in order to make this claim about themselves – that is, as belonging to the *una sancta* – Anglican churches do not dispute the claims of other churches to belong to the one church of Christ or devalue their ecclesial reality. Anglicans do not make exclusive claims for their church, nor do they unchurch others. Anglican ecclesiology is hospitable and inclusive. In recognizing in their ecumenical agreements that other churches are also authentic manifestations of the one church, Anglicans and their ecumenical partners are seeking to repair the visible unity of the church. And that unity remains an eschatological horizon in the light of which all denominational assertiveness, competitiveness and defensiveness must melt away.

31 See *Fresh Expressions in the Mission of the Church: Report of an Anglican-Methodist Working Party*, 2013, London: Church House Publishing.

3

Contested Legacy: Vatican II after 60 Years[1]

The Second Vatican Council (1962–65) was the most momentous religious phenomenon of the modern age. It has been described as 'the cataclysmic event of the twentieth century' for the Roman Catholic Church (RCC).[2] As a religious, ecclesiastical event within modern history, the impact of Vatican II can perhaps be matched only by the rise of Pentecostal forms of Christianity outside of the historic Christian communions and, rivalling them, the resurgence of an assertive, sometimes militant, Islam. But while the growth of Pentecostalism and the rise of Islam have both been spread over half a century of time and now cover large areas of the globe, the Second Vatican Council lasted for only a few years and took place in one European city, though it drew its episcopal members from all parts of the world (116 countries to be precise). Karl Rahner claimed that the Council turned the RCC from a Western church into a world church, but I think there was a large element of aspiration and future agenda in that claim.[3] I suspect,

1 This chapter is a much-expanded version of my article 'Contested Legacy: An Anglican Looks at Vatican II', *Theology* 118.3 (2015), pp. 188–95.

2 Guarino, Thomas G., 2018, *The Disputed Teachings of Vatican II: Continuity and Reversal in Catholic Doctrine*, Grand Rapids, MI: Eerdmans, p. 1.

3 Rahner, Karl, SJ, 1981, *Theological Investigations XX: Concern for the Church*, trans. Edward Quinn, London: Darton, Longman and Todd, chs 6 and 7. The global dimension of Vatican II is also discussed

however, that when sociologists of religion look back on the twentieth century from a vantage point 50 years or more from now, they may identify a different historical event as the most momentous religious phenomenon of the second half of that century, namely the relentless decline of Christianity – of Christian profession, organized practice and social influence – in the West, though that suggestion is speculative and depends on the straightforward extrapolation of recent and current trends into the future. Nevertheless, for the RCC the Council was, as Richard Gaillardetz puts it, 'an event of unparalleled significance in the history of modern Catholicism'.[4]

The momentum of the Council continues to reverberate within the ongoing process of the active reception of the Council.[5] In the third decade of the twenty-first century, the debate on Vatican II, its reception in the church and its interpretation in theology, shows no sign of diminishing. The repercussions of Vatican II impact not only Roman Catholics, but all Christians and churches, for we all have a stake in the continuing influence and effect of Vatican II. For many in the RCC – and indeed in the other major Christian traditions – the work of the Council is not yet done and much remains to be fully implemented; they are open to its deeper reception and indeed long for it.[6] For others, especially but not exclusively in the RCC, aspects of the Council are regarded as retrograde and anti-Catholic; for those who take this stance, there is a good deal that actually needs to be *undone*! The pontificate of Francis serves as the lightning conductor for these implacable

---

in Faggioli, Massimo, 2015, *A Council for the Global Church: Receiving Vatican II in History*, Minneapolis, MN: Fortress Press.

4 Gaillardetz, Richard R., 2015, *An Unfinished Council: Vatican II, Pope Francis, and the Renewal of Catholicism*, Collegeville, MN: Liturgical Press, p. ix.

5 Heft, James L. with John W. O'Malley (eds), 2012, *After Vatican II: Trajectories and Hermeneutics*, Grand Rapids, MI: Eerdmans.

6 An older, but compendious, assessment is Hastings, Adrian (ed.), 1991, *Modern Catholicism: Vatican II and After*, London: SPCK; New York: Oxford University Press; see especially ch. 10: F. J. Laishley, 'Unfinished Business', pp. 215–39.

opposing forces and at the time of writing the outcome of the contest seems uncertain.

The power struggle among Roman Catholics, at every level and in every part of that church, with regard to the legacy of Vatican II – compounded by the revelations of extensive sexual and other forms of abuse and the failure of some members of the episcopal hierarchy to deal responsibly with them – means that the largest church in Christendom is frankly an unreconciled church. The RCC is not at peace with itself. Its identity on the world stage is compromised and its witness is flawed. Studies of identity theory speak paradoxically of something being identical with itself, at one with itself, albeit in a dynamic and mediated way, not a static one.[7] This depiction of the unity and integration of identity is sadly not the case for the RCC in the early twenty-first century. Vatican II, however, was intentionally and consistently committed to reconciliation on three interrelated fronts: with other Christian traditions, with other world religions, and with the modern world generally. It looked for common ground and sought to build bridges with each of these constituencies, which it looked upon not as alien entities, but as dialogue partners whom it wished to invite into a shared conversation.

But the RCC is not unique in this predicament – far from it. All the major Christian world communions – the Orthodox Churches, the Anglican Communion, the Lutheran World Federation, the World Communion of Reformed Churches, the World Methodist Council, and the Baptist World Alliance – are riven by fierce arguments. These are accompanied by power struggles over the interpretation of tradition, the correct response to contemporary Western culture, morals and mores, the desirability of change and reform, and the ultimate location of authority. However, there is one major difference between all of these Christian world communions and the RCC: the latter is the only body, among those named, that is constituted

7 See, for example, Heidegger, Martin, 2002 (1969), *Identity and Difference*, trans. and intro. Joan Stambaugh, Chicago and London: Chicago University Press.

as a single church; the others are all families or communions of self-governing (autonomous or, in the case of a number of Orthodox Churches, autocephalous) churches. To my mind, that difference intensifies the significance, the problem, of disagreement. The degree of dissent that is probably bearable, because it is inevitable, in a global family of churches, provided it does not lead to schism, is not acceptable in a single church; this applies even when it is one spread throughout the world and embedded in many different cultures, especially when it is marked out among other Christian families by a powerful central authority.

In this chapter, I focus on the arguments and tensions within the RCC by interrogating a range of interpretations of the Council by Roman Catholic theologians writing in the English language. It is inevitably as an Anglican theologian and ecumenist that I have undertaken this study of the battles over the correct interpretation and right implementation of Vatican II, but as an Anglican theologian who is conscious of owing a significant historical, spiritual and theological debt to that church – and particularly to the Council – and so has an ongoing investment in it and in the outcome of the contested and chequered course of its reception.

The Council's ecumenical impact

Only the Protestant Reformation, 400 years before – when some fundamental tenets of Roman Catholic teaching were challenged by the Reformers, papal authority was repudiated and the Western Church broke into two parts – can compare with Vatican II in its impact on the RCC. The churches that emerged from the Reformation, or were shaped by it (Lutheran, Reformed, Anglican, Anabaptist), or arose subsequently (Baptist, Methodist, Pentecostal), have an existential interest in the reception of Vatican II and in the varying fortunes of that reception. To speak of reception is to engage with the dynamics of tradition and of history and therefore of process, change and development.[8] To navigate this realm, we need skills in historical interpretation and historical theology – the ability to begin (though not to end) an enquiry by locating everything in its historical context.

It is not feasible for me to describe how the Council has affected the Orthodox Churches, on the one hand, or the Lutheran, Reformed, Baptist, Methodist and Pentecostal churches, on the other. The intensity, duration, scope and productivity of the theological dialogue between these world communions and the RCC is testimony to the seriousness and hope with which all parties have approached the challenge of rapprochement and reconciliation since Vatican II. Nevertheless, I will briefly take Karl Barth as a representative of the non-Roman Catholic traditions (excluding the Orthodox, who would not be happy to be represented by Barth). Although Barth, who died in 1968, was not well enough to attend the Council, he journeyed to Rome shortly after it had ended, meeting Pope Paul VI and various conciliar theologians. Asked whether the Council represented a 'reformation' of the RCC, Barth replied that such a description would be going too far, though he did concede that it was a 'late flare up' of Reformation issues. If Barth were – *per impossibile* – still alive to be asked about the existence of reformation in the RCC today, the church of Pope Francis, I think his answer to the question would be an unqualified affirmative – though he (and we) might need to add that the outcome is not yet secure.[9]

There were eight observers – so a major presence – from the Anglican Communion at Vatican II.[10] The Council has also had an enormous impact on Anglicanism, especially on the Anglican understanding of the church, its liturgy, ministry, episcopal collegiality, social thought and approach to Christian

8 Points emphasized in Faggioli, *A Council for the Global Church*.

9 Barth, Karl, 1968, *Ad Limina Apostolorum: An Appraisal of Vatican II*, Richmond, VA; Norwood, Donald, 2015, *Reforming Rome: Karl Barth and Vatican II*, Grand Rapids, MI: Eerdmans.

10 Pawley, Bernard C. (ed.), 1967, *The Second Vatican Council: Studies by Eight Anglican Observers*, Oxford: Oxford University Press.

unity. By opening up the RCC to ecumenical dialogue it made the work of the Anglican–Roman Catholic International Commission (ARCIC) possible. With a few bumps along the road, ARCIC has achieved significant convergence in several areas that were previously believed to keep our two traditions apart doctrinally, notably eucharistic theology, ministry and ordination, justification, ecclesiology and authority. It is currently in the second phase of the third Commission (3/ii). In the spirit of ARCIC, Anglicans and Roman Catholics have come together locally in many practical ways and the two episcopates have held conversations in various parts of the world under the aegis of a parallel but more recent body, the International Anglican–Roman Catholic Commission for Unity and Mission (IARCCUM). Therefore a discussion, as in the present chapter of a work on reconciliation, about the legacy and significance of Vatican II – which may appear at first sight to be a purely internal issue for Roman Catholics – is actually vitally important to all Christians, not least to Anglicans such as myself.

A contested Council

Vatican II is, as Catherine Clifford puts it, 'one of the most extensively documented conciliar events in the history of the church' and 'the council texts themselves are more extensive than any other body of conciliar teaching in the history of Christianity'.[11] The massive archive of official and unofficial documentation, commentary and reminiscence, together with

11 Catherine Clifford, 'Appendix: Sources for the Study of Vatican II', in Richard R. Gaillardetz (ed.), 2020, *The Cambridge Companion to Vatican II*, Cambridge: Cambridge University Press, p. 339. An excellent introduction to the texts is Gaillardetz, Richard R. and Catherine E. Clifford (eds), 2012, *Keys to the Council: Unlocking the Teaching of Vatican II*, Collegeville, MN: Liturgical Press. A gem of an introduction for students, clergy and lay people is Sullivan, Maureen, 2002, *101 Questions and Answers on Vatican II*, New York/Mahwah, NJ: Paulist Press.

the substantial volume of official texts, is a recipe for ambiguity and consequent battles over interpretation. Every line of the Council's documents was fought over at the time and its reception has been a battleground for more than half a century. 'Progressive' Roman Catholic interpreters have tended to invoke the 'spirit' or 'mind' – that is, the underlying intention and tendency of the Council – rather than the letter of its teaching.[12] They emphasize the 'bringing up to date' (*aggiornamento*) aspect of Pope John XXIII's aspiration and agenda for his Council and attempt to push its trajectory further towards inclusive and democratic reforms. They tend to play up the *ressourcement* aspect of John XXIII's vision for the Council, the retrieval of Scripture and of patristic theology in order to resource the movement towards reform. 'Conservative' Roman Catholic interpreters, on the other hand, deplore any talk of a 'rupture' with tradition, specifically with the teaching of Vatican I (1869–70) which defined the (potentially) infallible teaching authority and immediate universal jurisdiction of the pope.[13]

These two conflicting lines of interpretation – progressive and conservative – are a very rough phenomenology of the continuing engagement of the RCC and its theologians with the Council. As Walter Kasper and others have pointed out, 'progressive' and 'conservative' statements are often simply juxtaposed in the conciliar texts, remaining unreconciled and so inevitably generating ambiguity.[14] We should not

12 See, for example, Rush, Ormond, 2004, *Still Interpreting Vatican II: Some Hermeneutical Principles*, New York/Mahwah, NJ: Paulist Press. See, concisely, Rush, 'Conciliar Hermeneutics', in Gaillardetz, *The Cambridge Companion to Vatican II*, ch. 6.

13 For a substantial account of reception in continuity with tradition, see Lamb, Matthew L. and Matthew Levering (eds), 2017, *The Reception of Vatican II*, New York: Oxford University Press.

14 Kasper, Walter, 1989, *Theology and Church*, trans. Margaret Kohl, London: SCM Press, pp. 166–76, at p. 170. See also Kasper, Walter, 2015, *The Catholic Church: Nature, Reality and Mission*, ed. R. David Nelson, trans. Thomas Hoebel, London and New York: Bloomsbury, pp. 10–15.

absolutize the polarity. Yves Congar, an interpreter *par excellence* of tradition, was a pioneering advocate of reform and ecumenical *rapprochement*, while a more conservative scholar such as Henri de Lubac is a major source of the eucharistic ecclesiology that has the potential for both reform and theological convergence. Pope Benedict XVI, as a young and rising *peritus* (theological adviser to the bishops) at the Council, on the side of reform and theological renewal, later became an arch-reactionary, emphasizing the continuity of the Council's teaching with the tradition of the church and deploring any talk of the Council as marking a watershed or 'rupture' with the past. The highly sophisticated theology of Karl Rahner, SJ, while ostensibly conservative and supportive of the established order and official dogma, had – and has – enormous subversive potential to radically change the shape of the RCC. The pigeon-holing of outstanding thinkers is seldom helpful.

A continuing Council

In 1959, Pope John XXIII astonished the world, including his own bishops and cardinals, when he announced that he would call an Ecumenical Council, the twenty-first according to the reckoning of the RCC, but the first for nearly a century. When the Council was convened, 2,400 bishops participated, together with about 500 theological advisers and (for the first time) about 50 observers from other Christian churches. Against all the odds, the outcome of the Council was to begin the gradual transformation of the RCC. As James Carroll has said of the participating bishops, 'They were old men (average age 60), temperamentally conservative, culturally detached ... they were schooled in anachronism in how they thought, spoke, dressed and lived – yet they presided at a climax of modernity ... Rigidly orthodox, they took instruction from innovators they had silenced.'[15] The Council trusted its theologians (*periti*)

15 Carroll, James, 'The Beginning of Change', in Tanner, Norman,

to instruct it (as well as to explain the Latin to those bishops who were struggling with it). Even more, it trusted the Holy Spirit to guide it. The Christian church today continues to look to the Holy Spirit to guide its continuing reception.[16]

On the one hand, we have to acknowledge the *singularity* of Vatican II. It was in several respects an unprecedented, unique event. Joseph A. Komonchak, John W. O'Malley, Richard Gaillardetz and Ormond Rush are among those interpreters who have typified Vatican II as an 'event' in history, a singularity, a watershed. It was different from all previous councils in its size and scope, its method of working, its mode of discourse and the fact that it addressed the challenges of modernity while standing on the cusp of postmodernity. On the other hand, we need to recognize the *universality* of Vatican II. Modern electronic communication and mass media not only gave the Council's impact an immediacy and a universality that no church council before it had enjoyed, it also constitutes Vatican II as a continuing council. The process of its reception has become more dynamic and more contested with every passing year; Vatican II continues, so to speak, in its ongoing reception history. The pastoral style and thematic coherence of the Council's teaching (in spite of inherent tensions) has aided its global dissemination and ongoing reception. Vatican II has become a theological and cultural watershed for the whole of world Christianity.

Sixty years since the inauguration of the Council in 1962, the commemorations are still in full swing. 'Commemorations'? The word 'contestations' would be more apt. The real significance of the Council, the correct interpretation of its teaching, and therefore its legacy for the RCC and for the whole Christian world, has been argued over ever since it happened and the argument is now more vociferous than ever. The dismissive

---

SJ (ed.), 2012, *Vatican II: The Essential Texts*, Pref. Edward P. Hahnenberg, Intros Benedict XVI and James Carroll, New York: Image Books, pp. 14–26.

16 As Ormond Rush emphasizes in *Still Interpreting Vatican II*, ch. 4 on 'reception pneumatology'.

comment of the eminent Roman Catholic theologian Charles Davis in 1978 that, 'The documents of the Second Vatican Council are already now chiefly of interest to the historian' and 'are of little or no use in tackling the present issues of theology and of even less help in the pressing questions of Catholic practice' looks singularly inept – and in fact incomprehensible from our present viewpoint.[17]

'Vatican II changed nothing'

One school of Catholic thought has emphasized the continuity of Vatican II with all that went before, especially Vatican I (1870–71) which solemnly defined the terms of papal infallibility and asserted the ordinary, universal and immediate jurisdiction of the pope over all churches. For these conservative popes, bishops, theologians and curial officials, Vatican II changed little: it simply applied traditional teaching to modern circumstances. It was not a revolution, hardly even a watershed. 'Business as usual' was and remains their motto. They refuse to allow the outworking of Vatican II to interfere with the business of running the RCC from the centre – in practice, by the Roman curia. The scholarly flagship of the conservative cause has been the journal *Communio*, founded in 1972 by Joseph Ratzinger, Hans Urs von Balthasar and Henri de Lubac.

An extremely robust and erudite presentation of the conservative position has been made by Serafino Lanzetta.[18] Clearly, Vatican II made some radical changes, he admits, but what is

17 Davis, Charles, 1980, *Theology and Political Society: The Hulsean Lectures in the University of Cambridge 1978*, Cambridge: Cambridge University Press, p. 1.

18 Lanzetta, Serafino M., 2016, *Vatican II: A Pastoral Council*, Leominster: Gracewing. Page references embedded in my main text. The translation from the Italian leaves much to be desired: the style is often inelegant, the sense is sometimes opaque and there is the occasional *faux pas*, as when 'duplicity' is used for 'duality', with reference to the relation of Scripture and Tradition (p. 66; cf. p. 94).

their status and authority? Are they the last word on the matter? He proposes some second thoughts (p. 361). Lanzetta's book mounts a powerful rearguard action. He regrets certain aspects of the Council and poses some challenges which, if successful, would serve to relativize its authority and put the ecumenical clock back. His approach is subtle, as well as learned. He wants to go behind the texts to the 'intention', the mind (*mens*) of the Council – which was, in his view, to remain in continuity with the tradition, especially as embodied in papal pronouncements and the decrees of earlier councils (pp. 33, 38).

Lanzetta's book is subtitled 'A Pastoral Council', but that is not meant as a compliment. For the author, its pastoral temper is the Achilles' heel of the Council. In the course of an extended, detailed excavation of how some key documents (on revelation, the Church and Mary) emerged, Lanzetta attempts to show that there was a bias to the pastoral, at the expense of the doctrinal, and that this seriously compromised the Council's teaching. Pastoral concerns 'dictated the agenda' (p. xlviii). The Council itself did not specify the respective authority of its documents, or reflect on the relation between the pastoral and the doctrinal aspects, or give any guidance about how its documents should be interpreted. For would-be interpreters to make the pastoral the key to interpreting the Council, he argues, would be to treat Vatican II as unique, as though it were the only council ever to have instructed the church. For this preponderance of the pastoral, as he sees it, Lanzetta blames the *periti* or experts, of whom there were more than 200 – including a galaxy of the greatest Roman Catholic theologians of the twentieth century. He dubs this 'a parallel Magisterium of the theologians' (p. 16). However, on the author's terms, it is hard to see how Pope John XXIII, who called the Council and set its direction and trajectory, can avoid censure – for the following reasons.

Pope John specifically designed the Council to be a 'pastoral' one. It would catch up with the modern world and its concerns (*aggiornamento*), drawing on the Scriptures and patristic theology (*ressourcement*). However, it would not be hidebound by tradition and would bypass scholasticism altogether. As Pope

John insisted in his opening address, *Gaudet Mater Ecclesia*, which he had written himself, the Council's teaching authority ('magisterium') would have a pastoral tone. He wanted the church to be reconciled to the modern world and to the separated communities.[19] That is what John XXIII wanted and that is how it turned out. Unlike many previous councils, Vatican II did not set out precise definitions of doctrine or pronounce anathemas on those who believed differently; it appended no canons to bring its teaching into effect (though revision of the Canon Law followed in 1983). It presented its teaching in a unique conciliar genre: engaging, persuasive, unthreatening, inviting its global audience into a friendly dialogue. The typical stance of the RCC towards the modern world for more than two centuries – one of confrontation – was replaced by overtures of reconciliation. The mode was basically narrative and expository, the style rising sometimes to a poetical level. The Council sought to ease the reception of its teaching by the engaging, persuasive and uplifting tone of its discourse. The price that the Council paid for its pastoral style was discursiveness, compromise and imprecision in the texts, so it has inadvertently offered many loopholes for contested interpretation ever since. Lanzetta wishes it had been more rigorous, as previous councils had been, defining doctrine precisely and condemning error uncompromisingly.

Vatican II addressed at large the 'modern world' and 'humanity', its society and culture, outside the church, at what it saw as a critical point in the history of human consciousness. But another part of its intended audience was the whole Christian world, the *oecumene* (οἰκουμένη) – in other words, the Christian traditions not in communion with the pope: namely, the Orthodox churches, the Anglican Communion

19 John XXIII's opening address, in Abbott, Walter M., SJ, 1966, *The Documents of Vatican II*, London and Dublin: Geoffrey Chapman, pp. 710–19. O'Malley, John, SJ, 'Vatican II Revisited as Reconciliation' and Theobald, Christoph, SJ, 'The Principle of Pastorality at Vatican II', both in Massimo Faggioli and Andrea Vicini, SJ (eds), 2015, *The Legacy of Vatican II*, Mahwah, NJ: Paulist Press, chs 1 and 2.

and the Protestant churches (the latter two groups being styled 'ecclesial communities'). Vatican II brought the RCC into the Ecumenical Movement, which it had previously condemned (formally in 1928), so that Roman Catholics had been excluded from participating in it. In Lanzetta's view, the Council – largely under the influence of the experts, though with Cardinal Augustin Bea, first President of the Secretariat (later Pontifical Council) for Promoting Christian Unity, also exerting pressure – bent over backwards to accommodate Protestants, so pulling its dogmatic punches. Lanzetta identifies a 'metaphysical deficit' (p. 129) in its teaching, claiming that pastoral concerns trumped doctrinal ones and that pragmatism, rather than theological principle, influenced what was said. Although the magisterium strictly consists of the college of bishops with the pope at their head, Lanzetta thinks that the authority of the bishops cannot be compared with that of the pope. So he marginalizes not only the experts, but also the bishops. Not surprisingly, he is also no friend of the conciliar tradition and is suspicious of the concept of representation, one of the pillars of the Conciliar Movement (p. 6).[20] Only the papacy is left. Naturally, Lanzetta admires the stance of Popes John Paul II and Benedict XVI (the book was written before Francis became pope), but he takes issue with Karl Rahner and Hans Küng. It is widely understood that, because of Protestant sensitivities, the Council was intentionally muted in what it said about the Blessed Virgin Mary (though it said more about her than any previous council). Lanzetta regrets this restraint and believes that the best thing that could still happen to the church would be a solemn papal definition of Mary as Mediatrix and Co-Redemptrix (pp. 452–3).

The conservative interpreters have looked to Popes John Paul II and Benedict XVI (the former Cardinal Ratzinger) to deter change and uphold continuity. In 1985 John Paul II convened an Extraordinary Assembly of the College of Bishops to

---

20 See Avis, Paul, 2006, *Beyond the Reformation? Authority, Primacy and Unity in the Conciliar Tradition*, London and New York: T&T Clark, and its bibliography.

take stock of the harvest of Vatican II. The official report of the Synod emphasized the continuity of the Council with all that had gone before. It insisted that the Council was 'a legitimate and valid expression and interpretation of the deposit of faith as it is found in Sacred Scripture and in the living tradition of the Church'. It condemned any attempt to play off the 'letter' against the 'spirit' of the Council. The report insisted, 'The Church is one and the same throughout all the councils.'[21] In other words, no change, but the *status quo ante*. In 2000 John Paul II warned, 'To read the Council as if it marked a break with the past, while in fact it placed itself in the line of the faith of all times, is decidedly unacceptable.'[22] Nevertheless, John Paul II spoke more warmly of Vatican II than did his successor, Benedict XVI, and notably embraced its affirmation of human rights and its openness to other world faiths. In his 1995 encyclical *Ut Unum Sint* ('That they may be one') John Paul II took up the Council's cordial approach to other Christian traditions and pushed it even further by inviting dialogue with non-Roman Catholic traditions on the meaning of papal primacy.[23]

Between 1988 and 2001, a five-volume *History of Vatican II* was produced under the editorship of Giuseppe Alberigo in Bologna.[24] By tracing the chequered career of the Council's

---

21 Quoted in Faggioli, Massimo, 2012, *Vatican II: The Battle for Meaning*, Mahwah, NJ: Paulist Press, pp. 12–13.

22 Quoted by O'Malley, John W., 'Vatican II: Did Anything Happen?', in John W. O'Malley et al., 2007, *Vatican II: Did Anything Happen?*, ed. David G. Schultover, New York and London: Bloomsbury, pp. 52–91 at p. 54.

23 John Paul II, *Ut Unum Sint*, www.vatican.va/content/john-paul-ii/en/encyclicals/documents/hf_jp-ii_enc_25051995_ut-unum-sint.html (accessed 19.05.2021).

24 Alberigo, Giuseppe, *History of Vatican II*, ET ed. Joseph Komonchak, 1995–2006, 5 vols, Maryknoll, NY: Orbis; Leuven: Peeters. The standard, authoritative translation is Tanner, Norman, SJ (ed.), 1990, *Decrees of the Ecumenical Councils*, 2 vols, London: Sheed and Ward; Washington, DC: Georgetown University Press, vol. 2 (in Latin and English).

debates and documents it enabled scholars to see the Council in full historical and political perspective as never before. Rather like modern historical-critical scholarship does with the Bible, the *History of Vatican II* brought out the contingent, human element in the emergence of the texts, including the elements of compromise and ambiguity in the drafting. In other words, the historical analysis had an inevitable relativizing and distancing effect. For this reason, the *History* became an object of suspicion to the conservatives and was attacked for liberal bias.

Benedict XVI: belated resistance to Vatican II

Since the conclusion of the Council, there has been a steady stream of reactionary voices within the RCC who have completely rejected the Council, seeing it as the epitome of all the heresies of the ages and therefore without legitimacy or authority. To some of them, like the late Archbishop Marcel Lefebvre, that was a reason to take the nuclear option and go into open schism by ordaining his own bishops. It was an act that led to Lefebvre's excommunication by John Paul II in 1988 – albeit Benedict XVI sought to woo back Lefebvre's followers in the Society of St Pius X (SSPX). Even a non-expert observer of the RCC, such as myself, can see a line of continuity running between the 'no change' interpreters of the Council during the past half-century and the recent and current critics and open opponents of Pope Francis – though Francis's method is not to constantly invoke the authority of the Council, but quietly to push forward its agenda by word and action.

As we have already noted, the younger Joseph Ratzinger took a different view of the Council to the Cardinal Ratzinger who was Prefect of the Congregation for the Doctrine of the Faith and then pope. At the time of the Council, Ratzinger saw it as a radical event, a *novum*, a watershed. 'It was undoubtedly a rupture', he said in 1966 after the Council, which he had attended as a theological adviser (*peritus*), 'but a rupture within a fundamentally common intention'; and in

1985 Ratzinger anticipated a renewal of the Council's impact through discovering the true 'spirit' of the Council beneath the actual texts (appeal to 'the spirit' of the Council being virtually a trademark sign of progressive views).[25]

However, in an address to the Roman curia in 2005, Benedict XVI rejected what he called 'a hermeneutic [i.e. method of interpretation] of discontinuity and rupture' and advocated instead 'a hermeneutic of reform and renewal'. In words reminiscent of John Henry Newman's argument in his *Essay on the Development of Christian Doctrine*, Benedict claimed that, while the church grows and develops through time, it always remains essentially the same.[26] Benedict deplored appeals to 'the spirit of the Council' that aimed to set up a trajectory of interpretation that would trump the actual texts. He called for 'a dynamic of fidelity' and invoked what Pope John XXIII had said at the opening of the Council: traditional teaching would be brought into relation with modern thought and modern research methods, without becoming changed in the process. Benedict interpreted Pope John XXIII's subtle statement on that occasion ('The substance of the ancient doctrine of the deposit of faith is one thing, and the way in which it is presented is another') to mean that the church's meaning and message are always the same. Benedict went on to accept that the world-view of the seventeenth- and eighteenth-century European Enlightenment, which (he held, erroneously) was typically hostile to the idea of divine revelation, had given way to a new openness on the part of modern science.[27] This fresh context, he believed, also opened up the possibility of a new

25 Cited in Faggioli, *Vatican II: The Battle for Meaning*, p. 136.

26 Pope Benedict XVI, 'What Has Been the Result of the Council?', in Tanner (ed.), *Vatican II: The Essential Texts*, pp. 3–13. Newman, J. H., 1974, *An Essay on the Development of Christian Doctrine: The Edition of 1845*, ed. and intro. J. M. Cameron, Harmondsworth: Penguin.

27 On the Christian and fundamentally orthodox identity of much of the Enlightenment (including the *Aufklärung* in Germany), see Avis, Paul, 2022, *Theology and the Enlightenment*, London and New York: T&T Clark.

partnership between church and state and a new attitude to other religions, especially Judaism. Benedict concluded, 'It is precisely in this combination of continuity and discontinuity at different levels that the very nature of true reform consists.' Benedict's boldest gesture of affirmation was to describe the effect of the Council as a 'process of innovation in continuity'. He did not deny, in this 2005 address, that the Council had 'reviewed or even corrected certain historical decisions' of the church, but he insisted that, in so doing, it had 'actually preserved and deepened her inmost nature and true identity'.

As is widely acknowledged, Benedict XVI's stewardship of the papacy was marked to a significant extent by caution, suspicion and defensiveness. The modern world was seen as basically alien and threatening. Change was to be deplored, even (one suspects) feared. It is unfortunate that Pope Benedict will be remembered, as far as his official teaching is concerned, more for his counter-cultural stern condemnation of modern Western liberal culture and morals, than for his edifying, indeed inspiring, theological encyclicals. For Ratzinger-Benedict, since the student riots across Europe in 1968, the West had been going to moral and intellectual rack and ruin. But it is rather poignant to recall that, in John XXIII's opening address of 1962 to the Council, he had actually taken to task those gloomy souls for whom (as he put it) 'the modern world is nothing but betrayal and ruin', characterizing them as 'prophets of doom who are forever forecasting calamity'. In a similar vein, Pope Francis's apostolic exhortation *Evangelii gaudium* of November 2013 deplored the 'disillusioned pessimism' that 'stifles boldness and zeal' and adopts a 'sour' attitude to life. If Benedict XVI represented a recurrence of suspicion, alienation and fear, a return of the repressed, Francis embodies a more relaxed attitude to the world, something of the humanity, joy and optimism of John XXIII himself. Francis has been described, with good reason, as 'good Pope John' *redivivus*.

'Vatican II changed everything'

For other Roman Catholics, though, the Second Vatican Council was a revolution and changed everything. For them, it brought the RCC into the modern world. It threw off the insularity, defensiveness – even paranoia – that had characterized the RCC since the eighteenth century, the era of the Enlightenment and the French Revolution, the lowest ebb of the RCC's fortunes until the recent and current sexual abuse scandals. One of the Council's chief merits in their eyes was that it adopted a pastoral tone, not hectoring but inviting, not condemning but persuading – the first general council in history to do so since the Council of Jerusalem in Acts 15. It pronounced no anathemas. It opened the windows of the RCC to fresh hope and renewed energies. The progressives embraced its two watchwords – one Italian, one French – *aggiornamento* (coming up to date, modernizing) and *ressourcement* (drawing on the neglected riches of ancient tradition, the Scriptures and the writings of the early Fathers). The theological flagship of the progressive tendency in the interpretation of Vatican II is the journal *Concilium* which first appeared in 1965 and has been associated in its history with Hans Küng, Yves Congar, Karl Rahner and Edward Schillebeeckx.

In spite of what some conservative interpreters might wish, it is perfectly clear that Vatican II made some radical changes in Roman Catholic doctrine and church policy. Let me mention some of the most startling ones.[28]

1 Vatican II patently reversed the traditional Roman Catholic rejection of the principle of religious liberty, emphasizing in its place freedom of conscience in religious belief and practice. In 1832, Pope Gregory XVI had condemned freedom of religion and freedom of the press as 'absurd' and a 'menacing error' in the encyclical *Mirari Vos: On Liberal-*

28 In brief, Tanner, Norman, SJ, 'How Novel Was Vatican II?', *Ecclesiastical Law Journal* 15 (2013), pp. 175–82.

ism and Religious Indifferentism. Later in the same century, in the *Syllabus of Errors* (number 80) that was attached to the encyclical *Quanta cura* (1864), Pius IX memorably denounced the idea that 'the Roman Pontiff can and should reconcile himself to and agree with progress, liberalism, and modern civilization'. The main instigator of this *volte face* at Vatican II and champion of the principle of religious freedom, the American Jesuit John Courtney Murray, insisted that the change of heart was a development of doctrine, sifting what was 'timeless' in the church's teaching from what was 'historically conditioned'. But it looked for all the world like a reversal, a contradiction, and was seen as such by Courtney Murray's opponents in the Roman Catholic hierarchy.[29]

2 Vatican II also modified the RCC's traditional stance on the relationship between church and state, namely that while the state had its proper, God-appointed sphere, it should ultimately be subordinate to the church which would provide it with its framework of beliefs and its moral compass. Drawing on the American democratic, pluralistic experience, the Council accepted the integrity of the state in its own sphere and the principle of pluralist democracy. This was a radical change; Leo XIII had condemned 'Americanism' in 1889.

3 In *Nostre aetate: Declaration on the Relation of the Church with Non-Christian Religions* (1965), the Council recognized aspects of divine revelation in other major religions and accepted the possibility that those who duly followed the light that they had received thereby would be saved. This actually contradicted the age-old mantra *Nulla salus extra ecclesiam* ('No salvation outside the church').

---

29 Hudock, Barry, 2015, *Struggle, Condemnation, Vindication: John Courtney Murray's Journey toward Vatican II*, Collegeville, MN: Liturgical Press, especially pp. 169–72. Guarino, *The Disputed Teachings of Vatican II*, takes religious liberty as the major touchstone of his enquiry.

4 In *Unitatis redintegratio*, the *Decree on Ecumenism*, the Council committed the RCC to the cause of Christian unity and to the ecumenical movement, which had previously been 'off limits' to Roman Catholics, so that they had not been permitted to participate in its gatherings, except occasionally as observers. Vatican II spoke in a friendly way of non-Roman Catholic Christians, acknowledging that they belonged to the body of Christ through baptism, and recognizing the elements of truth and grace in their churches.
5 The Council revitalized liturgical worship – the Constitution *Sacrosanctum concilium* was the first of its documents to be promulgated – affirming that all the faithful actively participate in, and indeed celebrate corporately, the liturgy – that is, especially the Eucharist, which should be celebrated in the vernacular.
6 It also set the vernacular Scriptures centre stage in worship and teaching and encouraged the faithful to study the Bible.

That list is more than sufficient to show that something radically new and decisively different took place in the Second Vatican Council.[30] It seems clear that, within an overall framework of continuity, there were indeed aspects of the teaching of the Council that should be regarded as revolutionary in comparison with traditional teaching. Guarino grasps the nettle, accepting that such discontinuities do indeed amount to 'reversals' of received teaching. But he argues that they are reversals not of 'doctrinal landmarks', as promulgated by the 'extraordinary magisterium', the pope and the other bishops, but of the teaching of the 'ordinary magisterium' which tends to be more time- and culture-bound than the former.[31] That clever apologia for contradictions of the traditional teaching of the RCC is intended to persuade doubtful Roman Catholics

---

30 O'Malley, John W., 2008, *What Happened at Vatican II*, Cambridge, MA: The Belknap Press of Harvard University Press, pp. 295–311, summarizes what the Council achieved and how it made a difference in both content and tone.

31 Guarino, *The Disputed Teachings of Vatican II*.

to accept the Council by claiming that it was not as radical as it seems.

Richard Gaillardetz as exponent of Vatican II

The American lay Roman Catholic ecclesiologist Richard Gaillardetz has particularly stressed that the Second Vatican Council intended to effect change.[32] He believes that Vatican II intended a thorough reform of the theology, structures and practice of the RCC, that the Council's intention was largely stifled under the papacies of John Paul II and Benedict XVI (indeed, that some actual reversal took place). But Gaillardetz is convinced that Pope Francis is wholeheartedly committed to implementing the Council's programme, noting that Francis has announced that intention and has begun, against concerted opposition, to put it into practice. Gaillardetz holds that, while Vatican II did not achieve a unified ecclesiology and, unlike earlier councils, was not concerned with the canonical implementation of its teaching, its impulse for reform is unchallengeable. Gaillardetz's aim is to attempt a 'synthetic theological interpretation' (p. xi) of the Council, 'in support of a robust program of ecclesial reform and renewal', which amounts to 'nothing less than an ecclesial conversion as regards the church's self-understanding, policies, structure, and conduct' (p. 137). The reform agenda was set by the Council; Pope Francis is the great reformer; and Gaillardetz is one of his prime interpreters.

The target of conciliar reform, so Gaillardetz believes, was (and is) the 'hierocratic ecclesiology' (Yves Congar's phrase) that began to be constructed in the late eleventh century under Pope Gregory VII (Hildebrand) and reached its peak of development in the immediately pre-conciliar period under Popes Pius X, XI and XII. Borrowing the metaphor of Vatican II as an unfinished building from Hermann Pottmeyer, Gaillardetz

32 Gaillardetz, *Unfinished Council*. Page references in my main text.

identifies five pillars of the hierocratic church, the edifice that Vatican II intended to deconstruct: 1) Divine revelation is imparted in propositional form rather than through personal communication. It manifests itself as the imparting of information rather than as a drawing into a relationship of communion. 2) Its ecclesiology is of a centralized church under a sovereign papacy, conceived and operated as a juridical structure, rather than as a community with sacramental bonds of communion. 3) The ordained ministry takes the form of a sacral priesthood, elevated above and standing apart from the laity in both holiness and wisdom. 4) Its theology of grace is quasi-mechanical, seeing grace as poured through the sacraments as its channels and placed at the disposal, so to speak, of the sacral priesthood. 5) It is marked by a defensive, confrontational attitude to the world and modern culture; it evinces a defensive, siege mentality.

Gaillardetz juxtaposes this oppressive ideology with what he believes to be the 'ecclesial vision' of Vatican II and does so in seven points: 1) A theology of revelation that is personalist, kerygmatic and trinitarian, distinguishing as John XXIII famously did (echoed by the Council itself), between the original deposit of faith and the way that it is presented at various junctures in history and culture. 2) A continual dialogical engagement of persons and ideas within the community of the church, with other churches and religions, and with the world. 3) The priority of baptism – the great equalizer – as the basis of the 'baptismal priesthood' of all Christians. 4) A working theology of grace that is consistently pneumatological, not mechanical, recognizing the presence and power of the Holy Spirit at every step. 5) The reality of episcopal collegiality, not merely in theory, but with structures, procedures and practices to implement it. 6) The identity of the church as 'missionary by its very nature' (as the Council put it), comprising a 'community of missionary disciples' (as Pope Francis presents it in *Evangelii gaudium*); and with that – in place of triumphalism and 'ecclesial arrogance' – 7) the pilgrim character, not only of the individual Christian, but of the whole body.

Gaillardetz's vision for the church invokes a 'virtue ecclesiology', stressing institutional humility as well as a proper confidence in the gifts of God (what Aquinas calls divine 'magnanimity'). The ethos of such a church will be one of 'non-competitive relationships' between, for example, the pope and the bishops, the clergy and the laity. To effect this transformation, the church's centre of gravity must move, he believes, from the centre to the periphery, to embrace the marginalized, including theologians and religious (both groups having been harassed under previous pontificates), as well as the poor and the oppressed. In his signature theme of 'mercy', Pope Francis has picked up what John XXIII said in his inaugural address to the Council about the church showing the face of mercy to the world, as well as to its own faithful: 'Nowadays however, the Spouse of Christ prefers to make use of the medicine of mercy rather than that of severity.'[33] Ecclesial subsidiarity, approved by the Council with regard to liturgical reform, but condemned by some leading prelates at the Extraordinary Synod of Bishops in 1985, must come into its own. At the same time, Gaillardetz is looking for a 'centrifugal church', marked by 'missionary discipleship'. In place of the 'confrontational rhetoric' of John Paul II and Benedict XVI, with their unbalanced denunciations of what they supposed to be a Western culture of self-indulgence and the 'dictatorship of relativism', Gaillardetz wants to see a positive engagement with modern culture.

Vatican II galvanized the RCC and made non-Roman Catholics look at that church with fresh eyes; some non-Roman Catholic Christians were bowled over and converted. For progressive Roman Catholics, Vatican II changed a great deal. It was about reform and renewal – themes on which the Council had spoken in uncanny echoes of the Reformers of the sixteenth century. As Gaillardetz insists, its reforming intention is unchallengeable. And as Pope Benedict rightly said, true

33 See also Faggioli, Massimo, 2014, *John XXIII: The Medicine of Mercy*, Collegeville, MN: Liturgical Press.

reform involves both continuity and discontinuity; but where to put the emphasis between the two remains hotly debated. John O'Malley points out that to insist exclusively on continuity 'is to blind oneself to the discontinuities, which is to blind oneself to change of any kind. And if there is no change, nothing happened.'[34] To deny change is to negate history, and if we do that we let tradition go. John Henry Newman worked out a concept of development, the development of church doctrine, no less – an idea that, though it was vehemently resisted by the RCC at the time, allowed Newman to convert to Roman Catholicism in 1845. It would be perverse to deny that development in the church takes place – that would be to shut our eyes to all of history. The crucial challenge is to find the criteria, or 'tests' (as Newman called them in the first edition of his *Essay on the Development of Christian Doctrine*), of authentic development, the kind of dynamic development that enables the church to respond to the demands of mission while remaining faithful to the gospel.

The Australian theologian and social scientist Neil Ormerod has taken a more radical approach, questioning whether the tussle over continuity versus discontinuity is even coherent in the way that it has been applied to the large-scale social and cultural changes that Vatican II reflected and responded to. Deploying Newman's *Essay on Development* and the writings of Alastair MacIntyre and Bernard Lonergan, Ormerod proposes that the real question to be put to Vatican II is not whether continuity or discontinuity preponderated in its outcomes, but whether the undeniable changes that it made are authentic or inauthentic. In answering that question, ethical criteria come into play, which are more relevant than ever in this age of clerical sexual abuse and its cover-up by those who held the responsibility for the holiness of the church.[35]

---

34 O'Malley, 'Vatican II: Did Anything Happen?', p. 56.

35 Ormerod, Neil, 2014, *Re-Visioning the Church: An Experiment in Systematic-Historical Theology*, Minneapolis, MN: Fortress Press: 'Postscript: Vatican II, Toward an Ontology of Meaning'.

For the 'progressive' interpreters of Vatican II, the Council remains in the category of 'unfinished business'. In some key areas, its agenda has not been followed through; its implementation has been aborted, most glaringly with regard to episcopal collegiality and the responsibilities of the laity. Its internal tensions and (even) contradictions have not been resolved.[36] Hermann Pottmeyer describes Vatican II as 'a building site'. He suggests that the Council has already built four great supporting columns for a renewed church and a renewed ecclesiology: 1) the idea of the church as 'the people of God'; 2) the idea of the church as the sacrament of the kingdom of God in the world; 3) the doctrine of the collegiality of the episcopate; and 4) the openness to dialogue with separated Christian traditions. But, Pottmeyer argues, the great dome that should rest on the four pillars has never been built. The pillars still await the dome that would draw them into a unity.[37] At the present time the Christian world waits in prayerful expectation to see how far Pope Francis will be able to complete the unfinished business of Vatican II. Without continually banging the Vatican II drum in public, Francis is deeply committed to its teaching and tone. Without unduly polarizing Francis and his post-conciliar papal predecessors, Gaillardetz is convinced that Francis is unique in his 'comprehensive and integrated retrieval of not just one teaching or another but of the council's deeper reformist impulse'.[38] We may add that, if Francis is given time, by God and humankind, to carry through his mission and to implement in a deep structural way the vision for the church that he has enunciated both in a number of magisterial statements, beginning with *Evangelii gaudium* and in many informal homilies and impromptu statements, the RCC as an institution will be eventually transformed. Francis and his interpreter Richard Gaillardetz believe that this will come about through 'pastoral conversion', as the institution

36 Lakeland, Paul, 2015, *A Council That Will Never End:* Lumen Gentium *and the Church Today*, Collegeville, MN: Liturgical Press.

37 Cited in Faggioli, *Vatican II: The Battle for Meaning*, p. 124.

38 Gaillardetz, *Unfinished Council*, p. 135.

is led by a radical commitment to mission, responding to the needs of the world: 'pastoral ministry in a missionary style' (*Evangelii gaudium* 35).

To bring together Vatican II and the pontificate of Francis, I will round off this section with Gerald O'Collins's list of seven positive themes that are common to the Council and to Pope Francis's teaching and practice – notice the order! 1) Confessing one's sinfulness and looking for continual conversion. 2) The centrality of Christ in the church's message. 3) The collegiality of bishops in communion with the pope. 4) The integrity and strategic importance of local churches (dioceses). 5) Pastoral sensitivity, especially towards those excluded from communion by their lifestyle. 6) Positive approaches to the Jews, other Christians and other religions. 7) The divine beauty revealed in Christ, the saints and the church.[39] There could be no better note than the divine beauty on which to conclude with a word about the personal significance of Vatican II for me.

Concluding reflection

The Council's two principles of action – *aggiornamento* and *ressourcement* – have the heart of the matter in them and remain valid. They are not in conflict, as though we could have 'today' without 'yesterday' or vice versa, but are complementary and mutually enriching. Both concepts – which are actually practices – require us to bring a historical consciousness to bear and they both point to the dynamic of tradition and the reality of change.[40] Coming up to date (*aggiornamento*) demands a sense of historical development, so that we know how we reached this point in time and what is different about 'today'. Recovering the treasures of the past (*ressourcement*) also requires a sense of historical perspective. For we are not talking about

39 O'Collins, Gerald, SJ, 'Towards a Truly Global Church', *The Tablet*, 15 March 2014, pp. 6–7.

40 See Rush, Ormond, 2019, *The Vision of Vatican II: Its Fundamental Principles*, Collegeville, MN: Liturgical Press, pp. 17–21.

'timeless truths', but about time-specific and culture-specific texts and practices, whether those of Scripture or of the early church. To know experientially that they are of the past and not of the eternal present (and therefore timeless) we need to feel a sense of critical distance from them and their difference from our present situation.[41] It is by means of this twofold, converging, hermeneutic that we seek to bring the teaching and practice of any historical institution up to date and to reform it precisely by going back to our roots and drawing on the resources of authoritative texts from the past. We recur to our origins and aim to recapture the initial impetus – the 'big bang' – that generated the institution and its historical trajectory in the first place. In the case of the church this initial impulse is both revelatory and redemptive, centred on the Paschal Mystery of the death, resurrection and glorification of Jesus Christ and the sending of the Holy Spirit. It is the mystery that is commemorated, celebrated and communicated in the church, especially in the celebration of the sacraments and, above all, the Eucharist.[42]

In conclusion, I take as a foil to my argument Christopher L. Lamb's and Matthew Levering's *Vatican II: Renewal Within Tradition*, which is designed as a riposte to the O'Malley camp and consists of expositions of the Council documents from the standpoint of the hermeneutic of continuity.[43] It adopts the Ratzinger/Benedict XVI line as the last word on the interpretation of Vatican II (Benedict was still pope when the book was written and published). It brands the 'progressive' view as 'ideological' (as though its own stance were ideologically

41 See Flynn, Gabriel, and Paul Murray (eds), 2011, *Ressourcement: A Movement for Renewal in Twentieth-Century Catholic Theology*, Oxford: Oxford University Press; Boersma, Hans, 2009, *Nouvelle Théologie and Sacramental Ontology: A Return to Mystery*, New York: Oxford University Press.

42 See further, Avis, Paul, 2020, *Jesus and the Church: The Foundation of the Church in the New Testament and Modern Theology*, London and New York: T&T Clark.

43 Lamb, Christopher L. and Matthew Levering (eds), 2008, *Vatican II: Renewal Within Tradition*, Oxford: Oxford University Press.

neutral) and accuses it of being in thrall to a crude media tactic of polarizing 'conservative' and 'liberal' interpretations of the Council. It is as though nothing in the church needs to change. Any suggestion that reform might be needed is conspicuous by its absence from the editors' own contributions. In an eloquent conclusion, Matthew Lamb quotes Paul Claudel's affirmation: 'everything of the good, the great and the beautiful from one end of the earth to the other' rightly belongs to the RCC (p. 442). Of course, there is much that is good, great and beautiful in that church, but evidently it also harbours much that is seriously out of order – in fact, despicable and sometimes criminal – though it is not of course the only church to which that judgement applies. Lamb's and Levering's romantic, complacent and rose-tinted vision of an unchanging church – and one that has no need to change – has been made to look not only woefully inadequate, but morally sick, by the sexual abuse scandals, exacerbated by the failures of the hierarchy in whom the traditionalists claim to put their trust. We need to accept that all the major churches have failed in this area and all are tainted to various degrees. All need to demonstrate penitence, to institute structural reforms and to make practical amends.

As an Anglican looking at Vatican II with admiration and gratitude and whose theology and spirituality has been profoundly shaped by its teaching, I am not the slightest bit interested in playing politics with the legacy of the Council or in taking sides in the battle of conservative versus progressive interpretations. It is not my argument or my business. But it is distressing to witness a great church so torn apart by conflicting reactions to this great council and needing to be reconciled to itself. But of one thing I am sure: any church – and I do mean *any* church – that, in the face of criticism, invests heavily in defensive tactics and in protecting its reputation and that of its senior representatives and is not manifestly committed to reforming itself on the basis of self-scrutiny before the word of God, and thus shrinks from expressing collective penitence for its failures – such a church has lost its way and missed its vocation, whether it be the Roman Catholic Church, the Church of England or any other. Humility, self-scrutiny and transparency are the prerequisites for a church becoming reconciled to the observing world, to its better self and to God. The church's leaders and pastors, whether the Pope or Archbishop of Canterbury, inevitably model the defining stance of their churches at a given time; and many Christians take their cue almost uncritically in these matters from them. What we look for in our senior pastors first of all and above all – before reckoning up their skills, learning and experience – are the virtues of humility, prayerfulness, self-examination and ethical transparency. Being a public role model for the faithful is not the least of the responsibilities that church leaders assume. And that fact raises far-reaching issues of actual leadership styles and questions regarding the theological and social-science understandings of power, authority and leadership that lie behind the practice. But that is another story.

4

Polity and Polemics

The one-time Bishop of Durham, the redoubtable Herbert Hensley Henson (d. 1947), who was notorious for his waspish put-downs, confided to his journal that he found the polity of the Anglican Communion 'a subject of portentous dullness', especially when it was being discussed by Anglican bishops.[1] Contrary to Henson's sardonic prejudice, I want in this chapter to affirm with enthusiasm the vital importance of ecclesiastical polity for any major tradition of the Christian church. Ecclesiastical polity, far from being a dull subject, is a highly contested field of debate and a site where the unreconciled state of the Christian church worldwide becomes especially apparent. I am conscious that, in using the phrase 'ecclesiastical polity', I am echoing the title of Richard Hooker's foundational work of Anglican ecclesiology – *Of the Lawes of Ecclesiasticall Politie*. In the spirit of Hooker, a contemporary of William Shakespeare and Francis Bacon, but who died before either of them, in 1600, I understand the study of the church's polity as a form of applied ecclesiology. Our understanding of the church, its nature and mission, is translated concretely into 'political' structures of practice, organization, oversight, authority and governance – that is to say, polity. And in all traditions it is underpinned and guaranteed by the law of the church concerned. I locate ecclesiastical polity, therefore, in the conceptual space between ecclesiology and canon law. I see polity, therefore, as a theological discipline with both theoret-

1 Henson, Herbert Hensley, 1943, *Retrospect of an Unimportant Life* [3 vols], *Volume 2, 1920–1939*, London: Oxford University Press, p. 277. Henson was commenting on the Lambeth Conference 1930.

ical and practical (including juridical) aspects, for which the term *praxis* is appropriate: the *praxis* of polity.

In this chapter, I consider ecclesiastical polity in a mainly methodological and programmatic way, though I also aim to make some connections with the received tradition of Anglican ecclesiology and the polity of the Anglican Communion and to set this discussion in an ecumenical context.[2] I point out that the Anglican Communion, though not constituted as a single worldwide church, nevertheless has a lightly structured ecclesiastical polity of its own, mainly embodied in the Instruments of Communion. I warn against short-term, pragmatic tinkering with church structures, while recognizing the need for structural reform from time to time to bring the outward shape of the church into closer conformity to the nature and mission of the church of Christ as that is understood and received within a particular Christian tradition. In discussing Richard Hooker's contention that the church is a political society, as well as a mystical body, I point out that the societal character of Anglican churches is distinguished from the traditional Roman Catholic conception of the church as a *societas perfecta*, a self-contained, complete and autonomous society. In the tradition of Hooker, I affirm the role of political philosophy in the articulation of ecclesiastical polity, precisely as a particular outworking of the theological relationship between nature and grace. The resulting method points to an interdisciplinary project in which ecclesiology, polity and church law, informed by the insights of political philosophy, serve and enhance the graced life of the church in its worship, service and mission, while underpinning its unity. Above all, we should remind ourselves, before embarking on the substantive discussion, that ecclesiastical polity is not an end in itself. Polity is entirely subservient to the purpose, goal and end of the church, which is to glorify God and enjoy God for ever. Polity finds its rationale solely in facilitating the participation of the Christian

2 An earlier, shorter, version of this chapter appeared, with the title 'Polity and Polemics: The Function of Ecclesiastical Polity in Theology and Practice', in *Ecclesiastical Law Journal* 18.1 (2016), pp. 2–13.

community in the blessed life, love and power of the eternal Trinity-in-Unity.

Polemical polity

Ecclesiastical polity has long been a flashpoint of controversial theology, to the extent that the terms 'polity' and 'polemics' seem to belong together and to deserve each other. The word 'polemical' derives from the Greek *polemikos*, hostile, and stems from the word for war, *polemos*. Rival claims for different political models of church government – particularly papalism, episcopalianism, presbyterianism and congregationalism – have been the stuff of polemical theology through many centuries. It is thanks to several factors, which I will indicate very briefly, that the discourse of ecclesiastical polity has softened in recent years: a) The influence of the ecumenical movement, bringing the churches into dialogue, deeper fellowship, and in some cases concrete cooperation, has softened debate on polity, which is now generally more courteous and respectful, more tolerant of differences, and more open to mutual understanding. b) The decline of the churches in the Western world – numerically, financially, institutionally and in terms of their public voice and presence – has brought about a reordering of priorities. Bickering over forms of polity, as in the past, seems a waste of energy and resources when the survival of an effective Christian presence is felt to be in doubt. Mission and growth are at the top of the agenda for most churches. c) Modern biblical and historical research has pulled the rug from under any exclusive claims for the divine institution of any particular form of church polity. I will expand this point at slightly greater length.

A key historical question for ecclesiology, and with it church polity, in any Christian tradition, is to ask whether Jesus of Nazareth founded the church, with its ministerial and sacramental structure, as an intentional act, as is still claimed in the official theology of certain churches, whether Roman Catholic or Presbyterian, for example. In these instances, there is an attempt to validate the hierarchical structure of the institutional church by an appeal to a historical act of Jesus in his earthly ministry. However, biblical and patristic scholarship during the past two centuries has called this purportedly historical claim seriously into question on several grounds which I will briefly summarize:

1 It is clear from the Gospels that Jesus' mission was almost entirely to 'the lost sheep of the house of Israel' (Matt. 10.6; 15.24), with a call to repent and to trust in the good news of the reign of God that was at hand in his person and ministry (Mark 1.14–15). In other words, his message was intended for the existing Jewish church. This was certainly a political theocracy but also – as such – a church. It was the assembly that understood itself to have been called together by God (Yahweh) for true worship; Israel is often referred to as the *ekklesia* in the LXX. Jesus did not need to found a new church – Jesus *could* not found a church – because the church of God already existed. Jesus and the apostles belonged to it and ministered within it. The alternative to accepting this picture of Jesus-already-within-the-church is to posit that a (putative) church founded by Christ was intended by him to replace and supersede the Jewish church (a position known as supersessionism) and to hold as a concomitant that God had at that point rejected God's covenant people – a view that is generally repudiated by the churches and that St Paul explicitly condemns in Romans 11.1.
2 The New Testament and other early Christian documents show little evidence of any settled or common institutional, political or ministerial structure of the community. Paul's early letters reflect a basically charismatic situation in which individuals were guided by the Holy Spirit to exercise Spirit-given gifts (1 Cor. 12 and 14; Rom. 12.3–8). Even in the Pastoral Epistles, where Paul (or 'Paul') is making provision for orderly oversight and management of the community, the structures are embryonic and pragmatic,

hardly the *Urkatholizismus* that some have detected in these letters.

3 Alongside the lack of evidence of any fixed institutional structure for the early Christian communities, we have to set the fact of the wide diversity of belief, creed, canon, worship, organization and oversight across the churches of the Roman Empire, a diversity that lasted for several centuries. There was no single template of faith and order. The evidence of the first-century church tells strongly against the claim that Jesus instituted a formal pattern – a polity – for his followers to adhere to.

4 In many places the New Testament writings testify to an imminent expectation of the *parousia* on the part of the apostles and their communities, an expectation that seems to have been shared even by Jesus himself. These texts speak of the manifestation of the kingdom, the return of the Son of Man, the judgement, the resurrection. The impending eschatological *denouement* is abundantly evident on the surface of the text, in the Gospels, the Epistles, the Acts of the Apostles and the Apocalypse, for all who read with their eyes open. The foreshortened timetable of New Testament eschatology also seems to rule out a specific founding of the church, in an institutional sense and set up for the long haul, by Jesus Christ.

However, the conclusion that Jesus of Nazareth did not found or institute a church in any political form that was intended to be permanent does not mean that he did not have intentions for his band of disciples in the limited time that was expected to be available to them before the advent of the *parousia*. The eschatological horizon of the thought-world of that time required that there should be an eschatological community of the last days. This community was the remnant, foretold by the Hebrew prophets, that would remain faithful to the reign of God and would in the end be vindicated by God. But the conclusion that Jesus did not found or institute a church in any enduring form does have several critical implications; the main one for our purposes being that it is no longer plausible to claim direct dominical institution or any other exclusive biblical warrant for any particular ecclesiastical polity or form of ministry or structure of authority. Such claims have never been purely historical; they have always been intended to serve certain power functions and to protect the privileges of a few; they have always been tainted by ideology. Of course, arguments can be put forward for particular forms of ministry and authority on other grounds, especially tradition, ecumenical usefulness, or pastoral effectiveness. But such claims cannot be absolutized. They cannot be made to serve the unchurching by one Christian body of other Christian bodies that has disfigured Christian history. All such anathemas are baseless.[3]

Whatever impact ecumenical rapprochement and church decline have made on how we view various models of ecclesiastical polity, the bottom line remains that no transcendent authority is available to support any exclusive claim with regard to polity. It is highly paradoxical, therefore, that it is the areas of authority, oversight and governance that continue to prove the most difficult – and sometimes intractable – in the agenda of ecumenical dialogue and that reconciliation on these issues seems as far off as ever.[4] While, as Norman Doe has shown extensively, there are broad swathes of common principles that can be identified by a comparative study of the bodies of law of the various churches, it remains the case that it is the structurally embedded polities of the churches, underpinned by their respective church laws, that continue to hold them unhappily apart in certain crucial respects. This lamentable state of affairs derives from the fact that polity expresses the concrete way that authority is understood and exercised in the respective churches. It is polity that channels

3 See further on this question, Avis, Paul, 2020, *Jesus and the Church: The Foundation of the Church in the New Testament and Modern Theology*, London and New York: T&T Clark.

4 Kasper, Cardinal Walter, 2009, *Harvesting the Fruits: Basic Aspects of Christian Faith in Ecumenical Dialogue*, London and New York: Continuum.

the exercise of authority, providing the conduits through which it is exercised.[5]

Similarly, within the Anglican Communion, there is a hugely impressive body of common principles pertaining to ecclesiology and polity that are largely shared by the member churches, being inscribed in the bodies of canon law of those churches.[6] But somehow all that common ground does not prevent energetic, and sometimes bitter and divisive, debate within the Anglican Communion with regard to the exercise of authority within the framework of its polity – precisely because the theological basis of authority, in Scripture, tradition and reason, is understood differently. Ecclesiastical polity has not caught up with biblical scholarship and continues to be a theological battleground, though today it is mainly a war of words, not swords.

At the present time there seems to be an openness within the major or mainstream Christian churches to revisit questions of polity afresh – especially the need for the reform and renewal of polity that is widely recognized by Roman Catholics. This applies particularly with regard to the centralization of authority structures in that church and the question of how episcopal collegiality, affirmed in principle by the Second Vatican Council, can be made more real in practice, especially with regard to the discretion given to local bishops' conferences and the weight accorded to meetings of the Synod of Bishops (recently, the Synod on the Family, 2015, and the Amazon Synod, 2019). At the same time the Anglican Communion has been engaged in reflection, through the Inter-Anglican Standing Commission

---

5 Doe, Norman, 2013, *Christian Law: Contemporary Principles*, Cambridge: Cambridge University Press; see also Doe, Norman, 'The Ecumenical Value of Comparative Church Law: Towards the Category of Christian Law', *Ecclesiastical Law Journal* 17.2 (2015), pp. 135–69; Koffeman, Leo, 'The Ecumenical Potential of Church Polity', *Ecclesiastical Law Journal* 17.2 (2015), pp. 182–93.

6 *The Principles of Canon Law Common to the Churches of the Anglican Communion*, 2008, London: Anglican Consultative Council, especially Principle 15 (p. 31), but also *passim*.

on Unity, Faith and Order, on the Instruments of Communion and how they can be made more representative and effective.[7] To come even closer to home, the Church of England is currently engaged in a comprehensive process of review, the 'Renewal and Reform' programme, that is presented as an attempt to simplify, reform and revitalize the structures and processes of governance and oversight.[8]

Ecclesiology, polity and church law

As a world communion of churches, the Anglican Communion has a certain ecclesial character and complexion, though one that is rather difficult to define. Although the Anglican Communion is not a global church, but a family of self-governing churches – and therefore is not properly referred to as 'the Anglican Church' – it does possess a common basic ecclesiology. Anglican churches share a basic theological understanding of the nature and mission of the church, which is derived from Scripture, patristic and medieval theology and from the theological insights and practical reforms of the Reformation era. This basic Anglican ecclesiology is inscribed in the 'historic formularies' of the Church of England, the substantive content of which is widely owned across the Communion: the *Book of Common Prayer*, 1662; the Thirty-nine Articles of Religion, 1571; and the Ordinal of 1550/1662. The shared inheritance of Anglican ecclesiology is inscribed especially in the various prayer books that stand in the lineage of the *Book of Common Prayer*, 1662, as that text has been received and adapted within

7 *Towards a Symphony of Instruments: A Historical and Theological Consideration of the Instruments of Communion of the Anglican Communion; Working Paper prepared by the Inter-Anglican Standing Commission on Unity, Faith and Order*, 2015, London: Anglican Consultative Council.

8 'Renewal and Reform', *The Church of England*, www.churchofengland.org/about/renewal-reform (accessed 11.05.2021).

the member churches of the Communion.[9] What the common Anglican ecclesiology contains in substance is not our main concern here.[10] My key point is that it is not enough for a church or a communion of churches to have, and to own, an ecclesiology (even one that is contested by some, continually debated and constantly evolving). In addition to an ecclesiology, a church or a communion of churches also needs an ecclesiastical polity – that is to say, a stable political order or structure that governs the distribution and uses of authority and facilitates its common tasks. But at this point we probably need to ask: What, more precisely, is ecclesiastical polity?

Polity defined

The realm of ecclesiastical polity embraces the political, pastoral and administrative structures of a church and its organizational shape. Polity has to do particularly with governance and therefore embraces such areas as the distribution and exercise of authority, the practice of oversight, the making of policy, the deployment of resources and the resolving of disputes. The fundamental intention behind an ecclesiastical polity is to enable a church or family of churches to discern God's will for it at a particular time, through the recognized practices of conciliarity, where the church addresses its responsibilities and challenges in synods and councils at various levels. Conciliarity involves consulting the *consensus fidelium* (the common mind of the faithful) through whatever representative channels are

9 See Avis, Paul, 2012, 'The Book of Common Prayer and Anglicanism: Worship and Belief', in Stephen Platten and Christopher Woods (eds), 2012, *Comfortable Words: Polity, Piety and the Book of Common Prayer*, Norwich: Canterbury Press, ch. 9.

10 Avis, Paul, 2013, *The Anglican Understanding of the Church*, 2nd edn, London: SPCK; Avis, Paul, 2002, *Anglicanism and the Christian Church*, 2nd edn, London and New York: T&T Clark; Avis, Paul, 2007, *The Identity of Anglicanism: Essentials of Anglican Ecclesiology*, London and New York: T&T Clark.

provided in a particular church, deliberation through prayerful Bible study and debate, the subsequent taking of decisions, and the ongoing process of reception – including the need to test decisions against the consent of the faithful.[11] A key principle of church polity is subsidiarity, according to which the so-called 'higher levels' of church authority are intended to serve the 'lower' and to give preference to it. It does not mean, as some conveniently assume, that the 'higher' level of governance delegates responsibilities to the lower level, but instead the reverse. The language of hierarchies of levels is invidious and ecclesiologically toxic, but difficult to avoid completely. The 'higher levels' are not there to serve themselves, though there is a kind of entropy in all institutions that tends in this direction. Subsidiarity in the church means that lay people (though never without their pastors) provide the centre of gravity, the focus of discernment, for all that is discussed, debated and decided in a church.

But polity is not confined to areas of governance; it is equally concerned with the abiding structures of a church's ministry in its preaching, sacramental and pastoral dimensions. Polity concerns, as John Milbank puts it, '"the rule" of the Church, its constitutional authority as established in canon law', which is itself mostly 'a digest of theology'.[12] The church of Christ cannot have a disembodied existence. It must be as real in space and time as the incarnation itself and the sacraments with their earthly, natural elements. The *form of the church* is the central preoccupation of ecclesiastical polity because that form is the structured expression of the church's mission. As A. G. Hebert

11 On the use of *consensus fidelium* and related concepts in the history of the church and in the Anglican tradition, see King, Benjamin J., '"The Consent of the Faithful" from Clement to the Anglican Covenant', *Journal of Anglican Studies* 12.1 (2014), pp. 7–36. On reception, see Avis, Paul, 2010, *Reshaping Ecumenical Theology*, London and New York: T&T Clark, ch. 5: 'Towards a Deeper Reception of "Reception"'.

12 Milbank, John, 2003, *Being Reconciled: Ontology and Pardon*, London and New York: Routledge, p. 108.

put it, 'The essential forms of the Church mark out its shape or structure, by mediating to us the Redemption on which the Church's existence is based.'[13] We may say that the polity of a church is the political form taken by the ecclesiology of that church, while allowing for the contingencies of history and the rough and ready way that principles find expression in practice in human affairs.

At this point we seem to invite the challenge that comes from spirit or charisma, which is often seen as opposed to – or at least in tension with – form or institution. The tension between the charismatic and the institutional dimensions of the Christian church – spirit versus structure – has generated a continuous theological and political dialectic throughout Christian history. Repeatedly, the primacy or superiority of the one or the other has been asserted in argument and fought for in violent action. The primacy of the charismatic was championed by Tertullian in the early church, by spiritual and mendicant movements in the Middle Ages, by radical elements in the Reformation – even in the mind and heart of Martin Luther himself – and by the eminent church historian Adolf von Harnack in the late nineteenth and early twentieth centuries.[14] Vatican II rehabilitated the concept of charism, but without really spelling out what it meant. The global Charismatic and Pentecostal movements of our times are of course predicated on the superior – even supreme – value of the charismatic compared with the institutional.

On the other hand, the institutional or structural dimension of the church began to be an embryonic subject of attention even in the New Testament (especially in 1 Corinthians and the Pastoral Epistles) and in the letters of St Ignatius of Antioch. In the later Roman Empire, the church inevitably became politic-

13 Hebert, A. G., 1946, *The Form of the Church*, London: Faber and Faber, p. 14.

14 See Pelikan, Jaroslav, 1964, *Obedient Rebels: Catholic Substance and Protestant Principle in Luther's Reformation*, London: SCM Press; Pelikan, Jaroslav, 1968, *Spirit Versus Structure: Luther and the Institutions of the Church*, London: Collins.

ally attuned through its association with the state and in the development of the papacy and of diocesan structures. In the sixteenth century, both John Calvin and the Council of Trent, in their very different and often opposed ways, took pains to safeguard the integrity of the institutions of the church. The rise of Protestant denominations in the Western world in the nineteenth century further hardened the institutional tendency within Christianity. But the trend was not confined to Protestantism. The encyclical of Pope Pius XII *Mystici Corporis Christi* (1943) sealed a century of centralization (it has gone much further since then) by asserting that ecclesial communion was exclusively embodied in the hierarchical institution of the (Roman) Catholic Church (RCC). In the early twenty-first century, a time when all historic institutions are viewed with suspicion as being incorrigibly self-serving and defensive, probably corrupt and almost certainly inefficient, the major Christian churches have been rocked to their foundations by clerical abuse scandals and their covering-up by those charged with the responsibility of oversight.

In this complex and disturbing situation, Judith Merkle, writing as a religious sister within a Roman Catholic context in the USA, but with relevance for all historic Christian traditions, offers a redefining and reframing of charism.[15] What is charism and what is its place within the institutional church? Can the institutional church be redeemed by charism? Running together theological, philosophical and sociological enquiry, she draws mainly on Max Weber, the master of the sociological analysis of the issue, Charles Taylor, the current philosophical guru for Christians wrestling with secularity, and the sturdy twin pillars of Karl Rahner and Bernard Lonergan for the theology. Charism is defined by Merkle as the Holy Spirit's gift to an individual to enable them to fulfil their calling from God – not for their own gratification or

15 Merkle, Judith A., 2016, *Beyond Our Lights and Shadows: Charism and Institution in the Church*, London and New York: Bloomsbury/T&T Clark.

self-aggrandizement, but for the common good of the church and of all people. She points out with helpful insight that it is charism that brings people in touch with the gospel. It gives insight into their hurts, wounds and fears and has a therapeutic effect. The fact of charism in a person's life points obliquely to its transcendent source in mystery. But charism cannot operate in a vacuum, without channels and structures. Charism flows through the church as an institution according to the key principles of mediation, sacramentality and communion. So charism cannot be effective without the body, which means the institutional church. Merkle explores the dialectic of spirit and structure from several perspectives, offering eventually some modestly expressed practical prescriptions for the reform of the RCC. Alongside what Merkle provides, there is also much to be learned from the Eastern Orthodox tradition about the possibility of an *epicletic* ecclesiology, in which the (necessary) structures of the church serve as channels for the life-giving energy of the Holy Spirit.

It is fair comment that ecclesiology, as an area of disciplined theological reflection, is always at risk of remaining abstract, theoretical and ungrounded unless it is translated into polity. It is continually in danger of taking off into the stratosphere, elaborating theories without having to put them to the test in practice. The Second Vatican Council set up various ecclesiological trajectories, without elaborating a fully unified, coherent ecclesiology itself. But, unlike most earlier 'ecumenical' councils, it did not immediately follow its teaching through into canonical reform. The Catholic Code of Canon Law of 1983 is widely judged to fall short of the Council's intentions. Similarly, the agreed ecclesiological statements of formal ecumenical dialogues are widely perceived to be weak in practical application, often remaining at the abstract and theoretical level. They tend to hover at this level because normally they do not have to be translated into concrete proposals for the reform of polity in the churches concerned. While they often have a degree of moral and persuasive authority and can help to shape a church's stance vis-à-vis other churches, they do not, in themselves, normally serve as an agenda for change and reform.

Ecclesiology is rather helpless – certainly toothless – without polity. It lacks purchase and efficacy. As Norman Doe puts it, 'Theology shapes law, and law implements theology.'[16] Theology, in the form of ecclesiology, comes first, but polity forms a necessary second; polity is dependent on theology (ecclesiology) but claims a sphere of its own. However, there is a third level: the polity of a church, in its turn, rests on a body of church law (canon law), which generally gives legal status to key ecclesiological principles and also prescribes the parameters of their application in practice in the realm of polity (while not purporting to legislate for every circumstance or eventuality). Canon law consists of *norms of action* derived from ecclesiology and applied in the sphere of enacted polity.[17]

As Ladislas Örsy puts it, ecclesiology is *constitutive*, while the rules of polity are *regulative*; so it falls to theology to evaluate and critique polity and with it the laws and practices of the church.[18] Although the ecclesiastical polity of a church is in principle subsidiary to its official ecclesiology, and is intended to translate that ecclesiology into practice, it seems to me that it is important to affirm, as Leo Koffeman does, that polity is – just as much as ecclesiology – essentially a theological discipline, taking its rise from theological reflection certainly, though not stopping there, but bringing such reflection to bear on political realities in the church with the aid of juridical expertise and

16 Doe, *Christian Law*, p. 385.

17 Wijlens, Myriam, 1991, 'Theology and the Science of Canon Law: A Historical and Systematic Overview', *Louvain Studies* 16.4, pp. 292–311. Wijlens follows Ladislas Örsy in emphasizing the cognitive or conceptual dimension of canon law (rather than its epistemological, procedural dimension), which of course strengthens its connection to theology (see my next footnote, 18).

18 Örsy, Ladislas, 1992, *Theology and Canon Law: New Horizons for Legislation and Interpretation*, Collegeville, MN: Liturgical Press, ch. 10: 'Theology and Canon Law: An Inquiry into their Relationship'. Also Reuver, Marc, 2000, *Faith and Law: Juridical Perspectives for the Ecumenical Movement*, Geneva: World Council of Churches, p. 3.

sound jurisprudential judgement.[19] Koffeman writes: 'Church polity is a theological (sub)discipline: it aims at the critical analysis, systematic study, and practical development of positive church polity (i.e. church polity as it is in force ... in, for instance, a church order ...) from an ecclesiological perspective.'[20] Since its raw material substantially includes the corpus of law pertaining to a church, polity sits between the theoretical discipline of ecclesiology and the practical discipline of ecclesiastical jurisprudence (the practice of church law as a component of pastoral oversight and the work of church courts).

But there is an authority higher than theology and that is Holy Scripture, through which the Head of the church, Jesus Christ, teaches, guides, admonishes and sustains his ecclesial body. Ecclesiology is basically an exegesis and elaboration of the biblical teaching on the church. It follows that ecclesiology, and with it polity, must be true to biblical revelation and brought continually to the touchstone of Scripture, to which they are accountable. As Karl Barth says, 'Although it consists entirely of human beings, the Church is not a human polity ... The Church is governed. As it is created and maintained by the Word of God, it is also governed by the Word of God ... To say that Jesus Christ rules the Church is equivalent to saying that Holy Scripture rules the Church.'[21]

So here we have a hierarchy of descending levels: Holy Scripture, ecclesiology, polity, church law. But the traffic, the influence, is not all one way; it is reciprocal. We may equally say that there is a hierarchy of ascending levels: church law, church polity, ecclesiology, Scripture. We should never forget

19 Koffeman, Leo J., 2014, *In Order to Serve: An Ecumenical Introduction to Church Polity*, Zurich and Berlin: LIT, part 1.

20 Koffeman, *In Order to Serve*, p. 23. An insightful analysis of ecclesiastical government, with a bias towards the American scene, is Long, Edward LeRoy, JR, 2001, *Patterns of Polity: Varieties of Church Governance*, Cleveland, OH: Pilgrim Press.

21 Barth, Karl, 1975–, *Church Dogmatics*, ed. Geoffrey W. Bromiley and Thomas F. Torrance, Edinburgh/London: T&T Clark, I/2, p. 693.

that, underlying all these, there is the vibrant reality of the life and practice of the church of Jesus Christ as it goes about its everyday business of prayer, worship, sacrament, proclamation, witness, pastoral care, service and ministry in a multiplicity of ways. It is the energy generated by Christian practices that validates law, polity and ecclesiology and makes them necessary. As Hebert underlines, '[T]he Church has its forms and its whole outward institutional order ... apart from which there cannot be the Church; but it is only by the presence of the Holy Spirit within it that the Church lives.'[22]

Polity and praxis

So it would be a mistake to think of polity as a purely theoretical matter and therefore as inevitably having the tendency to become arid and devoid of spiritual energy (though often intellectually demanding and fascinating at the same time). Polity is a living subject. It provides patterns, connections and models for personal and group interaction and channels of mutual fidelity within the church. Polity has a key relational function in enabling the ordered intercourse that comprises the intentional life of a church or family of churches.[23] Church law, which both underlies and inscribes ecclesiastical polity, is also intended to facilitate the interpersonal interaction and cooperation of members and office holders in the service of God's mission through the body of Christ; it should therefore be regarded as a salutary, enabling and supportive provision, though in need of periodic revision or reform in the face of changing circumstances.

As the concrete expression of a theological – specifically ecclesiological – discipline, a church's polity should conform to the nature of the Christian church, to its divine commission and ordering and to its place in the mission of God. The

22 Hebert, *Form of the Church*, p. 11.
23 See Koffeman, *In Order to Serve*, p. 63.

polity of any church or family of churches intends to be consonant with the fundamental ecclesiology and missiology of the church. Its function is primarily to serve the one church, the church catholic, not merely 'our own' particular, favoured expression of the church. Karl Barth's emphasis, in his discussion of church order, is strongly on the primacy of service: polity enables us to serve the Lord and one another, not only in the local parish or congregation, but in the communion of saints (*communio sanctorum*).[24] As an aspect of the church, polity is ordered to mutual service and needs to be oriented in practice to that end. The way that the churches structure themselves and their common life cannot be divorced from the total mission of God (*missio Dei*), into which the particular churches are called, as expressions of the one church. As Dan Hardy has put it with reference to the Anglican Communion, 'Anglican polity is based on a humble confidence in Anglican Christianity as a mediation of the engagement of the triune God with the world.'[25] This aspiration is certainly not exclusive to Anglicanism, but applies to all those bodies that see themselves as churches of Christ.

Above all, church polity should reflect the trinitarian reality of communion (*koinonia*), which is the very essence of the church's life. The Joint International Commission for Theological Dialogue between the Roman Catholic Church (RCC) and the Orthodox Church said in its Munich document of 1982: 'The institutional elements [of the church] should be nothing but a visible reflection of the reality of the [trinitarian] mystery.'[26] The polity of a church should, therefore, derive from

24 Barth, *Church Dogmatics*, IV/2, pp. 693–5.

25 Hardy, Daniel W., 2001, *Finding the Church*, London: SCM Press, pp. 158–9.

26 Joint International Commission for Theological Dialogue between the Roman Catholic Church and the Orthodox Church, *The Mystery of the Church and of the Eucharist in the Light of the Mystery of the Holy Trinity* (Munich, 1982), II, 1: www.ecupatria.org/documents/the-mystery-of-the-church-and-of-the-eucharist-in-the-light-of-the-mystery-of-the-holy-trinity/ (accessed 11.05.2021).

and express in concrete terms the ecclesiological principles of that church, which of course the church in question believes to be consonant with the basic ecclesiological principles of the one church of Christ. Polity is based on theological principles that are fundamental to the authentic existence of a church. As Karl Barth insists, church order, polity and law must stem from the church's corporate faith, its 'confession', applying that faith to the sphere of human action.[27] So it is not for us to invent or dream up a blueprint for church polity; nor is it acceptable to play around with an inherited form of polity simply because we have had a few bright ideas or to meet a passing need. Polity cannot be arbitrary, nor is it a purely pragmatic matter, though a certain pragmatism, in the sense of realism and the art of the possible, must play a part. Polity is the outcome of applied theology, a salient example of theological *praxis*.

Anglican and Roman Catholic aspects

Some instructive comparisons can be made between the polities of the RCC and the Anglican Communion (which Martyn Percy aptly terms a 'somewhat patchwork polity').[28] The term 'Anglican Communion', whatever more it may imply, certainly suggests a communal dimension to the worldwide Anglican family of churches. As an organized, lightly structured community it inevitably has a political aspect. Its polity is shaped by the four 'Instruments of Communion': the Lambeth Conference, the Primates Meeting, the ministry or office of the Archbishop of Canterbury, and the Anglican Consultative Council. Alongside the constitutional Instruments are many

27 Barth, *Church Dogmatics*, IV/2, p. 707.

28 Percy, Martyn, 2017, *The Future Shapes of Anglicanism: Currents, Contours, Charts*, London and New York: Routledge, p. 94. For variations of polity within the Communion, see Doe, Norman, 1998, *Canon Law in the Anglican Communion: A Worldwide Perspective*, Oxford: Oxford University Press; Doe, *Christian Law*, ch. 4: 'The Institutions of Ecclesiastical Governance'.

less formal initiatives and organizations: commissions set up by the Instruments, such as the Inter-Anglican Standing Commission on Unity, Faith and Order (IASCUFO), networks and consultations, mission societies and the Mothers Union. These impart energy and dynamism to the Communion and without them the formal Instruments would remain rather distant. If the Instruments provide the skeleton of Anglican Communion polity, the many networks and projects put flesh on the bones.[29] To say that the Anglican Communion is a political *community* is a softer, slightly warmer, way of saying that it is a political *society*. A society (*societas*) is a community of people bound together by common values and organized in pursuit of a common goal, which – other things being equal – it has the means to achieve. It is, therefore, a term that is applicable to particular churches within the one church. As we shall see in a moment, 'society' is the language of Richard Hooker. But to call a church or a communion of churches a 'society' risks some contamination from the history and import of the phrase 'perfect society' (*societas perfecta*), which the RCC has applied to itself, at least in the past.

A church conceived as a perfect or complete society (the Latin adjective *perfecta* has both senses) is one that is self-contained and self-sufficient, independent of, or superior to, other societies. It enjoys sovereignty – that is, supreme power to make

29 On the Instruments of Communion, see *Towards a Symphony of Instruments*; *The Windsor Report*, 2004, London: Anglican Consultative Council; Pickard, Stephen, 2012, *Seeking the Church: An Introduction to Ecclesiology*, London: SCM Press, ch. 7; Markham, Ian S. et al. (eds), 2013, *The Wiley-Blackwell Companion to the Anglican Communion*, Malden, MA, and Oxford: Wiley-Blackwell, chs 4 (Norman Doe), 7 (Robert Prichard) and 8 (Samuel Van Culin and Andrew Bennett Terry); Avis, Paul, 2015, 'Anglican Conciliarism: the Lambeth Conference as an Instrument of Communion', in Mark D. Chapman, Sathianathan Clarke and Martyn Percy (eds), 2015, *The Oxford Handbook of Anglican Studies*, Oxford: Oxford University Press, ch. 3. A stimulating study of the polity of the Anglican Communion is Ross, Alexander, 2020, *A Still More Excellent Way: Authority and Polity in the Anglican Communion*, London: SCM Press.

and apply its own laws and to apply punitive sanctions to both laity and clergy for breaches of church law. The concept of the RCC as a perfect or complete society first emerged in the contest between church and state, pope and emperor, in the Middle Ages. Aristotle had described the *polis* or city-state as a perfect society and Augustine had used societal language of the church. Following Aristotle, Thomas Aquinas defined the state as a perfect community (*communitas perfecta*). In defensive reaction against the Reformation, the Jesuits, notably Robert Cardinal Bellarmine, repristinated the language of *societas perfecta*. It became the default rhetoric of the RCC from the Council of Trent in the mid-sixteenth century onwards, especially in response to the critique of that church by the secular, anti-clerical aspect of the Enlightenment. While the dogmas of the First Vatican Council (Vatican I, 1869–70) do not use the term *societas perfecta*, it figured prominently in the debates on the draft schemata of that Council and continued to be the currency of Roman Catholic apologetic until the mid-twentieth century.[30] Leo XIII's encyclical *Immortale Dei* (1885), in the wake of Vatican I, expounded the unconditional sovereignty of the RCC, understood as coterminous with the universal church of Christ. The concept of the RCC as a *societas perfecta* dominated the now superseded 1917 Code of Canon Law (*Codex Iuris Canonici*), though the actual term is not used there. Almost the last gasp of the *societas perfecta* ecclesiology occurs in Alfredo Ottaviani's massive exposition of the institutional, juridical nature of the RCC, published on the eve of the Second Vatican Council (1962–65). That Council rejected the draft Schema *Aeternum Unigenite Pater* containing the term.

30 Granfield, Patrick, 'The Church as Societas Perfecta in the Schemata of Vatican I', *Church History* 48.4 (1979), pp. 431–46; Witte, Henk, 2012, '"Ecclesia, quid dicis de teipsa?" Can Ecclesiology Be of any Help to the Church to Deal with Advanced Modernity?', in Staf Hellemans and Josef Wissink (eds), *Towards a New Catholic Church in Advanced Modernity*, Zurich and Berlin: LIT, pp. 121–45, especially pp. 123–8; Leys, Adrianus C. N. P., 1995, *Ecclesiological Impacts of the Principle of Subsidiarity*, Kampen: Kok; KTC no. 28, pp. 120–34.

Although only vestiges of this conception are to be found in the teaching of Vatican II, which largely breathes a different spirit, Paul VI used the expression in 1969 and the post-Vatican II revision of Canon Law (1983) is still substantially informed by the notion of the RCC as a complete, sovereign society, the one true church.[31] However, in his words, actions and demeanour, Pope Francis has repudiated the *societas perfecta* conception of the RCC. He has stepped into the shoes of the fisherman, not the emperor.

In contrast to the historical Roman self-definition, Anglican churches generally see themselves as more porous, less self-contained, and not entirely self-defining. They do not play up their sovereignty. The larger Anglican churches locate themselves as public institutions, alongside other institutions within civil society; and thus by inclination, as well as by obligation, subject to the law of the land, but without abrogating their apostolic credentials. The Church of England, as the established church in England, has negotiated over time (and taking the rough with the smooth) a relationship of partnership and critical solidarity with the state.[32] In that sense, we might say, it has broadly perpetuated the historical pattern of church–state relations in England.[33] Today the General Synod makes public law (subject to certain constraints and safeguards), and about half of the Church of England's diocesan bishops sit in the second chamber of the legislature, the House of Lords. The Anglican consciousness, whether in England or elsewhere, does not normally think in terms of self-sufficiency or sovereignty or competition, but instead in terms of service and mission, partnership where possible, and loyal citizenship. I think that that is also precisely how most Roman Catholics in England

31 Reuver, *Faith and Law*, pp. 3, 16–17, 44, 103–4.

32 Avis, Paul, 2001, *Church, State and Establishment*, London: SPCK, 2001.

33 See Kaye, Bruce, 2018, *The Rise and Fall of the English Christendom: Theocracy, Christology, Order and Power*, London and New York: Routledge.

today think too, although in the view of many members of that church, certain structures and teachings of their church remain inimical to that ethos, as we shall mention shortly. But if we choose to speak of Anglican churches, or of the Anglican Communion as a whole, as a 'political societies', that is intended to bring out the dimension of polity, which is necessary for all collective enterprises that endure as historical institutions. Such terminology need not have the connotations of *societas perfecta*.

The form of the church

In the present era of post- or late-modernity, polity, like politics itself, is widely distrusted. So, the churches struggle to do their work in the face of the pervasive post-modern suspicion of historic institutions, which is accompanied by a culture of spontaneity and individualism that militates against collective action – all of which pervades the churches and the thinking of their members. In the face of the prevailing scepticism with regard to historic institutions, we have to insist that polity is a proper concern of the church and deserves its best study, reflection and leadership skills. If, as the proverb has it, a bad worker blames their tools, it is equally true that an inadequate leader blames the structures and diverts the energies of his or her followers to rejig them, though to no avail (this is frequently observed). The church needs to take form in every age, a form that will enable it to respond coherently and effectively to challenges, especially when they are hostile to Christianity and to human well-being.

John Calvin, possibly influenced by Luther's notion of the hiddenness of the church, especially under the persecuting reign of Antichrist, entertained the possibility that the church could exist temporarily without form; it may be hidden from human gaze, being known only to God. However, for Calvin, as for Luther, the visible form of the church is normally to be known by the pure preaching of the word of God, and the due administration of the sacraments. In his 'Prefatory Address to Francis, King of the French', Calvin said:

> We ... maintain, both that the Church may exist without any apparent form, and moreover, that the form is not ascertained by that external splendour which they [the papists] foolishly admire, but by a very different mark, namely by the pure preaching of the word of God, and the due administration of the sacraments ... as God alone knows who are his, so he may sometimes withdraw the external manifestation of his church from the view of men. This, I allow, is a fearful punishment which God sends on the earth ...[34]

In the light of Calvin's remarks, I think it is not for us to rule out the possibility that God may allow the visible form of the church on earth to be hidden for a time. But the ecclesiological norm is that the church takes form.

Some purport to cavalierly disparage ecclesiastical polity, to look down on it as basically unspiritual. But as Ephraim Radner has argued in his disturbing book *A Brutal Unity: The Spiritual Politics of the Christian Church*, no collective body of human beings can presuppose that it lacks form.[35] Radner shows that a major reason why all the churches failed abysmally and culpably to intervene, as far as they could, against murderous, genocidal actions, in Nazi Germany in the 1930s and in Rwanda in the 1990s, was lack of unified organization and cohesive action. The church is paralysed in its mission when it lacks defined political form (that is, ecclesiastical polity). Theological reflection on polity calls for the church's best spiritual gifts and insights. These have not been lacking in the history of Anglican thought.

A great classic of Anglican theology, Richard Hooker's *Of the Lawes of Ecclesiasticall Politie*, written in the late sixteenth

---

34 Calvin, John, 1962, *Institutes of the Christian Religion*, trans. H. Beveridge, 2 vols, London: James Clarke, vol. 1, pp. 14–15.

35 Radner, Ephraim, 2012, *A Brutal Unity: The Spiritual Politics of the Christian Church*, Waco, TX: Baylor University Press, p. 403.

century, models this high calling. Hooker insists that the church has two dimensions to its existence: it is a 'politic society' as well as a 'body mystical', a 'natural society' as well as a 'society supernatural'.[36] According to Hooker, the church of Christ is not correctly described as simply a supernatural or mystical communion (he is combating the notion of the 'invisible church'). It is also a political body or society, with structures of governance that are informed by the practical wisdom of political philosophy. In the divine economy, according to Hooker, there exists a sphere of human law within the church, pertaining to its outward fabric, mainly its governance, discipline and worship. This body of law is mutable, related to changing circumstances and subject to corporate judgements that are not absolute but basically pragmatic. This does not mean that they are devoid of principle; the pragmatism lies in applying permanent principles to changing circumstances in appropriate ways, which are discerned by the practical reason. For Hooker, ecclesiastical polity cannot be reduced simply to political structures of authority and governance. It rests on a profound biblical, theological, philosophical and juridical foundation. It embraces liturgy and the sacraments, the form of the ordained ministry, and church–state relations. The core of Hooker's presentation of ecclesiastical polity is his exposition of the connection between Christology and sacramental theology in Book V of the *Lawes*. In Hooker, ecclesiastical polity emerges from reflection on the profoundest, most central truths of biblical revelation as they are brought into conversation with political philosophy.

---

36 Hooker, Richard, 1977, *Of the Lawes of Ecclesiasticall Politie*, I.xv.2–3: *The Folger Library Edition of the Works of Richard Hooker*, ed. W. Speed Hill, vol. 1, Cambridge, MA and London: The Belknap Press of Harvard University Press, pp. 131–2; Cargill Thompson, W. D. J., 1972, 'The Philosopher of the "Politic Society": Richard Hooker as a Political Thinker', in W. Speed Hill (ed.), *Studies on Richard Hooker: Essays Preliminary to an Edition of his Works*, Cleveland, OH and London: Case Western Reserve University Press, ch. 1.

Ecclesiology, polity and political philosophy

Richard Hooker's approach to the political dimension of the church, which has become normative for Anglicanism – namely, the connection between ecclesiology and political philosophy – has recently been capably defended (though, surprising to Anglican eyes, Hooker himself is not mentioned) by Luca Badini Confalonieri, in *Democracy in the Christian Church: An Historical, Theological and Political Case*.[37] Confalonieri, a Roman Catholic, argues that the present state of governance in the RCC is not simply an organizational challenge but also an ethical issue – in fact, a moral scandal, bearing on the question of the responsible stewardship of the church's mission. In terms of Bernard Lonergan's methodology (his philosophy of intentionality), which Confalonieri employs throughout, the twin imperatives for the church are to think intelligently, drawing on all relevant sources of knowledge and insight, and then to act responsibly for the common good.[38] When these ethical imperatives are flouted, when thinking is not done intelligently and acting is not carried out responsibly, an ethical failure has occurred and the conscience of the faithful, as well as the conscience of (the rest of) the world, is offended. Confalonieri could have argued – against the general drift of modern sociological reasoning – that the body of ethical principles and moral teaching, which forms the ethical consensus and moral centre of gravity of any given society, should be seen as a concrete structural element within it, no less important than its political or economic structure.[39] Roman Catholic social teaching (CST)

37 Confalonieri, Luca Badini, 2012, *Democracy in the Christian Church: An Historical, Theological and Political Case*, London and New York: T&T Clark.

38 Lonergan, Bernard J. F., SJ, 1983 [1957], *Insight: A Study of Human Understanding*, London: Darton, Longman and Todd; Lonergan, Bernard J. F., 1973 [1971], *Method in Theology*, London: Darton, Longman and Todd.

39 As does Morgan, Teresa, 2015, *Roman Faith and Christian Faith:* Pistis *and* Fides *in the Early Roman Empire and Early Churches*, Oxford: Oxford University Press, especially ch. 12.

exalts justice and endorses the principle of subsidiarity when applied to situations outside the church. But subsidiarity needs to be applied within the church by the church. It is subversive of the hierarchical principle: it means that the 'higher' level is subsidiary to the 'lower', not the other way round, and that it is within the remit of the lower to decide whether responsibility should be passed to a higher level. The author believes that it is 'immoral' that the subsidiarity principle, exalted in papal social teaching, is systematically negated in the internal polity and practice of the RCC.[40] Like Adrianus Leys,[41] Confalonieri believes that the principle of subsidiarity, translated into concrete structures and processes, needs to be called into play to counteract the centralizing, hierarchical tendencies of *communio* ecclesiology that, notwithstanding the personal example and public gestures of Pope Francis, are still largely operative within that church.

Confalonieri refutes the claim, associated with Cardinal Bellarmine in the sixteenth century and Cardinal Ratzinger/Pope Benedict XVI in the twentieth, that because the church is a divinely-created mystery, a *communio*, its organization cannot be compared or assimilated to human, earthly, political structures and that what political philosophy has to teach about the nature of societies has no bearing on the matter.[42] Drawing mainly on secondary sources at this point, particularly on Francis Oakley's valuable work on the conciliar tradition,[43] Confalonieri has no difficulty in demonstrating that throughout history the church has borrowed, without apology, from both the theory and the practice of political philosophy. In the early church, the house churches were modelled on the Roman *domus* and the first church councils took their cue from the

40 Confalonieri, *Democracy in the Christian Church*, p. 123.

41 On subsidiarity and the polity of the RCC, see Leys, *Ecclesiological Impacts of the Principle of Subsidiarity*.

42 Confalonieri, *Democracy in the Christian Church*, p. 101.

43 Oakley, Francis, 2003, *The Conciliarist Tradition: Constitutionalism in the Catholic Church 1300–1870*, Oxford: Oxford University Press.

Graeco-Roman public assemblies. Medieval canonists drew on the legacy of Roman corporation law to formulate the concept of *plenitudo potestatis* (fullness of power) as an attribute of the papacy, while conciliarists seized on the corporationist axiom *quod omnes tangit, omnibus tractari et approbari debet* (what affects all must be approved by all). The validity of natural law for church law was an unquestioned axiom. While papalists drew on natural law to support papal authority, conciliarists appealed to it to challenge what they saw as oppressive man-made (positive) laws in the church.[44]

The historical indebtedness of ecclesiology to political philosophy respects the traditional Catholic, Thomistic doctrine of the relation of nature and grace, reason and revelation, namely that the latter presupposes and perfects the former (*gratia non tollit naturam sed perficit*). The cognitive and moral operations that enable us (in Lonergan's terms) to think intelligently and then to decide responsibly are one and the same in all aspects of human life and in both civil and Christian communities. We are not given a new brain when we are baptized. The structure of human intentionality is, as Lonergan insisted, generic and universal. Just as personal Christian ethics presupposes and builds on natural ethical principles, so too Christian social ethics – including the ethical dimension of the exercise of authority and the taking of decisions – should presuppose and build on natural social ethics. Social ethics is, as it were, the applied form of political philosophy, just as ecclesiastical polity is the applied form of ecclesiology. Ecclesiology and political philosophy exist in a symbiotic relationship because the structure of intentionality and action in each is analogous. The church is a society (*societas*) and what is true of societies is true of the church. Ecclesiology needs political philosophy in order to do its work, to operate (as Confalonieri puts it) at a critical, explanatory and systematic level.[45] That is to say that

44 See also Avis, Paul, 2006, *Beyond the Reformation? Authority, Primacy and Unity in the Conciliar Tradition*, London and New York: T&T Clark.

45 Confalonieri, *Democracy in the Christian Church*, p. 130.

ecclesiology is dependent on political philosophy *methodologically* and one cannot get much more fundamental than that.

There is a ferment going on within the RCC with regard to authority and governance, with formidable organized opposition to the change of direction that Pope Francis has been trying to bring about. There is work going on within the Church of England also with regard to authority and governance, but there are few signs that those who lead it have much grasp of the basic principles that apply in this sensitive area. So we have a challenging but rewarding interdisciplinary task ahead of us as we continue to reflect, always ecumenically and with the aid of political philosophy, on the nature and mission of the church (ecclesiology), the political structures that enable that mission (ecclesiastical polity), and the canonical regulation that helps to give it stability, coherence and integrity (church law).

5

Unreconciled Church: Counter-sign of the Kingdom

The impending arrival of the kingdom or reign of God was the core of Jesus of Nazareth's preaching. This assessment is almost universally agreed by New Testament scholars.[1] As J. D. G. Dunn emphasizes, 'The centrality of the kingdom of God (*basileia tou theou*) in Jesus' preaching is one of the least disputable, or disputed, facts about Jesus.'[2] The opening of Mark's Gospel provides the key: 'After John [the Baptist] had been handed over, Jesus came into Galilee proclaiming the gospel of God and saying, "The time has been fulfilled and the reign (*basileia*) of God is at hand (*ēngiken*); repent and believe in the gospel"' (Mark 1.14–15). The imminence of the kingdom was the content of the 'good news' (*euangelion*, 'gospel'). The Hebrew background, especially the term *malküt*, royal authority or rule, strongly suggests a dynamic, rather than territorial understanding of the kingdom. It is primarily a state of affairs, an event or action, rather than a place, and is therefore well expressed as the 'reign' of God.[3] We do not need to

1 This chapter is a revised and expanded version of my 'Overcoming "The Church as Counter-sign of the Kingdom"', in Mark D. Chapman and Vladimir Latinovic (eds), 2021, *Changing the Church: Transformations of Christian Belief, Practice, and Life*, Cham, Switzerland: Palgrave Macmillan, pp. 243–9.

2 Dunn, James D. G., 2003, *Jesus Remembered, Christianity in the Making, Volume 1*, Grand Rapids, MI: Eerdmans, p. 383.

3 Jeremias, Joachim, 1971, *New Testament Theology* [2 vols; vol. 1], *Part One: The Proclamation of Jesus*, trans. John Bowden, London: SCM Press, p. 98.

examine here the various theories of New Testament eschatology, whether 'future', 'realized' or 'inaugurated', or any combination of them, in order to recognize the centrality of the coming reign of God for the mission and preaching of Jesus Christ. The theme of the nearness or imminence of the reign of God is pivotal for Jesus' destiny from beginning to end.[4]

As early Christian theology evolved during the apostolic and post-apostolic periods, Jesus Christ came to be seen as the personification, the personal embodiment, of the reign of God. King and kingdom were one and indivisible. The Alexandrian theologian Origen (AD c. 184–c. 253) described Jesus Christ as *autobasileia*, the kingdom itself, an idea that was revived in modern times by Karl Barth.[5] The one who came proclaiming the kingdom was soon being proclaimed by the apostolic church as the content, meaning and personal manifestation of the kingdom. As Rudolf Bultmann put it, '*The proclaimer became the proclaimed.*'[6] The steady development of a high Christology in the New Testament period enabled the church to speak of the kingdom of Christ, as well as of God (2 Pet. 1.11; Rev. 20.6). Nevertheless, St Paul speaks mysteriously of Christ 'handing over the kingdom to God the Father' at the 'end' (*telos*), because he [Christ] must reign [as king] until he has subdued all his enemies (1 Cor. 15. 24–25).

The reconciling reign of God

In the New Testament, the one kingdom of Christ and of God is presented as the kingdom of reconciliation. The imminent

4 Avis, Paul, 2020, *Jesus and the Church: The Foundation of the Church in the New Testament and Modern Theology*, London and New York: T&T Clark, especially pp. 42–5.

5 See Barth, Karl, 1975–, *Church Dogmatics*, ed. G. W. Bromiley and Thomas F. Torrance, Edinburgh: T&T Clark, IV/2, pp. 655–8.

6 Bultmann, Rudolf, 1952, *Theology of the New Testament*, trans. Kendrick Grobel, 2 vols, London: SCM Press, vol. 1, p. 33; italics original.

revealing of the reign of God has a twofold reference to reconciliation: it both calls for reconciliation among human beings (as in the ethical preaching of John the Baptist: Matt 3.1–12; Luke 3.1–20) and effects reconciliation – the restoration of Israel to a faithful covenant relationship with its God, which was the central purpose of Jesus' mission. In the preaching of Jesus, as in that of John the Baptist, repentance and faith are the essential steps towards reconciliation with the God of Israel. The kingdom is both invitation and command, offer and demand, salvation and judgement. According to the New Testament, one may 'discern' the kingdom, 'receive' the kingdom, 'enter' the kingdom and rejoice in the kingdom, but never 'build' the kingdom or 'extend' the kingdom, as in much dubious modern preaching and mission rhetoric. For Paul, the gospel is the message of reconciliation with God and with one another in the body of Christ. God has reconciled us to himself through Christ and has given us (presumably 'us' means Paul and his fellow apostles) the ministry (*diakonia*) of reconciliation. In Christ, God was effecting the reconciliation of the world to Godself and entrusting the message to the apostles. Remarkably, Paul presents Christ's saving work and the apostolic ministry as a single divine-human redemptive act or continuum (2 Cor. 5.18–20). Apostolicity consists in being the bearer and proclaimer of God's reconciling work in Christ.

Wolfhart Pannenberg wrestles with the nature of the connection between the kingdom, the church and God's act of reconciliation in Christ: 'As the body of Christ the church is the eschatological people of God gathered out of all peoples, and it is thus a sign of reconciliation for a future unity of redeemed humanity in the kingdom of God.' Pannenberg continues: 'Jesus Christ is the revelation of the divine mystery of salvation because from his death and resurrection proceeds the reconciliation of humanity with a view to God's kingdom.' The church is constituted as a sign of reconciled humanity, but it is, as Pannenberg puts it, a 'broken sign' precisely because of its own unreconciled divisions. However, Pannenberg believes that because the church is held 'in Christ' through faith and the liturgy, there are God-given 'forces of reconciliation' constantly at work in its history which act to bind Christians together into the unity of Christ's body in order to overcome division and remake the church as a sign of humanity's destined unity in God's kingdom.[7]

The relationship, whether as connection or as opposition, between the kingdom of God and the church has been a constant subject of debate in the history of theology.[8] Augustine of Hippo was inclined to identify church and kingdom, while Protestant theology has tended to hold them apart, trying to avoid any hint of a divinization of the church. In modern ecumenical theology the church is not identified with the kingdom, but is closely related to it, being seen as the sign, instrument and foretaste of the kingdom – witnessing to the kingdom and serving kingdom purposes, but in dialectical tension with it.[9] The church depends on the kingdom for its existence, being 'constituted' by the kingdom, as Pannenberg puts it. The church spearheads the kingdom in the world, but should not be identified with it. The church both participates in the kingdom and is judged against the kingdom. Modern theologians of various traditions, and the Second Vatican Council itself, designated the church as 'a' or 'the' sacrament of salvation.[10] But since the kingdom or reign of God is the sphere of God's salvific action, we may also say that the church is the sign or sacrament of the

7 Pannenberg, Wolfhart, 1997, *Systematic Theology, Volume 3*, trans. Geoffrey W. Bromiley, Edinburgh: T&T Clark, pp. 43–4.

8 See Pannenberg, *Systematic Theology, Volume 3*, pp. 26–38, on the historical theology of kingdom and church.

9 Lesslie Newbigin expounded the theme of the church as sign, instrument and foretaste in 1976 and the formula has since been received into ecumenical discourse: www.wcc-coe.org/wcc/who/crete-03-e.html (accessed 24.05.2021).

10 *Lumen gentium* 48; *Gaudium et spes* 45. It is not appropriate to give substantial documentation here, but see, briefly, Kasper, Walter, 1989, *Theology and Church*, trans. Margaret Kohl, London: SCM Press, ch. 6; Kasper, Walter, 2015, *The Catholic Church: Nature, Reality and Mission*, ed. R. David Nelson, trans. Thomas Hoebel, London and New York: Bloomsbury, pp. 78–81.

kingdom. However, this affirmation, justified and necessary in itself, immediately raises a horrendous problem for theology.

The unreconciled Church

One of the most agonizing questions of ecclesiology is, What does it mean when the church, by its actions, obscures the kingdom of God? How can we accept the fact that the church sometimes counteracts the kingdom, thwarting the redemptive purposes of God? Paul says that 'the kingdom of God is ... righteousness and peace and joy in the Holy Spirit' (Rom. 14.17). Hence the reign of God is sometimes called 'the peaceable kingdom' because it is the sphere where reconciliation has been accomplished and brings forth the fruits of peace, harmony and concord. But, in stark contrast to the character of the kingdom, the Christian church confronts us as an *unreconciled* reality, not a token of peace, harmony and concord, but of division, faction and dispute. The unreconciled church as a *counter-sign of the kingdom* confronts us with a major theological anomaly, a ghastly *aporia*, a black hole of meaninglessness. It amounts to the question whether the unreconciled church can be the *church*?

With regard to the failings of the church, we should distinguish between ordinary human moral frailty and weakness, on the one hand, and intentional, premeditated human wickedness, on the other. To be a Christian is to know weakness as well as strength. The sign of a sanctified life is an overpowering sense of how far we still have to travel into the holiness of God. As the old hymn puts it: 'And those who fain would serve thee best / Are conscious most of wrong within' (H. Twells, 'At even when the sun was set'). The first sign of true sainthood is self-abasement. Typically, the saints are moved by an overpowering sense of unworthiness and that is the necessary condition for receiving God's grace. God's power is made perfect in human weakness. 'When I am weak, then I am strong', writes Paul – and *only* 'when I am weak' (2 Cor. 12.9–10).

Christian moral weakness, Christian sinfulness or 'falling short' are unavoidable (Rom. 3.23; 7.14–25). We are steeped in sinfulness at the same time as we are being transformed by grace, by the glory of God in the face of Jesus Christ (2 Cor. 3.18). Karl Barth – as flawed a Christian as the rest of us – writes of Christians even as they draw near to God in worship: 'They know also that they are God's sinful creatures; that because of their own corruption their activity is a corrupt activity.'[11] In their weakness, Barth continues, they 'know that they cannot avert the sorrow and suffering of the world; that they cannot avoid their own misery; that they cannot alter the human situation ... that they cannot hallow God's name as they should [etc.] ... they can only pray ...'

However, the serious misdemeanours and crimes of the church corporately, such as those being uncovered in the current global sexual abuse scandals, belong to another league altogether. Not only do they harm and ruin countless human lives, but they also obliterate the presence of the kingdom of God and of Christ in the perception of many both within and beyond the church. Where does that leave our credal belief in the church, *Credo in unam, sanctam, catholicam et apostolicam Ecclesiam*?

Because the church is the body of Christ, crucified and risen, its weakness as well as its strength is apparent. Just as Christ's risen body bore the marks of crucifixion (John 20.20, etc.), so the church bears all the marks of human imperfection and fallibility, even of sin (which cannot be predicated of Christ). As Martin Luther reminds us, Christ is veiled and hidden in the church. It is not easy to perceive him there. In the eyes of the world, Luther writes, 'the church is like its bridegroom Christ: hacked to pieces, marked with scratches, despised, crucified, mocked'; but in the eyes of God the church is a holy, spotless dove.[12] Notoriously, Luther called the church 'the

11 Barth, *Church Dogmatics*, IV/2 (§67), p. 704.

12 Luther, Martin, 1967, *Luther's Works*, ed. Helmut T. Lehmann, vol. 54, *Table Talk*, trans. Theodore G. Tappert, Philadelphia, PA: Fortress Press, p. 262.

greatest sinner'. Just as there is no one who is a greater sinner than the Christian, so 'there is no greater sinner than the Christian church', and that is why, Luther added, the church prays daily, 'Forgive us our trespasses'.[13] Unlike some modern theologians, including Pope John Paul II, Luther refuses to make a qualitative difference between the Christian and the church on this score. For Luther, the church is at the same time sinful and justified, *ecclesia simul iusta et peccatrix*, just like the individual Christian.

But it may well trouble us to use that sort of language about the body of Christ. Some Christian traditions cannot accept it. Many Orthodox scholars would condemn it as blasphemous. Some Anglicans are certainly uncomfortable with it. Roman Catholics also struggle to admit that the church is sinful. But let Luther's statement stand alongside St Paul's confession (or one attributed to him) that he was 'the chief, or foremost of sinners' (1 Tim. 1.15). Paul is not being merely rhetorical. He is the number one sinner because he was 'formerly a blasphemer, a persecutor, and a man of violence' (1 Tim. 1.13). He tried to strangle the infant church at birth (Acts 8.1–3; 26.10; Gal. 1.13). But we need to ask: Is Paul's the kind of language that should ever be applied to an apostle of Jesus Christ and a saint of the church? I think we are faced with basically the same issue in both cases: holy church and holy apostle; sinful church, sinful apostle.

There is an unavoidable ambiguity about the church as we know it and as we see it in history. It is at once sign and counter-sign of Christ and of the kingdom of God. Like John the Baptist in Grünewald's Isenheim altarpiece, the church points people to Christ crucified and that is a vivid depiction of its true role. But the church often drives people away from Christ, pointing them in the opposite direction. It deters people from coming to him in faith and gives them an aversion to

---

13 Luther, Martin, 1883–, *D. Martin Luthers Werke*, Kritische Gesamtausgabe, Weimar, vol. 34/1, p. 276: *Non est tam magna peccatrix ut Christiana ecclesia.*

Christianity. Today many people of integrity and goodwill experience a sense of revulsion at the church and are deeply suspicious of its clergy. How many people today are outside the church precisely because of the church? How many who once were regular worshippers and communicants are now distanced or alienated? In our own small worlds, we are probably all aware of numerous acquaintances who once went to church and no longer do so. It is my hunch, based on pastoral and personal experience, that there are more people around who have rejected the church than currently feel that they belong to it.

Paul's expression 'the mystery of iniquity' (2 Thess. 2.7, KJV) can stand for the fact that the church, the historical vehicle of Christ's mission in the world and the privileged instrument of his kingdom, can be the means of turning people away from him. We struggle to understand how God could permit that reality to stand within God's good purposes for the world and the church. It is part of the great unanswerable question of theodicy, of why a just and loving God allows evil, suffering and pain in the creation. Sin in the church is the question of *ecclesial theodicy*. We do not know why God allows such depths of depravity in God's church, any more than we understand why God allows such depths of depravity in the world at large.

The brute fact is that the church and its ministers sometimes actively obscure Christ's presence in the world. The public profile of the church can become a counter-sign of Christ, averting people from him. In our own time, because of serious abuses committed by clergy and culpable acts of cover-up by those entrusted with oversight, the church itself has become – and here is the tragic irony – a major instrument of the *de-Christianization of Christendom*. The church has been digging its own grave. The church as a human institution is capable of great evil and can perpetrate enormous wrong. As Paul says, 'Antichrist makes his throne in the temple of God' (2 Thess. 2.4), a text often cited by Luther. How difficult it is at such times to say with the Ceylonese Methodist bishop and evangelist D. T. Niles (1908–70): 'The answer to the problems of the world is the answer that Jesus Christ provided, which is the church.'[14] The church carries so little credibility today that even many Christians would hesitate to affirm this claim.

The church is, by definition, a community of sinners and no others, though sinners who are being sanctified through word and sacrament. When their sins get the upper hand and lead the church as an institution to commit great wrong, I think that we have no alternative but to say that the church itself is sinful. I have noted that it is almost impossible for Christians of some traditions – Orthodox, Roman Catholic or Anglo-Catholic – to bring themselves to say that. Karl Rahner, SJ, who calls the question of the sinfulness of the church 'one of the most agonising questions of ecclesiology', is prepared to assert without equivocation that 'the church is sinful'. For Rahner, it is dissembling and self-deceiving to say that flagrant sinners and wrongdoers are 'in' the church but not 'of' it, that their actions do not touch the character of the church, that the church remains spotless while its representatives commit appalling crimes. As Rahner puts it, 'The church is a sinful church: this is a truth of faith ... and it is a shattering truth.'[15] Vatican II acknowledged that the church is always in need of penitence, purification, reformation and renewal.[16]

When the sins of the church eclipse the glory of God, we have to say with Luther, 'The face of the church is the face of one who is a sinner, troubled, forsaken, dying and full of distress.'[17] Henri de Lubac puts it similarly: 'On the one hand

14 Niles, D. T., 1966, *The Message and Its Messengers*, Nashville, TN: Abingdon Press, p. 50.

15 Rahner, Karl, SJ, 1969, *Theological Investigations*, vol. 6, Baltimore, MD: Helicon Press; London: Darton, Longman and Todd, pp. 253, 256–60 ('The Church of Sinners').

16 *Lumen gentium* 8; *Unitatis redintegratio* 6. See also Rahner, Karl, 'The Sinful Church in the Decrees of Vatican II', *Theological Investigations*, vol. 6, ch. 18; Avis, Paul, 2006, *Beyond the Reformation? Authority, Primacy and Unity in the Conciliar Tradition*, London and New York: T&T Clark, pp. 200–3.

17 Cited in Elert, Werner, 1962, *The Structure of Lutheranism*, St Louis, MO: Concordia Publishing House, p. 262.

we see an assembly of sinners, a mixed herd, wheat gathered with the straw, a field with tares growing in it: *Corpus Christi mixtum*, the ark which shelters clean and unclean animals; on the other [hand] we have an unspotted virgin, mother of saints, born on Calvary from the pierced side of Jesus … the very assembly she has made holy … known only to God.'[18] Thus both Reformation and Roman Catholic sources are prepared to confess the sinfulness of the Church, though with different nuances.

Rahner and de Lubac were writing half a century or more ago. Now Brian Flanagan, a lay Roman Catholic academic based in the USA, has responded to the scandal of child sexual abuse, as well as to other sins and crimes within his church, and has done so with learning, clarity and moderation.[19] His discussion is relevant to all Christian traditions because the topic is troubling the faithful in all the churches at this time. In truth, Flanagan's theme of sin and sanctity in the church is a constant concern, for history shows us that the church, in all its branches, has never been without moral failure, error, sin and crime, to one extent or another, notwithstanding many wonderful examples of holiness, dedication and virtue, both known and unknown to us. When Paul addresses the Christians in his churches, he calls them 'saints', but then he tells them to stop stealing and lying, hating and slandering, fornicating and committing adultery, and so on. There is nothing new about the church being mired in moral failure and turpitude. There can be no expression of the church on earth that is not institutional in form and there is no institution that is not prone to corruption, self-serving and abuse of power and position. The crisis of endemic sexual abuse and its flagrant cover-up touches most of Christendom, but in the over-clericalized, hierarchical,

---

18 De Lubac, Henri, 1950, *Catholicism: A Study of Dogma in Relation to the Corporate Destiny of Mankind*, trans. L. C. Sheppard, London: Burns, Oates and Washbourne, p. 26.

19 Flanagan, Brian P., 2018, *Stumbling in Holiness: Sin and Sanctity in the Church*, Collegeville, MN: Liturgical Press Academic. Page references in my main text.

secretive and unaccountable polity of the Roman Catholic Church (RCC) it is proving catastrophic.[20]

Nevertheless, Flanagan's voice is not shrill and his tone is not alarmist. In a systematic yet pastoral way, he takes a steady, discursive approach to the problem, providing expositions of the key concepts – holiness, sin and the church – along the way. He is not crushed by iniquity in the church and its officers. He wants to put the matter into theological perspective, to offer hope and reassurance.

What does it mean for a person to be 'holy'? The biblical concept of holiness has a dual aspect: first, holiness refers to divine calling and election – knowing oneself called by God to live one's life in fellowship with God and for God; second, holiness means following the calling to become conformed progressively to the moral character of God as seen in Jesus Christ. Holiness means both set apart or consecrated (by the word of God and baptism) and transformed or sanctified (through the word of God and the Eucharist), so as to become a morally better person, manifesting the virtues of faith, hope and charity. Flanagan proposes that to call something 'holy' means 'to ascribe to it a certain closeness to God, a transparency of encounter with God's glory in and through encounter with the created reality, a saturation of the reality with the presence of God's Spirit that confers a kind of borrowed divinity upon it' (p. 2). This definition does justice to the first aspect of the biblical understanding of holiness: the call of God to be 'set apart' for God's worship and service. But, on its own, it seems to overlook the ethical dimension of holiness: the progressive moral conforming of the person to the character of Christ, including Jesus' goodness, purity, selflessness and compassion, as we see him portrayed in the Gospels. Flanagan does not completely overlook the ethical dimension, but I wonder whether his argument fully faces up to 'the exceeding sinfulness of sin' (Rom. 7.13) and the depths of 'the mystery of iniquity' (2 Thess. 2.7). He is working with a

20 See, further, Miller, Virginia, 2021, *Child Sexual Abuse Inquiries and the Catholic Church: Reassessing the Evidence*, Florence: Firenze University Press.

definition of sin as a 'failure in love for God and for neighbor' and he acknowledges that sin participates in 'the irrationality of evil' (p. 71). Following an honourable theological tradition, Flanagan defines sin as a negative quality, an absence of goodness, justice and rationality. He argues for holding holiness and sin together in a dynamic tension in the process of spiritual growth in the church, pointing out that the holiness of the church is eschatological: already present, but not yet complete. But is the notion of sin as a lack or failure, and as something that resists rational explanation, adequate to the challenge of intentional, predatory evil in the church, such as we see in the calculated, habitual, long-term sexual abuse of children by priests? I feel that Flanagan's approach is not uncomfortable enough, not sufficiently troubled in spirit, about the *status quo*. There is plenty of sin around – we live with it in ourselves and all around us every day – but in the church and among its clergy and bishops there is also the presence of crime and deliberate evil. And that raises the hoary problem of theodicy – in this case, ecclesial theodicy. Why does God allow so much that is wrong in God's church? Why does God permit God's kingdom to be compromised and the church's mission to be undermined? Why (as the Psalmists often complain) should the name of God be blasphemed on account of God's professed servants? To this question we will return shortly.

Flanagan's main theological sources and influences, apart from Scripture, are the salutary names of Yves Congar, Karl Rahner, J. M. R. Tillard, Joseph Komonchak and Francis A. Sullivan. As we have noted, Rahner was raising the question of sin in the church as early as 1947 and cutting through the standard equivocation – promoted later by Pope John Paul II – that while Christians certainly sin, the church remains sinless. With Rahner and against John Paul II, Flanagan insists that that gambit represents 'a mistaken hypostatization and dehistoricization of the church' (p. 11), by postulating a church that has an existence separate from its members. The faithful, deceived by such ideological rhetorical slogans as 'Holy Mother Church', 'the spotless Bride of Christ', and so on (and

Flanagan critiques the distorted gender stereotyping at work in that language) are shocked and sickened when blatant iniquity within the priesthood and episcopate is uncovered. Rahner and Flanagan insist that the church itself, not merely certain individual members, is at the same time both sinful and holy. Sin on the part of the clergy is the cause of the current troubles of the church, the RCC particularly. But if Flanagan had cast his theological net a little wider than his own tradition, he would have found rich treasures: the daring insights of Martin Luther who followed Scripture in pointing out that Satan poses as an angel of light and that Antichrist takes his seat in the very temple of God.

Having touched on some Roman Catholic voices, I now want to mention a powerful Anglican contribution. Ephraim Radner's *A Brutal Unity: The Spiritual Politics of the Christian Church*[21] is a plea for rethinking ecclesiology in a way that takes the history of division in the church – and the tragic and sometimes criminal consequences of division – with greater seriousness. Radner argues for a 'realistic' ecclesiology, rather than an idealistic one that does not reflect the state of the church as it is. He has not provided such an ecclesiology – at least not in a systematic way – but he has given us a crucial methodological prolegomenon to it. It takes some dedication to work through its 482 pages, but those who do so will probably never be able to think about the church – in other words, to do ecclesiology – in the same way again. Radner's realism means looking at the church without our customary rose-tinted spectacles. The church that goes wrong, commits sins and crimes, is none other than Christ's church. It is not merely the earthly shadow of the real heavenly church, nor is it simply the visible tip of an invisible iceberg. Neither is it the ecclesial mirror-image of the social Trinity, as in some *communio* ecclesiology. The church is not a politically uncontaminated mystical body, but is political through and through, inescap-

21 Radner, Ephraim, 2012, *A Brutal Unity: The Spiritual Politics of the Christian Church*, Waco, TX: Baylor University Press. Page references in my main text.

ably involved with issues of power and justice or injustice. The sinful church that we see *is* the church. The only church that exists is a sinful church. In Radner's view, such ecclesiological realism does not eradicate the church's potential to be an instrument of the mission of God. The two aspects exist in tension. As Radner puts it, the fact that 'disordered failure and redemptive capacity' coincide in the church's life is 'one of the most anguished centres' of Christian experience. But disunity, leading to further failure and wrong-doing, constantly threatens to undermine the Church's God-given *raison d'être*, because a disunited Church cannot point unequivocally – indeed, can hardly point at all – to the unity of God, the most fundamental theological truth of all.

Christian disunity and division is not only an appalling evil in itself but it gives birth to even worse evils. Through an analysis of the late medieval and post-Reformation religious wars in Europe, the church in Hitler's Germany, massacres in Burundi and genocide in Rwanda, Radner shows that the failure of the churches to stand together, to speak and act as one against a common foe, proved to be their undoing and led in some cases to direct involvement in killing, or at least complicity in it. He rejects the recent Roman Catholic apologetic which protests that, while individual members have sinned grievously, 'the church as such' or 'the church in itself' (John Paul II) remains immaculate. He also faults the Barthian, German Confessing Church model which, he argues, evacuated the institutional dimension from the Church (p. 145). Radner's approach is not anti-institutional; no body of humans can suppose that it lacks form. He disputes what he takes to be William Cavanaugh's thesis that religion is usually employed as a pretext for violent action by other powers.[22] No, it is religion itself that is sometimes lethal. The unpalatable fact is that 'religious violence has

---

22 Cavanaugh, William, 2009, *The Myth of Religious Violence*, Oxford: Oxford University Press; Juergensmeyer, Mark, Margo Kitts and Michael Jerryson, 2015, *The Oxford Handbook of Religion and Violence*, Oxford: Oxford University Press; Burridge, Richard A. and Jonathan Sacks (eds), 2018, *Confronting Religious Violence: A*

a horrendous character peculiar to itself'. It finds opportunity when a distorted version of religious identity 'empowers evil'. The religious wars in Europe have been characterized as 'killing people for God's sake'.[23] In the sixteenth century Montaigne observed, 'There is no hostility that exceeds religious hostility.' And Pascal's *pensée* is well known: 'No one does evil so fully and happily as when done for the sake of conscience'. As one of Montesquieu's Persian travellers put it: 'I can assure you that no kingdom has ever had as many civil wars as the kingdom of Christ.'[24]

Even in modern times, Christians have prepared themselves by prayer or even by receiving Holy Communion to slaughter the innocent. Radner points to the Rwanda genocide to argue that there is a kind of Christianity, one that is not at all uncommon, that lends itself to this kind of perversion. It stresses obedience to religious authority; plays up religious differences, stereotyping and – ultimately – demonizing the other; revels in power play and political jockeying; and manipulates powerful indigenous sacral forces for its own purposes. That toxic cocktail makes forgiveness, reconciliation and sacrifice between separated Christians impossible. Certain recognizable types of Christian mindset are congenitally receptive to being taken over for evil purposes.[25] Religious division and violence are not so much cause and effect as 'consanguineous'. The church as a 'killer' is an almost unbearable thought, a prime cause of theological vertigo, but a wholesale catalogue of horrors would probably make the third article of the Apostles' Creed, 'I believe in ... the holy catholic church', stick in the throat.

Counternarrative, London: SCM Press; Waco, TX: Baylor University Press.

23 Housley, Norman, 2002, *Religious Warfare in Europe, 1400–1536*, Oxford: Oxford University Press.

24 Montesquieu, 1973, *Persian Letters*, trans. C. J. Berrs, Harmondsworth: Penguin, p. 81 (Letter 29).

25 Radner draws on Longman, Timothy Paul, 2010, *Christianity and Genocide in Rwanda*, Cambridge: Cambridge University Press.

There is, therefore, a profound challenge for theological work here: 'the reality of Christian division ought to be the topic of a central theological discipline' (p. 125). Ecumenical theology as we know it, Radner suggests, does not do this because it is focused on the healing of divisions. The ecumenical movement today is far too tolerant of division. The urgent imperative of unity has been replaced by a view of Christian division as 'a collection of multiple benignities' (p. 139). While eschatologically-oriented ecclesiologies that project unity into the future are blind to the past, the Church only truly knows itself by looking backwards to see what it has become over time (pp. 141, 160). Unless there is passion, desire and radical intentionality there will never be unity. But that intention must be expressed in action, in a common life of activity. It is practice that shapes the Church. Unity is 'a *life* that is shaped by a single desire' (p. 171). To be of one mind, as the apostle exhorts, is not a mental attitude, but an *act* or series of acts in time (p. 399). Radner's definition of unity is 'charity lived in distinction' (p. 88). Charity is self-giving, self-emptying (*kenosis*) – not a giving away of our identity, but of power and privilege.

The antidote to division, for Radner, begins with *conciliarity*, the practice of the Church coming together in a representative way to wait on God in prayer and Bible study. He lays down the principle that the subject of conciliar activity is always the Scriptures (p. 211). The Church in council seeks to indwell the Scriptures. To do that, individuals must perforce accept the Benedictine discipline of remaining together in one place, as on the Day of Pentecost (pp. 213–14). The metaphor of walking with Jesus as his disciples in the Gospels sheds light on synodality ('together on the way') (p. 218). The very process of conciliarity contains a drive towards convergence and agreement (pp. 248–9). Conciliarity is intrinsically personal and relational; person-to-person interaction – 'extended and intimate engagement' – is the key (p. 261). The mark of a true council is the outgoing charity that seeks to share the gospel more widely (p. 212). Never has disunity been exposed to such a damning indictment as in *Christianity and Genocide in Rwanda*. Rarely has the conciliar path to convergence been portrayed with such insight. But what to do when warring Christians will neither meet nor talk, is a further – and seemingly intractable – question.

So we have an institution fraught with ambiguity and our response to that ambiguity is one of acute ambivalence. We are in two minds about the church. We know that if we love Christ, we should love his church. If we love his church, we should spend ourselves for its unity and devote ourselves to its mission. But we also sense that Christ grieves over the church. Pascal says, 'Christ will be in agony until the end of the world.'[26] We would defend God's church to the death, but we are heartbroken with grief at its failings. Only God is perfect; only God never fails. Nevertheless, there is much that we can and should do:

1 First, for corporate sin there should be corporate penitence and it should be expressed liturgically at every level of the church, led by the episcopate. Repentance includes not only confessing our sins with sorrow and remorse, but also restructuring our understanding of what has happened in the past, the purification and rectification of the collective memory. We now see things differently, not only the past, but also the present and the future.[27]
2 Second, there should be structural and practical reformation, setting right what has gone wrong, extirpating abuses, and putting in place structures of effective oversight and accountability. Like love in 1 Corinthians 13, reform 'never ends', hence the Reformation watchword *ecclesia reformata semper reformanda* (the reformed church is always reforming).

26 Pascal, Blaise, 1966, *Pensées*, trans. A. J. Krailsheimer, Harmondsworth: Penguin, p. 313.

27 See, further, Bergen, Jeremy, 2011, *Ecclesial Repentance: The Churches Confront their Sinful Pasts*, London and New York: T&T Clark.

3 Third, the possibility of further development. Adapting doctrine and practice to meet fresh challenges should be openly and responsibly explored, not closed down *a priori*. Development has been a continuous feature of the church in history and is a proper function of the church. Development is part of the church's business and not something to be defensive about. The more we protest, like Newman, that the church only changes in order to remain the same, the more we become captive to false consciousness. As Roger Haight insists, the church actually changes most when it strives to remain the same by defending to the last supposedly unchanging structures and formulae, which are actually illusory constructions and projections. To postulate sameness is radically contrary to the nature of the church as revealed in history. The church has always sought to respond and react to its social, cultural and political environment. This responsiveness is unavoidable because the church is part of its own environment, not separate from it, and – even more significantly perhaps – the environment is within the church.[28]

4 To return to where we began: John the Baptist and Jesus himself were scourges of Pharisaical hypocrisy. They called on their hearers to be reconciled to their God and to one another by practising ethical integrity. In like manner, the churches today, spiritually chastened and taught institutional humility by heart-felt penitence and concrete reformation, should take theologically informed development as their liberating pathway out of this present quagmire – this 'Slough of Despond', to borrow John Bunyan's phrase.[29] Then, as Vatican II intended, they would be pilgrim churches indeed.[30]

---

28 Haight, Roger, SJ, 2021, 'The World Mission of the Christian Church', in Chapman and Latinovic (eds), *Changing the Church*, ch. 14, at p. 123.

29 Bunyan, John, 1935 (1678, 1684), *The Pilgrim's Progress from this World to that which is to come, Delivered under the Similitude of a Dream*, London: Oxford University Press, pp. 14–16.

30 *Lumen gentium* 8 and many other references and allusions.

The reconciling Spirit

The biblical term 'reconciliation' has sometimes been used to describe the process of *rapprochement* between the churches that begins with the project of seeking mutual recognition of ecclesial authenticity. Ecumenical reconciliation works for sufficient agreement in faith, order and practice for two or more churches if there is the will to do so; to begin to live *as one*: to worship, preach, discern, decide and evangelize *as one*, for their mutual enrichment, empowerment and effectiveness. These churches remain distinct, embedded in their enduring traditions and structures and steadfast in their received identity; what they believe and practise makes them what they are and not something else. But at the same time, they are learning to be mutually receiving communities, actively receptive, not only to what concretely they can learn from and emulate in their partner church(es), but also from the deep fund of their less tangible wisdom, insight, perspectives, priorities and energy. These churches are now organically interacting; interlocking in all possible ways; not enclosed and sealed up; not manning the barricades against one another; not defining themselves 'over against'; not fearing and stereotyping the other; not saying to themselves or even to God (to adapt the smug words of the Pharisee in the parable): 'We thank thee that we are not as other churches' (cf. Luke 18.9–14). By working *as one*, even before they are organizationally or structurally one, they are moving towards the organic relationship that has sometimes been described in dialogue involving Anglicans and Roman Catholics as 'full visible communion'.[31]

As several popes have said, there can be no turning back from the adventure of Christian unity, no losing hope, because

31 Here I am very much in tune with the 'Receptive Ecumenism' project, emanating from Durham University; see Murray, Paul D. (ed.), 2008, *Receptive Ecumenism and the Call to Catholic Learning: Exploring a Way for Contemporary Ecumenism*, Oxford: Oxford University Press; Avis, Paul, 'Are we Receiving Receptive Ecumenism?', *Ecclesiology* 8.2 (2012), pp. 223–34.

as Christians and churches we are called to the apostolic ministry of reconciliation (2 Cor. 5.18). If charity begins at home, so does reconciliation. But we humans are not the reconcilers. In this ministry, the triune God is the reconciler – the initiator, actor and empowerer in the process of reconciliation. We – the churches and their faithful – may by grace become the instruments of God's work of reconciliation: 'Make me a channel of your peace.' Through the word of the gospel God calls us, beseeches us, commands us, to be reconciled and to reconcile. Pursuing the cause of unity involves a purposeful ministry of reconciliation with regard to the assumptions, beliefs and prejudices of parties who seem to stand far apart on certain matters. Such a ministry of reconciliation is an inescapable stage on the path that leads to the ultimate goal of ecclesial communion (*koinonia*) or sacramental fellowship (*communio in sacris*) in which the divine blessings of charity, harmony and unity can be experienced even in the midst of diversity.

Finally, we might take a warning from the fact that reconciliation also has a more passive sense: to be reconciled to something can mean to acquiesce in a state of affairs, to be resigned to it, to live with it without repining too much. Edmund Burke wrote, 'Custom reconciles us to every thing [sic].'[32] No feature of Christianity is more *customary* to us, more *taken for granted*, than the divided state of the church, of ecclesial separation and fragmentation. But no state of affairs in the church is more contrary to the will of God and the mind of Christ, because it is the antithesis of reconciliation. As Joan Crewdson, a disciple and expositor of Michael Polanyi's personalist philosophy, succinctly put it, 'Redemption is a process by which things that are fragmented come to wholeness.'[33] It is

32 Burke, Edmund, 1834, *On the Sublime and the Beautiful*, IV, xviii, *The Works of the Right Hon. Edmund Burke with a Biographical and Critical Introduction and Portrait after Sir Joshua Reynolds*, London: Holdsworth and Ball, vol. 1, p. 65.

33 Crewdson, Joan, 1994, *Christian Doctrine in the Light of Michael Polanyi's Theory of Personal Knowledge: A Personalist Theology*,

not only wilful sin, but custom, what we are used to, *habitude*, that has reconciled us to the scandal, shame and disaster of church disunity. What has happened to the Christian church over 2,000 years – the progressive dismemberment of the body – does not trouble our conscience overmuch; it does not keep us awake at night; it does not make us tremble before the altar. That is an intolerable fact – theologically, spiritually and morally intolerable. To pray, study and work for the reconciliation of the church of Christ to itself, to God and to the world, is to cease to tolerate the intolerable.

All kinds of justification have been put forward that serve to numb the Christian conscience to the scandal of an unreconciled church: a) There is the familiar claim of *exclusivity*: 'Our church is *the* church'; therefore, other ecclesial bodies are 'not churches in the proper sense', 'lack the fullness of the church that we enjoy', and so on. That gambit, which is deployed in traditional Roman Catholic and Orthodox ecclesiological rhetoric, attempts to put division outside the boundaries of the church thus defined and so serves to obviate the guilt of division. But the question of who is in the church and who is not is not for humans to decide. b) Then there is the ultra-Protestant – it is not true of the major Reformers – appeal to an *invisible* church: 'Unity belongs to the invisible church and therefore it is indestructible; so division in the visible church does not matter very much.' According to this tactic, division does not touch the essence of the church; it is superficial and almost trivial. But the dichotomy between the visible church and the invisible church creates a grossly dualistic and incoherent ecclesiology. c) Finally, there is the – rather startling – *added value* argument in favour of separation: 'Division brings variety and variety brings enrichment and generates energy, so the church actually benefits from being disunited.'[34] That is perhaps the most perverse justification for disunity that I have ever come across;

Toronto Studies in Theology, vol. 66, Lewiston/Queenston/Lampeter: The Edwin Mellen Press, p. 320.

34 Ingle-Gillis, W. C., 2007, *The Trinity and Ecumenical Church Thought*, Aldershot and Burlington, VT: Ashgate (discussed in ch. 1).

it reminds me of St Paul's parody in Romans: 'Let us sin that grace may abound' (Rom. 6.1).

The answer that, I believe, refutes all those evasions of the imperative of unity is found in eucharistic ecclesiology, the theology of *koinonia*, *communio*, *sobornost*. It rests on a realist understanding of the sacramental principle and draws out its implications. It begins by affirming that the baptismal unity of Christians in the body of Christ is both mystical and visible – in other words, sacramental. Through sacramental initiation (catechesis-baptism-confirmation-Eucharist, though not always in that order), Christians are placed in ontological union with Jesus Christ and to one another through the power of the Holy Spirit (1 Cor. 12.13). Christian initiation places us within the realm of sacramentality, inserted into the church as the body of Christ. David Jones quoted Maurice de la Taille that, at the Last Supper, Christ 'placed himself in the order of signs'.[35] The Holy Spirit, through the sacraments of Christian initiation, has placed us also, with Christ, in the order of signs – signs that mediate and convey what they signify – and has brought us into sacramental communion with the Holy Trinity and with every other baptized Christian in the communion of saints. That sacramental communion is grounded in baptism and finds its continual expression, renewal and completion in the Eucharist (1 Cor. 10.16–17). Eucharistic communion is the birthright of all the baptized. When, for whatever reason, Christians are unable to consummate their baptismal communion in eucharistic communion, they are deprived of their birthright. That state of affairs applies, in one way or another, to all Christians, all the baptized, all the faithful, in the world. None of us is in full visible communion with all our fellow members of the body gathered in their own communities.

35 Jones, David, 1959 (1955), 'Art and Sacrament', in David Jones, 1959 (1955) *Epoch and Artist*, London: Faber and Faber; la Taille, Maurice de, SJ, 1941, *The Mystery of Faith: Regarding the Most August Sacrament and Sacrifice of the Body and Blood of Christ, Book I: The Sacrifice of Our Lord*, London: Sheed and Ward.

There is no church that is in full visible communion with all other churches.

We should not point the finger at any particular church. All the churches are implicated in this fall from grace, this great historical Fall of the church. All churches have fallen short of the baptismal vocation to 'maintain the unity of the Spirit in the bond of peace' (Eph. 4.3). Surely we cannot reconcile ourselves to an unreconciled church? What are we going to do to build ecclesial communion in the power of the Spirit? The Holy Spirit is the spirit of communion (2 Cor. 13.13). What William Wordsworth wrote about the integrating, harmonizing power of the human spirit, doing its work deep within the psyche, can be applied to the Holy Spirit working in the church. Wordsworth elicits a gradual build-up of harmony in the human spirit: 'Dust as we are, the immortal spirit grows / Like harmony in music; there is a dark / Inscrutable workmanship that reconciles / Discordant elements, makes them cling together / In one society.'[36] The poet's words seem to echo what Paul says in 1 Corinthians 2.10–11 about the divine Spirit: 'the Spirit searches everything, even the depths of God. For what human being knows what is truly human except the human spirit that is within? So also no one comprehends what is truly God's except the Spirit of God.' As we work for deeper Christian unity, in prayer, thought and deed, let us put our faith in the reconciling Spirit.

36 Wordsworth, William, 1972, *The Prelude: A Parallel Text*, ed. J. C. Maxwell, Harmondsworth: Penguin, pp. 53, 55 (1850 version).

6

To Heal a Wounded Church

In the Old Testament book that bears his name, suffering Job, sitting in dust and ashes and licking his wounds, both literal and metaphorical, asks, 'Where shall wisdom be found? And where is the place of understanding?' Then Job answers his own question, saying, 'Mortals do not know the way to it, and it is not found in the land of the living' (Job 28.12–13). What Job desired above all, in order to understand his personal tragedy of undeserved and therefore (according to the dominant theological worldview of the Hebrews) inexplicable affliction, and to be able to answer the accusations of his friends, the 'false comforters', was the gift of divine wisdom. Job's cry is not one of cynical desperation; it reflects the confidence, characteristic of the rich Wisdom literature of the Hebrew Bible and the Apocrypha, that all created things and all worthy human endeavour are infused with divine Wisdom, that 'she' is available to all who seek her as the gift of God and that the search for truth will be rewarded. Job does eventually receive his answer; it is God's abiding word to humankind: 'Truly the fear of the Lord, that is wisdom; and to depart from evil is understanding' (Job 28.28).

In a similar mood to Job, I want to ask, in a spirit of searching, not cynicism, and of confidence, not despondency: 'Where shall unity be found? And where is the place of reconciliation?' In other words, I am asking, 'How can the wounds of division in the body of Christ be healed?' And I will add to that: 'What does Christian unity look like? How would we know it?' More radically, I want to enquire, 'When, if ever, has the church been united? Has Christian unity ever in fact existed?' But then we must face the challenge of how greater unity and deeper communion between separated Christians and churches can be realized and brought about. So, the agenda of my enquiry in this chapter can be summarized as: 'Christian Unity: Where? What? When? How?' I offer it as a preliminary essay in applied or practical ecclesiology – no one will be able to say that it is theoretical or abstract – preparing the ground for the last two chapters of the book which tackle the 'How?' question (the question of dynamics) in some depth.

The mind of Christ

Just as Job is representative of the Wisdom tradition in his conviction that wisdom is the gift of God and at the heart of God's providential administration of the created order, so I hold fast to the axiom that unity is grounded in the divine nature and is God's will for humankind and especially for God's church. 'O God, who art the author of peace and lover of concord, in knowledge of whom standeth our eternal life, whose service is perfect freedom', begins the Second Collect, for Peace, at Morning Prayer in the *Book of Common Prayer*, 1662: 'author', 'lover', 'life-giver', 'liberator'. The church also prays, 'Lord Jesus Christ, who said to your Apostles, "Peace I leave with you, my peace I give unto you", look not on our sins, but on the faith of your Church, and grant her that peace and unity which is in accordance with your will.'

In the same vein, the Apostle Paul appeals to the Philippians: 'If there is any encouragement in Christ, any consolation from love, any sharing in the spirit, any compassion and sympathy, make my joy complete ...' But how are they to do this? 'Be of the same mind, having the same love, being in full accord and of one mind. Do nothing from selfish ambition or conceit, but in humility regard others as better than yourselves.' It is striking how Paul reiterates the point about unanimity of mind: 'the same mind', 'of one mind', and then drives this home with his final and greatest appeal: 'Let the same mind be in you that was in Christ Jesus', the words that introduce the hymn of Christ's self-emptying descent into the form of a slave and a death by crucifixion, followed by his glorious exaltation (Phil. 2.1–11). It was Paul's signature appeal and heartfelt longing: 'Now I appeal to you, brothers and sisters, by the name of our Lord Jesus Christ', he writes to the Corinthian Christians, 'that all of you be in agreement and that there be no divisions among you, but that you be united in the same mind and the same purpose' (1 Cor. 1.10).

The mind of Christ, revealed in the Gospels, will lead us to a working definition of the unity of Christ's church. Such a definition needs to reflect the imperative of unity that we find throughout the New Testament, especially in John 17.21–23, the 'High-Priestly Prayer' of Jesus. On the eve of his Passion, Jesus prays that his disciples, then and in the future, will be one – that is, united in heart and purpose, as he and the Father are united in heart and purpose. He prays that theirs will be a unity of love that, in itself, will reveal to the world that he has been sent by the Father for the world's salvation. What could be more constraining for us, more imperative and more impelling, than the prayer of Jesus at the Last Supper? Those Christians, including bishops and other church leaders, who are not impelled by the prayer of Jesus to seek the unity of his body are not in tune with the heart of Jesus; they have turned aside from his declared will and are alienated from his central purpose.

So it will not be sufficient for our theological account of Christian unity to be merely descriptive of the current state of affairs ('How far are our churches united now and how far are they still actually divided?'), though that purely phenomenological approach has its uses. Our idea of unity must be prescriptive, articulating a vision of God's revealed will, expressing an aspiration for the future, and instilling a motivation for present action. Since the unity of the empirical church is evidently radically incomplete – I will not say non-existent – and a 'work in progress' at best, our definition needs to contain a dynamic thrust. So I wish to propose a rather practical definition of Christian unity with some cutting edge: *Christian unity is the quest to re-unite what belongs together but has come apart*. To put it more concisely, it means, *Bringing back together what belongs together*. Ecumenical theology, which is a branch of ecclesiology, aims to provide the theological building blocks for this re-uniting endeavour. My programmatic statement of intent contains two main elements, and both are verbs, action words: 'Belonging together' and 'Bringing together'. I will now look at each of these in turn.

In 'belonging together', I postulate both an 'original' and an 'essential' unity of the church. To postulate the church's 'original' unity points to its origin in time and is therefore a *historical* statement and an *empirical* claim. As such, it gives several hostages to fortune and is vulnerable to ongoing developments in historical research, so it needs to be examined. On the other hand, to affirm the church's 'essential' unity is a *theological* statement and a *dogmatic* claim, because it affirms that unity belongs to the irreducible essence or being of the church, so that unity is intrinsic to the church's very nature. As a theological statement and dogmatic claim, it is always open to critique and challenge, or at least refinement. But to affirm the church's essential unity remains a confession of faith, as in the Nicene Creed: 'I believe (or believe in) one holy catholic and apostolic Church.'

In the following two chapters, which are devoted to the notion of 'bringing together', I will approach the theme via the twin concepts of 'recognition' and 'reconciliation'. The nursery rhyme of Humpty Dumpty is a gloomy warning that, once something has shattered, the very best endeavours of the highest authority ('all the king's horses and all the king's men') may not be able to put it 'together again'. But that does not mean that there is nothing we can do. Step by step we can work for the greater unity, unanimity and harmony of Christ's church.

Reconciliation effects a new relationship

To reconcile, in any sphere of human life, ranging from fraught domestic situations to conflict-ridden international crises, is to bring estranged parties together in friendship and concord. Reconciliation is much more than pragmatic conflict-resolution because it aims to build an ongoing new relationship between formerly estranged parties. Reconciliation does this by resolving differences and bringing opponents to be at peace with one another in such a way that, in seeing one another differently, their own identity is changed. Reconciliation means to bring two opposed realities – which may be persons, communities, nations, beliefs, demands or states of affairs – into accord, harmony, a common mind and unity of purpose.[1] Christian theology holds that peace and harmony have their source in God and that the Holy Spirit is the bringer of concord. As I have already mentioned, the Second Collect at Morning Prayer in the Anglican *Book of Common Prayer* (1662) calls upon God 'the author of peace and lover of concord'.

Pre-Copernican cosmology spoke of 'the music of the celestial spheres'. In John Henry Newman's 'The Dream of Gerontius', the soul approaching the presence of God in heaven exclaims: 'But hark! A grand mysterious harmony: / It floods me, like the deep and solemn sound / Of many waters.' Gerontius' accompanying Guardian Angel informs him that the sound is that of 'a band of mighty angels … [who] hymn the Incarnate God'.[2] In Anthony Powell's captivating sequence of 12 novels

1 Bar-Siman-Tov, Yaacov (ed.), 2004, *From Conflict Resolution to Reconciliation*, Oxford: Oxford University Press, especially ch. 5: Herbert C. Kelman, 'Reconciliation as Identity Change: A Social-Psychological Perspective'. Deeper issues affecting the possibility of reconciliation are powerfully explored in Schimmel, Solomon, 2002, *Wounds Not Healed By Time: The Power of Repentance and Forgiveness*, Oxford: Oxford University Press. See also Bash, Anthony, 2007, *Forgiveness and Christian Ethics*, Cambridge: Cambridge University Press.

2 Newman, J. H., 1908 (1865), *The Dream of Gerontius*, London: Bagster, p. 68.

A Dance to the Music of Time, the last of them bears the title *Hearing Secret Harmonies*.[3] I suspect that those who heed the call to work for reconciliation between Christians and between churches do so because they hear, dimly and distantly, something akin to the imagined music of the spheres. They believe that unforced harmony in the church is a sign of the presence of the Holy Spirit and of the approach of the kingdom of God. To effect reconciliation is to perform a perfect human work; but it is also to do the work of God. Because there will always be misunderstandings, irrational fears and aggressive tensions, there will always be a need for reconciliation, for bringing into harmony and concord. To be reconciled after estrangement is the sweetest thing we know.

Clearly, there is a mountain of reconciling work to do between Christians and between churches. The array of ongoing theological dialogues, both internal to churches and external, between churches, testifies to this fact. But some may question whether the word 'reconciliation' is appropriate for the state of inter-church relations today, after a century of the ecumenical movement. It is true that mutual persecution and the trading of insults and anathemas has largely ceased between churches (though it still goes on within them!). Churches are talking to one another at all levels of their life, including official theological dialogue. There are innumerable personal friendships across denominational boundaries. Eucharistic hospitality is offered by the mainstream Protestant and Anglican churches. It might seem that reconciliation has already been accomplished; but 'reconciliation' need not imply that the parties concerned have been living in a state of permanent mutual enmity or hostility. While this has obviously often been the case in the past, today – though this also is nothing new – hostility mainly manifests itself *within* churches and world communions, rather than between them, in the form of ideological warfare for the dominant ground and place of power in that church or com-

3 Powell, Anthony, 1975, *Hearing Secret Harmonies*, London: Heinemann.

munion. To that extent, reconciliation in the strong sense is still required within all the major Christian traditions.

But even when churches already show respect for one another, perhaps already consulting and cooperating with one another to some extent, a fuller and stronger form of reconciliation is still needed because crucially they remain out of full sacramental communion and the visible wounds of division in the body of Christ remain unhealed. Reconciliation is often called for between friends, or family members, or married couples, or lovers, who have become estranged. They must learn – and they can be helped to learn through skilled mediation – to relate to one another in a fresh and positive way. Reconciliation, grounded in intentional mutual recognition, is the pathway that the ecumenical movement follows towards the goal of full visible communion. To be reconciled can mean to be brought together, to interface, to stand four-square with one another, to be positioned vis-à-vis. Reconciliation flows out of recognition and results in the healing of division, in the church made whole.

Avenues of reconciliation

The Archbishop of Canterbury, Justin Welby, has used the phrase 'good disagreement', and this is both stimulating and provocative. Stimulating because, given the state of violent disagreement within the churches, we are bound to ask, 'What style of disagreement is acceptable among Christians?' But the phrase is also provocative, because the word 'good' is just not *good* enough to characterize the kind of disagreement that, as Christians, we should aspire to have, given that disagreement there is going to be. Others have attempted to improve on the mantra 'good disagreement' with versions of 'gracious', 'virtuous' and 'loving' disagreement. In this section I will harvest, from a selection of recent studies, insights that will enrich our reflection on what may well be judged the major ecclesiological question of our time: the ethical dimension of ecclesial communion or, to put it another way, the ethical impediments to ecclesial communion. Ethics is undoubtedly the new frontier of ecumenical dialogue. Convergence on Faith and Order – the standard ecumenical agenda – is no longer enough. Agreement in moral teaching now presents an additional hurdle to churches moving closer together. It is, as Robert W. Jenson puts it in the symposium edited by Michael Root and James Buckley, 'the next great ecumenical stumbling block'.[4] This symposium is our first candidate for discussion.

The Morally Divided Body: Ethical Disagreement and the Disunity of the Body reflects the increasing realization that divisive ethical issues – especially how Christians understand gender, sexuality, marriage and reproduction – are also and at the same time doctrinal and moral questions. As F. C. Bauerschmidt insists, knowing and doing, doctrine and ethics, are one thing. To try to keep the doctrinal and the moral in separate compartments is to play false with Christian theology. Thomas Aquinas and Karl Barth equally insisted, from their different perspectives, that these two areas of theology are inseparable. Although they are certainly intertwined in the Bible, a straightforward appeal to Scripture will not get us very far. As Beth Barton Schweiger shows, both the opponents of slavery and its defenders in nineteenth-century America not only read the same Bible but read it in the same way (p. 17). Neither will invoking Reformation principles help very much: Joe Small deplores the fissiparousness of the Reformed family of churches and the way that the method of binary, 'yes or no', voting in church synods contributes to this. Small expounds an attractive vision, drawn from Václav Havel, of 'living within the truth'. Susan K. Wood, investigating the connection between ethics and ecclesiology, the moral body and the eucharistic body, shows that deep Christian divisions over moral

4 Root, Michael, and James Buckley (eds), 2012, *The Morally Divided Body: Ethical Disagreement and the Disunity of the Body*, Eugene, OR: Cascade Books, p. 1. See also Avis, Paul, 2010, *Reshaping Ecumenical Theology*, London and New York: T&T Clark, ch. 9: 'Ethics and Communion: The New Frontier in Ecumenism'.

teaching raise questions about whether the church can fulfil its God-given mission. As she puts it, ‘A morally divided body creates serious cognitive dissonance with the sacrament that represents the moral life in completion’ (p. 75).

David Yeago approaches the matter from another, actually Lutheran, angle, arguing that ‘we cannot agree about Christ if we disagree about substantial matters of moral teaching’ (p. 78). His thesis – surprising from a Lutheran point of view – is that we cannot agree about the gospel of Christ if we do not agree about the law of God. I think this claims too much. I suggest that it may be possible to agree on an ethical vision and ethical principles or values, while diverging somewhat on the specific moral application of the vision and values, as the Anglican–Roman Catholic International Commission report of 1993 *Life in Christ* shows.

In his survey and analysis of how ethics has featured in ecumenical dialogues since the 1960s, Michael Root identifies that ARCIC report as the most substantial discussion of its topic, though he points out that ecumenical dialogues have not generally neglected to at least touch on ethical and moral questions. But Root finds fault with the ARCIC report for seeming to suggest that ethical values and visions are somehow more fundamental than moral rules and disciplines. He does not believe that a ‘differentiated consensus’ approach – ‘We agree on the basics, but not on every aspect of their application’ – will work on this front because he assumes that any shared life between churches with different moral rules will come up against the very concrete issues that actually embody and apply the values and visions.

However, I doubt whether Root’s challenge to ARCIC takes sufficient account of the diversity of individual moral conviction and practice *within* all the churches today and – which amounts to much the same thing – whether it reckons adequately with the principle of the supremacy of conscience. There is already immense diversity of moral practice, based on diversity of moral conviction, within the major Christian traditions, whatever the churches’ official teachings may be.

So to insist on unanimity about moral rules before we can move towards ecclesial communion seems unreal. On the other hand, Root has pointed up once again the challenge posed by this collection as a whole: how can the churches attain visible unity, above all at the Eucharist, when there is moral disunity between them? The challenge is posed in Jenson's essay when he asks what moral issues justify separation – that is to say, what moral issues are church-dividing. My own rule of thumb in ecumenical theology is that to persist in a state of wilful or complacent sacramental separation within the body of Christ is a much greater sin – a heinous sin – than any falling short in moral teaching or in the day-to-day moral life of Christians. Therefore, some degree of accommodation or economy in the moral sphere needs to be built in to any proposals for steps towards unity.

Sex, Moral Teaching, and the Unity of the Church: A Study of the Episcopal Church, by Timothy F. Sedgwick, offers a different approach to that of Jenson and Root.[5] Sedgwick combines a historical narrative of recent conflicts within the Anglican Communion and the Episcopal Church over human sexuality with a calm analysis of issues of unity and difference and a profound vision of the path to healing through moral discernment. In place of bitter, inconclusive, binary arguments about 'who's right' and 'who's wrong', Sedgwick offers a pathway of moral discernment. We need to ask ourselves, 'How do we teach?' and 'How do we learn?' in the area of moral truth. This reflection on the *methods* of moral pedagogy itself depends on how we understand the *purpose* of inculcating moral awareness in the light of the gospel. In turn, our *structures* of moral authority in oversight (*episkopé*) must be shaped by the purpose and pedagogy of moral insight in place of political and ideological posturing. The organic process of moral shaping is always interpersonal and communal and therefore carries with it an imperative and momentum towards unity. The assertion

5 Sedgwick, Timothy F., 2014, *Sex, Moral Teaching, and the Unity of the Church: A Study of the Episcopal Church*, New York: Morehouse.

of identity in separation, by schismatic action, in order to preserve purity, is illusory, argues Sedgwick, because identity is always identity-in-difference and presupposes a living relationship, albeit one that exists in tension. If we concentrate our energies on the New Testament call to die to self and to embrace Christ's risen life in the community of the church, differences will simply not be allowed to divide us. As Sedgwick perceptively observes, in its divided state the church is not a place of welcome for a spiritual journey of trust and love. 'You can't trust or love what is divided' (p. 1), only what is unified and has integrity. Where that is lacking, evangelization is undermined and the church fails in its God-given task.

Third, *Good Disagreement* consists of essays by Anglican evangelicals for Anglican evangelicals, but contains much that is relevant to all who are troubled by the problem of glaring disunity among Christians.[6] The focus of the book is on the ethical integrity of debate, along with principled questions of unity and communion; it does not enter into the substantive issues within the culture of late modernity that are generating tensions within the churches, particularly gender roles in the church and same-sex unions. The joint editors, Andrew Atherstone and Andrew Goddard, historian and ethicist respectively, explore the notion of 'disagreeing with grace'. They pinpoint that we are dealing fundamentally with divergent interpretations of Scripture and of what truth and holiness, in the light of Scripture, might mean in practice. While these two editors explicitly countenance 'some form of separation among professing Christians' in extreme circumstances, Michael B. Thompson's study of 'Division and Discipline in the New Testament Church' (chapter 3) importantly finds no New Testament authority for churches breaking away from one another, pointing out that 'every case of discipline in the New Testament concerns the failings of individuals who profess the faith – there are no examples of the apostles excluding entire

6 Atherstone, Andrew and Andrew Goddard (eds), 2015, *Good Disagreement: Grace and Truth in a Divided Church*, Oxford: Lion Books.

congregations'. Ian Paul's chapter on reconciliation in the New Testament concludes that 'it is not possible to argue that the only thing which matters is the truth'. He shows that, alongside proclaiming the truth of the gospel, Jesus devoted himself to the restoration and rebuilding of relationships. But these are not two separate elements in Jesus' ministry: reconciliation comes through attending to his word – for us, attending together to God's revelation in Jesus Christ, embodied in the Scriptures.

Tom Wright sets out to deal with 'how Paul sees the question of *adiaphora*, "things indifferent"'. But Paul never uses the word *adiaphora* which comes rather from Reformation concerns with Christian unity and the scope of salvation. The idea may resonate with some Pauline concerns, but the word is not his.[7] For Paul, special foods and days and, crucially, circumcision were examples of things that did not 'make a difference' to salvation. These were more than 'cultural taboos', as Wright calls them; they were cultic inscriptions of the theological doctrine of the unique election of Israel among the nations; so it was no light matter to relativize them and to move them out of the category of salvation, as Paul did. Wright highlights Paul's use of the distinction between 'the strong and the weak' in one's attitude to things indifferent, where conscience must be the arbiter. Wright is spot on in urging Christians to learn the Pauline wisdom of holding back if their proposed action is likely to prove a stumbling block (*skandalon*) to the faith of others 'for whom Christ died'. The problem is that the question of same-sex unions is not regarded as a 'thing indifferent' either by progressives – who see it as a matter of love and justice, and therefore connected to the revealed character of God – or by conservatives, for whom same-sex unions are forbidden by God's revealed law. So who are 'the strong' and who are 'the weak' in this case? Both are 'strong' and that fact reflects the intractable nature of theological disagreement.

---

7 On *adiaphora*, see Verkamp, Bernard J., 1977, *The Indifferent Mean: Adiaphorism in the English Reformation to 1554*, Athens, OH: Ohio University Press/Detroit, MI: Wayne State University Press.

Ashley Null surveys attempts at conciliation in the sixteenth century – between the various Protestant Reformers themselves and between Protestants and Roman Catholics. Null points out that, for the Reformers, 'things indifferent' (*adiaphora*) were theological tenets or liturgical practices – intensely practical matters – that made no difference to salvation. For the reconciler Martin Bucer, the theological description of the mode of Christ's presence in the eucharistic elements was an *adiaphoron* that should not keep Christians apart. But for Martin Luther, the words of Christ at the Last Supper – in the mass, *Hoc est corpus meum* ('This is my body') – were the pledge and the means of salvation itself; therefore, there could be no compromise. The Reformers were adamant that separation from a church was never justified, not even by serious scandal or mistaken beliefs, but only when the very way of salvation (the gospel) was at stake. Null sometimes suggests that the sixteenth-century dialogue partners were looking for 'a form of words' or 'a formula' that would facilitate agreement and that was certainly sometimes the case. However, I think that agreement 'on paper' was always more than a cynical political ploy. But what the Reformers were actually working for was agreement with integrity, not papering over the cracks. Null sets out four principles that enabled genuine, though fragmentary, accord to come about in Reformation times. All concerned recognized that i) division in the church was a scandal; ii) theological truth deserved concentrated study and debate; iii) not all theological issues were equally important; iv) personal interaction around the dialogue, in order to build trust and respect, was vital.

Christians engaged in controversy have typically dipped their pens in vitriol. To learn to disagree graciously, as the contributors to this symposium advocate, would be to step into a new and unfamiliar dimension, to inhabit in fact the 'new creation' that God's work of reconciliation has brought about in Jesus Christ (2 Cor. 5.17). Disputing Christians need to move beyond so-called 'good disagreement' to find ways to actually narrow the gulf of division – a theological, emotional, relational and political gulf – on the way to deeper convergence on those points where it is possible. I need to reserve exploration of methods and tools – one of them being the subtle concept of 'differentiated consensus' which will always be associated with the ecumenical theologian Harding Meyer of the Lutheran Strasbourg Institute – for another occasion (astonishingly, the method of 'differentiated consensus', so important for the Lutheran–Roman Catholic *Joint Declaration on the Doctrine of Justification* of 1999, is not discussed in this symposium). But for any progress to be made, Christians of strongly opposed convictions need to be willing to talk to one another face to face. For some in entrenched positions, that is asking more than they are willing to give.

In *Disagreeing Virtuously: Religious Conflict in Interdisciplinary Perspective*, by Olli-Pekka Vainio, we move from 'disagreeing graciously' to 'disagreeing virtuously', from the theology of grace to philosophical ethics.[8] The grace of God, working through human channels, does not bypass ethical virtue, but is at home with it, strengthening and directing it. The churches today are experiencing the truth of John Henry Newman's dictum, in his 1841 essay 'The Tamworth Reading Room': 'You cannot have Christianity, and not have differences.'[9] If you cannot have Christianity without differences, you certainly cannot have a church either. Deep difference of conscientious conviction cannot be smoothed away by talking up 'good disagreement', exhorting all concerned to be on their best behaviour. These disputes can only be managed, negotiated and perhaps lifted up into a new framework and perspective where their potential for destruction is reduced. Difference is a function of pluralism, and the plurality of convictions and practices within the Christian church and within the particular churches themselves mirrors the plurality of ideologies and

8 Vainio, Olli-Pekka, 2017, *Disagreeing Virtuously: Religious Conflict in Interdisciplinary Perspective*, Grand Rapids, MI: Eerdmans.

9 Newman, J. H., 1948 (1841), 'The Tamworth Reading Room', in J. H. Newman, *Essays and Sketches*, ed. C. F. Harrold, 2 vols, New York: Longmans, vol. 2, p. 197.

life-forms in the world at large – all of which are necessarily politicized and carry 'clout'.

The value of Vainio's study of virtuous disagreement is that it sets the churches' problems, of managing and negotiating differences, within an interdisciplinary perspective, bringing forward a wide range of studies from the human sciences that have a bearing on how churches and theologians approach questions of difference, controversy and conflict. Starting from the premise, borrowed from Peter Berger's *The Heretical Imperative* (1980),[10] that 'we are all heretics now' because of pluralism and individual freedom, Vainio shows, on the basis of interdisciplinary study, that difference and disagreement are absolutely integral to human existence and essential to life in community – in a word, ineradicable. He devotes his first major section to a survey of how philosophers and theologians, from Plato and Aristotle, through Augustine and Aquinas, to Kant and Nietzsche, have handled theories of difference or disagreement. Vainio demonstrates that they disagreed with one another about every aspect of the problem, even disagreeing over what disagreement is (the exact opposite of the jejune saying, 'Great minds think alike'). This section ends with a brief discussion of what modern thinkers such as Rawls, Rorty and Wolterstorff have proposed about the place of difference in the public square of liberal democracy.

The discussion moves on through cognitive science and social psychology (including the question of how beliefs are formed and propagated) to an exposition of the classical virtues, particularly in connection with theories of identity and narrative that serve to bring the discussion closer to ecclesiology. The fundamental question that Vainio identifies – and it is a therapeutic one – is how all of us may attain a more true and more just perspective on the world, how we may learn to interpret our own lives and our environment more correctly. What disciplines are entailed in order to be 'true to life'? The hub of the issue is located in questions of interpretation, perspective

10 Berger, Peter L., 1980, *The Heretical Imperative*, London: Collins.

and framework. The relevant disciplines that Vainio covers bring out how our view of the world is prone to subjective distortion and structural bias. But there are skills available in 'debiasing', leading to deeper self-knowledge or (in religious terms) enlightenment. Studies reveal what an alarmingly tiny proportion of the population in the West is capable of avoiding absolutist positions and adopting an 'evaluative' stance, one of critical appreciation, in relation to issues that arise in the social and political culture. At this juncture, I think more could have been said about *empathy*, which is vital to historical and social insight. But Vainio does includes a nuanced discussion of tolerance, a much-misunderstood virtue and one that truly lies somewhere between two extremes: apathetic negligence, on the one hand, and uncritical acceptance, on the other, of whatever issue needs to be confronted.

A Theology of Disagreement: New Testament Ethics for Ecclesial Conflicts, by Christopher Landau, has the heart of the matter in it – all disagreement should be held within the love of God – but sadly it ultimately fails to achieve its promise.[11] Landau apparently does not know Tim Sedgwick's *Sex, Moral Teaching, and the Unity of the Church* (2014) or Olli-Pekka Vainio's *Disagreeing Virtuously* (2017). But Landau's approach is different from those mentioned above, being more of a biblical theology than any other kind, though insight from extra-biblical Christian resources is welcomed in principle. Landau's argument takes its rise from his response to Richard B. Hays's classic *The Moral Vision of the New Testament* and he relentlessly spars with Hays all the way through.[12] He understandably finds fault with Hays's approach for a procrustean hermeneutic that excludes both inconvenient biblical texts and insight from non-biblical sources.

11 Landau, Christopher, 2021, *A Theology of Disagreement: New Testament Ethics for Ecclesial Conflicts*, London: SCM Press.

12 Hays, Richard B., 1996, *The Moral Vision of the New Testament*, New York: HarperCollins.

Landau works through extensive biblical material from the Gospels and Epistles to see how Jesus and Paul dealt with disagreement. In spite of the wealth of exposition that Landau provides, his method is flawed in two ways. First, the texts are mainly taken at face value, without critical, contextual probing into what may lie behind them in the transmission and shaping of the Gospel narratives within the histories of early Christian communities. For example, a snippet from the Synoptics will be naively related to the Pauline image of the body of Christ. Second, not all the examples given from the New Testament are of disagreements; some are simply conversations – examples of human interaction and interpersonal rapport (e.g., Jesus and the Samaritan woman at Jacob's well in John 4). In addition, Landau concedes that there are examples of Jesus dealing angrily, scornfully and provocatively with opponents. He points out that these are situations where the mission of Jesus with regard to the coming of the reign of God was being fundamentally challenged, and not pastoral situations with needy people or teaching opportunities for the disciples. This anomaly needed addressing in relation to the Evangelists' possible rationales for their inclusion and their portrayal of the character of Christ. Incidentally, Landau speaks repeatedly of the 'biography' of Jesus in the Gospels and of the 'narrative' status of the love-commandment texts, which – without denying that there are biographical elements in the Gospels or that a narrative-genre approach has its place – does not strike quite the right note. What the author may be groping for is the theological-ethical concept of the 'character of Christ'.

Landau rightly points to the double love commandment (God and neighbour) in Matthew 22.36–40, reinforced by the 'new commandment' that Jesus gives his disciples in John 13.34–35, that they should love one another as he has loved them. However, Landau does not examine the meanings of 'love', or expound its cognitive, conative and affective dimensions. He does not point out that love is essentially a steadfast disposition and intention of the will selflessly to seek the good, the well-being, of the other. It is not possible to do this while disrespecting, insulting and caricaturing the other, as we find in so much intra-Christian discourse.

A major strength of the book is that it brings us back to the love commandment that runs, in various forms, throughout the New Testament. In practice, love does not normally form the reference point for disagreeing Christians. They often do not speak or act in love but in hate. A related concern is that all too often disagreeing Christians ignore the work of the Holy Spirit – the pneumatological dimension. Are all parties who are engaged in disagreements consciously dependent on the Holy Spirit of God? If they were, it is implied, disagreements would be kinder and more loving. But we might wonder whether the Pentecostal churches and other charismatic groups, for whom the Holy Spirit is pivotal to their faith, are less prone to bitter and divisive disagreements? I think not. Looking to the Holy Spirit cannot be a panacea; it cannot override other factors that need to be addressed. Another strength of Landau's work is the emphasis given to various practices of church life, especially liturgical worship, as inculcating a virtuous response to disagreement. Yes, liturgy is a building block, but liturgical churches are not preserved from damaging disagreements by their liturgies.

The feebleness of exhortations to 'good' or even 'gracious', 'virtuous' or 'loving' disagreement is exposed when one is dealing with professing Christians who will not even sit down to talk with those with whom they disagree, as the Episcopal absences from the 2008 Lambeth Conference revealed. An even more dire situation is created when they condemn to hell those with whom they disagree (usually on questions of gender and sexuality). This is sometimes the case on the extreme right wing of the Anglican Communion.[13] It is a posture that invites an adaptation of John-Paul Sartre's saying, *L'enfer c'est les autres*: 'Hell is [for] other people'.

13 See Raven, Charles (ed.), 2014, *The Truth Shall Set You Free: Global Anglicans in the 21st Century*, London: The Latimer Trust.

Belonging together

The underlying conviction of the ecumenical movement, from its beginning more than a century ago, up to the present day, has been that the separated parts of the Christian church *belong together*, notwithstanding the fact that, for whatever reason, they have drifted apart. I suggest that this deep sense that we belong together, that we belong to one another, is the basic intuitive affirmation underlying all ecumenical endeavour. Why else would all the major churches confer together in the Faith and Order Commission of the World Council of Churches or in missiological gatherings, or take part in international theological dialogues, unless they believed, at some deep level, that they ultimately belonged together? It is axiomatic for all ecumenical theology that division and separation between baptized Christian believers, gathered in their worshipping, witnessing communities, is wrong in principle and cannot be justified. Ecumenism is premised on the belief that disunity, especially sacramental disunity, contradicts the nature of the church and is contrary to the will of God. The erecting of altar against altar is the ultimate blasphemy against the Paschal Mystery of the cross and resurrection of Christ which is made present in the world, to the world and for the world in the church's celebration of the Eucharist.

The conviction that Christians and churches indissolubly belong together contains two elements and includes a twofold affirmation. First, the statement affirms that *originally* the church was undivided; second, it affirms that *essentially* the church is indivisible. Thus, in both its origin and its essence the church is affirmed as *one*. But what does the rather abstruse formula 'in its origin and essence' mean? This double question, concerning origin and essence, needs to be answered in a correspondingly twofold way: *historically*, with regard to origin, and *theologically*, with regard to essence. However, the historical and theological answers are intertwined: ultimately, origin and essence are not two different things, but two ways – diachronic and synchronic respectively – of affirming the indestructible unity of Christ's church. I will now look a little more closely at the historical approach to the unity of the church, the question of its *original* unity, before addressing the question of its *essential* unity.

Historically speaking

In the Creed of Nicea-Constantinople we affirm one holy catholic and apostolic church. Each of these attributes, notes or dimensions of the church – its unity and its holiness, its universality and its grounding in the mission and teaching of the apostles – involves empirical elements, though these attributes or notes cannot be reduced to the empirical, but also have an eschatological reference. Together the notes of the church involve a historical claim that, in the beginning, the church was not only holy, potentially universal and inclusive, and true to the apostolic foundation of the faith, but was also single and undivided. It would be straining faith to say, 'I believe *(Credo)* in the unity of the church, though I recognize that it has never actually been united.' The creed seems to me to imply that there was originally and at the beginning only one church. 'But when exactly was that?', one might well ask; 'When did division first kick in?'

Many of us will probably jump straight away to the sixteenth century and the Protestant Reformation in the Western church as the source of our divisions. But a moment's reflection will remind us that it is not true to say that the church first became divided at the Reformation.[14] That would be to overlook the fact that the split between East and West, so long coming to the boil, was finalized five centuries earlier, in 1054, so that the Reformation was a split within the Western church, not the whole church; it did not directly affect the Eastern churches. But we need to be very careful about claiming that

14 Radner, Ephraim, 1998, *The End of the Church: A Pneumatology of Christian Division in the West*, Grand Rapids, MI: Eerdmans.

the church was fully united before the Great Schism of 1054. Throughout the patristic period, communities that could not accept the doctrinal decrees of the ecumenical councils were condemned and excluded and became estranged from the unity of the church. The Councils of Nicaea (AD 325), Ephesus (431) and Chalcedon (451), whatever their merits, virtues and gains, were particularly destructive of church unity. Some of those schisms have recently been repaired through ecumenical dialogue, but the fact remains that even the early church, in the age of patristic Christianity, was not fully united. The period of the early councils was hardly the golden age of Christian unity. It was a time of bitter and sometimes violent strife. The superficially attractive notion of 'the undivided church', so often invoked by our ecumenical forebears, with reference to the first millennium, is a romantic illusion. But supposing we go right back to the apostolic age, the first century, what do we find there? There is plenty of evidence in the New Testament of bitter schisms within the communities founded by the apostles. We read accusations of people laying 'other foundations' (1 Cor. 3.11) and preaching 'a different gospel' (Gal. 1.6) and we hear of those unnamed persons who 'went out from us, but they did not belong to us' (1 John 2.19), and so on. So, by a process of continual historical regression, we are forced to place the original unity of the church further and further back. The quest for the historical 'one church' is just as problematic as the quest for the historical Jesus – it never quite reaches its goal!

Perhaps, in our historical quest for the undivided, fully united church, we should home in on the Day of Pentecost, when the Holy Spirit came upon the church, bringing wisdom, eloquence and power? We are told in the Acts of the Apostles that the Spirit came when the disciples were 'all together in one place' (Acts 2.1) or 'were all with one accord in one place' (KJV). We must allow for the possibility that Acts 2 may be an idealized scenario, designed as a reversal of the Tower of Babel when human speech and human community became fragmented, and signalling that the gospel was meant for all nations and peoples, to bind them together in the praise of God. All the same, I think we can affirm that when the apostles, Mary the mother of Jesus, Mary Magdalene and others were gathered together – in an upper room or wherever – in the period between the ascension and Pentecost, awaiting in prayer 'the promise of the Father', there was one church. The undivided church existed at that *pinpoint* in time.

When I say that I believe that we must hold to the original unity of the church, its unity in its origin, I am probably using 'original' and 'in origin' in a similar way to the book of Genesis (in the Septuagint, LXX) and the Gospel according to St John when they both begin with the words *En archē* – 'In the beginning'. The beginning that Genesis and John's Gospel both invoke cannot be historically specified, but is postulated as lying at the very start, or even before the start, of the created historical process. So, by analogy, we may say that before all the vicissitudes of church history, at point zero, there was one church. Before all the ways in which, through twenty centuries, the empirical unity of the church has been assaulted, compromised and fragmented, the church was one church. I think it is necessary to posit the original unity of the church as a historical fact, even if that affirmation is lacking in both precision and assurance. If this way of looking at it seems unsatisfactory, there may be an analogy in the resurrection of Christ. We may – and I think must – affirm that the resurrection is a historical fact, an event in time and space, even though we can say almost nothing about what actually happened in – and to – the physical body of Jesus. While the resurrection of Christ has to be historically grounded and posited as a historical (even if also a trans-historical) event, it eludes and transcends historical enquiry. Similarly, the unity of the church, while it is historically grounded and needs to be posited as such, eludes and transcends historical enquiry.

However, in saying that 'it is necessary to posit the original unity of the church as a historical fact', I have already crossed the line that demarcates history from theology, historical research from theological affirmation. I have moved the argument from historical enquiry into theological reasoning. The 'necessity' in question is not a historical compulsion, but a theological one. In passing, I would like to make it clear that I am not advocating any kind of methodological disjunction or dichotomy between historical enquiry and theological reflection. I do not think it is possible to do theology without input from historical research. I hold that historical perspective is a vital pathway to theological understanding. But, conversely, I also do not believe that it is possible to pursue historical enquiry without importing our ideological presuppositions, which in the case of church history are largely theological ones. So work in the field of church history is imbued with theological (and non-theological) assumptions, and correspondingly constructive theology – including ecclesiology – is informed by what we think we know about history. So there can be no watertight separation of theology and history, but rather a cross-fertilization of varying degrees of intimacy, of cooperation and mutual interrogation, according to the topic and the particular method being employed. For me, the connection between the two is very close. My starting point – though not my finishing point – in any theological project tends to be within the history of theology and the history of the church. But to return now to the main thread of the argument: I have spoken about 'origin' that belongs in the category of history; I now move to the language of 'essence', which belongs in the category of theology.

Theologically speaking

It is an imperative of Christian faith to hold that the church is essentially, even if not empirically, one. Insofar as the church, as the mystical body of Christ (Eph. 5.21–33), derives its existence from its source in the Triune God, it must be one as God is one. But insofar as the church is embedded in the historical process, it must also be diverse. The historical process contains social, economic, geographical and political factors, to look no further, and these necessarily pull in different directions.

Therefore, not merely differences, but also tensions and oppositions, are inevitable. Nevertheless, unity and diversity are not in principle incompatible. Every social entity or social form is marked by an intriguing combination of unity and diversity. We may think of a marriage, a family, a congregation, a local community, a college, a nation. Diversity, multiplicity, difference must be acknowledged and respected in the church, as everywhere else, but they can be lived with – as in a marriage, a family, a congregation, a local community, a college, a nation. No ecclesiological justification is available, or ever has been, for deliberate exclusion, the fomenting of division and the setting up of sacramental separation. So often these are the malign fruits of the vices that St Paul deplores in the texts with which we began this discussion: spiritual pride, self-aggrandizement, binary thinking, paranoia and party spirit. Lack of visible unity is the result of the church's failure – and its members' failure – to *be* the church. To fully be the church means to be fully one.

The church is one because Christ is one. The church is one because it is Christ's body. As Ephesians puts it, 'There is one body and one Spirit ... one hope ... one Lord, one faith, one baptism, one God and Father of all' (Eph. 4.4–6). This statement, with its seven instances of 'one', could hardly be more emphatic. Richard Hooker, the prime architect of Anglican ecclesiology, writing towards the end of the sixteenth century and speaking of the church's unity, echoes Ephesians 4 when he writes: 'The unity of which visible body and Church of Christ consisteth in that uniformity which all several persons thereunto belonging have, by reason of that *one Lord* whose servants they all profess themselves, that *one faith* which they all acknowledge, that *one baptism* wherewith they are all initiated.' Hooker continues: 'The visible Church of Jesus Christ is therefore one in outward profession of those things which supernaturally appertain to the very essence of Christianitie [sic] and are necessarily required in every particular christian [sic] man [sic].'[15] For Hooker, the unity of the church resides in

15 Hooker, Richard, *Of the Lawes of Ecclesiasticall Politie*, III, i,

the profession of those matters that 'supernaturally appertain to the very essence of Christianitie'. The essence of Christianity (such a modern-sounding expression), for Hooker, is given supernaturally – that is to say, by divine revelation in Scripture and includes the unity of the church. In Hooker's theology, that unity is grounded Christologically (two natures in one person), sacramentally (through real participation in Christ's body and blood in the Eucharist) and confessionally (all Christians make outward profession of the one essential faith).[16]

In the High Priestly Prayer of John 17, Jesus prays that his own, whom the Father has given him, may be one as he is one with the Father – one in such a way that the world may be enabled to believe that the Father has sent him into the world. This prayer suggests that the unity of the church was already fragile and under threat when the fourth Gospel was composed. But it is also clear that we are meant to understand that the intention of Jesus, with all the authority of his divine mission, was that his community should be visibly one. So the essential unity of the church is secured and underpinned by the prayerful intention of Jesus at the most solemn moment in his destiny. Christ continues, in his heavenly intercession (Heb. 7.25), to pray for the unity of his body on earth, and this intercession is represented and actualized in the Eucharist, the sacrament of unity (Heb. 13.15).

Putting together these three sources – Ephesians 4, Hooker's statement, and the prayer of Jesus – we can say that the church is single *by definition*. That the church is one church is an analytic proposition. The church cannot exist except as one

---

3–4; Speed Hill, W. (gen. ed.), 1977, *The Folger Library Edition of the Works of Richard Hooker*, 7 vols, vol. 1, Cambridge: MA and London: The Belknap Press of Harvard University Press, p. 396. Hooker not only uses the expression the 'essence' of Christianity, which is still current, but also refers to baptism as 'initiation', which today is basically an anthropological term.

16 See further on Hooker's ecclesiology, Avis, Paul, 2002, *Anglicanism and the Christian Church: Theological Resources in Historical Perspective*, 2nd edn, London and New York: T&T Clark, ch. 2.

church. The church of Christ cannot be many churches. As Karl Barth put it, 'A plurality of churches in this sense means a plurality of lords, a plurality of spirits, a plurality of gods', which is patently impossible.[17] Barth is saying that unreconciled disunity in the church strikes at the very heart of the Christian faith as it is given in divine revelation. It shatters the integrity of God's work in and through the church.

At the deepest level of all, the church is one because God is one. William Temple's teacher, the philosopher Edward Caird, wrote: 'God is a word that has no significance, unless by it we mean to express the idea of a living Being who is the principle of unity presupposed in all the differences of things, and in all our divided consciousness of them.'[18] Temple himself said: '[T]he unity of the world, its principle of rational coherence, is the Divine Personality in self-expression.'[19] It was this profound conviction and assurance of the transcendent and immanent unity holding the world together that enabled Temple to proclaim, in his Opening Address at the Second World Conference on *Faith and Order*, in Edinburgh, in 1937: 'The unity of the Church, on which our faith and hope is set, is grounded in the unity of God and the uniqueness of His redeeming act in Jesus Christ ... The unity of the Church of God is a perpetual fact; our task is not to create it but to exhibit it.'[20]

The confession of faith that the church makes with regard to itself and its essential unity in the creed is not only a 'time-

---

17 Barth, Karl, 1975–, *Church Dogmatics*, ed. Geoffrey W. Bromiley and Thomas F. Torrance, Edinburgh/London and New York: T&T Clark, IV/1, p. 675.

18 Caird, Edward, 1904, *The Evolution of Theology in the Greek Philosophers*, vol. 1, Glasgow: Maclehose, p. 257, cited in Edward Loane, 2016, *William Temple and Church Unity: The Politics and Practice of Ecumenical Theology*, Cham, Switzerland: Palgrave Macmillan, p. 23.

19 Temple, William, 1934, *Nature, Man and God: Gifford Lectures*, London: Macmillan, p. 302.

20 Temple, William, 1958, *Religious Experience and Other Essays and Addresses*, ed. A. E. Baker, London: James Clarke, ch. 'Christian Unity', pp. 153–9, at p. 153.

less truth' regarding the nature of God, but is also temporal and eschatological, looking forward to what is promised. That means at least two things. First, the church's credal affirmation of unity is filled with a sense of wistfulness, regret and incompleteness for the present lack of the unity that is being affirmed as original and essential – and the more strongly we affirm it, the more we grieve and lament for its absence in the church today. But, second, the affirmation is also filled with a sense of hope, anticipation, expectation and intercession, that it might once again be possible to experience the unity of the church – and the more strongly we affirm it, the more we feel that it could be restored. The confession of original and essential unity contains an 'already' and a 'not yet'. It says something about the beginning which demands that we say something about the end, but also about the end which says something crucial about the beginning. 'In my beginning is my end', T. S. Eliot began 'East Coker' in *Four Quartets*, and he finished the poem with, 'In my end is my beginning.'[21] In the creed we affirm the church's essence – its original unity – with the intention that the church's existence can be different. When we say the third article of the creed, we are bound to hope that the original unity of the church can be restored. Will its disunity one day be healed? If there is promise, found above all in the prayer and intention of Jesus, there must surely be fulfilment?

But at that point we have to remind ourselves that, while the promises of God in Scripture are irrevocable (Heb. 11.29), they are not unconditional. For their fulfilment, they require us to conform our lives and our abilities to the purposes of God and to allow ourselves to become instruments of that purpose – all too unworthily and ineffectually, of course. The gospel promises are not guarantees; they will not come to pass regardless and in any case. So when we speak of eschatological fulfilment, I suggest we need to gloss that phrase as 'the possibility of fulfilment'. The ecumenical movement has consistently seen

21 Eliot, T. S., 1974 (1963), *Collected Poems 1909–1962*, London: Faber and Faber, pp. 196, 204.

Christian unity as at once grace and calling, 'gift and task'.[22]

We have been exploring the notion of 'belonging together' in connection with a divided church. Things in the world may belong together in different ways. Cut an apple in half and you have two items that clearly belong together, because they are virtually the same; they fit together and make a whole apple. A left and right shoe also belong together, not because they are virtually identical – in one sense they are opposites – but because they make a pair and it is necessary to have both before you can walk in them. Two siblings belong together, not normally because they are the same – they may be of different sexes, sizes, ages, characters and appearances – but because they are (usually) offspring of the same parents and members of the same family. A wife and husband belong together, not because they are identical, but because of other weighty factors: they have solemnly and joyfully committed themselves to each other emotionally and physically; their union has perhaps been sealed and blessed by the Holy Spirit in the liturgy of the church; they have entered into joint ventures such as bringing up children, the purchase of property, and battling through adversity together – but particularly because they each know themselves to be incomplete without the other. So there is a sliding scale of 'belonging together' from the trivial and mundane to the ontological and mystical. Needless to say, the 'belonging together' of the church is firmly at the mystical, ontological end of the spectrum. But that in no way implies that the belonging together of the church is not physical, visible and tangible as well.

---

22 See especially the statement of the Fifth Assembly of the World Council of Churches, Canberra 1991: 'The Unity of the Church as Koinonia: Gift and Calling', in Kinnamon, Michael and Brian E. Cope (eds), 1997, *The Ecumenical Movement: An Anthology of Key Texts and Voices*, Geneva: World Council of Churches; Grand Rapids, MI: Eerdmans, pp. 124–5. www.oikoumene.org/en/resources/documents/commissions/faith-and-order/i-unity-the-church-and-its-mission/the-unity-of-the-church-gift-and-calling-the-canberra-statement (accessed 3.11.2021).

In belonging together there is always a dimension of unification and a dimension of differentiation. So the belonging together of the church cannot be monolithic or monochrome and any suggestion of uniformity of opinion and practice is quite out of court. So the corresponding process of bringing back together must be a reunion that does not destroy difference and diversity. It must respect the capaciousness, richness and hospitality that belong to the credal catholicity of the church. With his characteristic spiritual profundity, Baron Friedrich von Hügel described the catholicity of the church as 'the greatest possible multiplicity in the deepest possible unity'.[23] In line with von Hügel's dictum, Miroslav Volf has argued that the work of the Holy Spirit in the church is twofold: unifying and differentiating; both are equally valid and equally vital. If we take the church as a totality, writes Volf, we see that it must comprise a 'differentiated unity'. So any church that sees itself as 'catholic' (and what sort of church would it be, we might ask, that did not wish to be catholic, but instead 'uncatholic'?) must adopt a vision of unity that includes multiplicity; it must seek unity in multiplicity.[24]

Can multiplicity be brought into unity without ceasing to be multiplicity? How can radical diversity be held together? Can communion include conflict and even contradiction? These are the intractable questions that are endemic to ecumenical theology and indeed to all ecclesiology in the divided *oikouménē* (οἰκουμένη). There is a daunting agenda here for ecclesiologists and ecumenical theologians to get to grips with for the good of the church. I cannot embark at this point on any further discussion of difference and diversity, conflict and contradiction, in the church, though I wrestle with them continually and plan to return to them on another occasion. But I

23 Von Hügel, Friedrich, 1927 (1908), *The Mystical Element of Religion*, 2nd edn, 2 vols, London: Dent, vol. 1, pp. 66–7. See also Avis, Paul, 2010, *Reshaping Ecumenical Theology*, ch. 1: 'The Church – Unity and Multiplicity'.

24 Volf, Miroslav, 1998, *After Our Likeness: The Church as the Image of the Trinity*, Grand Rapids, MI: Eerdmans, pp. 282, 262.

hope I have said enough to prepare the ground for the last part of this book, which is concerned with 'bringing back together what belongs together'. This is the 'How?' question, concerning the pathway to deeper communion and fuller unity. I will look at the *motif* of 'bringing back together' under the rubrics of 'recognition' and 'reconciliation' in the following two chapters.

7

Mutual Recognition – Gateway to Reconciliation

'Seeing-you-seeing-me' sums up our experience of the social world. It is a world of reflections, a hall of mirrors – many of them distorting ones. To recognize others with empathy and to be recognized with positive regard by them are the keys to our state of being in the social world. These reciprocal actions weave the fabric of our existence in community and impart a moral value to our personhood that nothing else can give. Freely and autonomously to recognize others as who they are in the integrity of their personhood is a constitutive act of our own personhood. And to be recognized as who we are and on our own terms by others is to find the reality of our personhood enhanced. What kind of 'me' exists without the 'me' that exists in the perception of others? Recognition by the other has the making of our self-consciousness and of our sense of identity, even on those occasions when it may be unfriendly, hostile or even predatory. There is no identity until we are identified and no being without being recognized.[1]

Mutual recognition is also pivotal in building up fellowship among Christians, as we learn to see Christ in one another: 'I see that you are as I am – in Christ.' On a larger canvas, mutual recognition is a building block of theological dialogue and a key stage in the journey of churches into closer communion. When churches reach the point of formally recognizing the presence of the one church of Jesus Christ in one another, those

1 Searle, John R., 1995, *The Social Construction of Reality*, London: Allen Lane.

churches receive an enhanced reality from the other and a new status in the *oecumene*. They will have taken an incremental step towards full ecclesial communion and are now poised to move towards ecclesial reconciliation.

Social-science perspectives

In this chapter I am intertwining reflection on individual-social recognition and ecumenical-ecclesial recognition, so that they may shed light on each other. 'Recognition' is one of the most pivotal concepts in academic discourse, especially in social science, philosophy, critical theory, psychology and theology. But it is also one of the most over-determined of notions, a bloated concept, one of infinite capaciousness. Ricoeur points out that no widely accepted philosophical theory of recognition is available.[2] The all-embracingness of 'recognition' is not surprising, given the fact that the phenomenon of recognition permeates our individual and social existence. It stands for the vis-à-vis dimension of human life, sociality itself. But as a concept, 'recognition' is made to do more work than it can bear. It is so promiscuously applied that it lacks shape and boundaries, focus and precision. The result is that we cannot know for sure exactly what is meant when a particular moment in social experience is claimed as 'recognition'.

A case in point is the critical theorist Axel Honneth's capacious use of 'recognition' (*Anerkennung*), in his suggestively titled *The I in We*, to encompass ideals of equality, social justice and the rights of workers in a capitalist economy. Helpfully, Honneth equates recognition to the giving of respect and affirmation, and rightly sees it as a major building block of groups, communities and society. But then he makes it do too much work, so that everything becomes recognition. For example, he exposes a negative, ideologically suspect

2 Ricoeur, Paul, 2005 (2004), *The Course of Recognition*, trans. David Pellauer, Cambridge, MA: Harvard University Press, pp. ix, 1.

form of 'recognition', subjecting it to ideological critique and deconstruction – where the representatives of the prevailing socioeconomic structures award some kind of public 'recognition' (commendation, praise, applause) to prominent members of a suppressed social class. However, they do this cynically to reconcile them to their unjust treatment, their oppressed state, and thereby bolstering the existing structures of domination.[3] A kind of recognition is certainly in there, but it is not the kind of recognition that builds social and individual well-being.

Similarly, in ecumenical dialogue the language of recognition is often ladled generously on to what two churches say to each other: there is a sincere desire to offer some kind of recognition to the other, but this offer of 'recognition' is seldom accompanied by much definition or precision. Ecumenical reports have used 'recognition' promiscuously, as equivalent to various degrees of closeness or unity between churches. They have employed 'recognition' language not only for mutual acknowledgement of ecclesial reality and authenticity, but also for the further, distinct steps of the 'interchangeability' of ordained ministries, the 'reconciliation' of churches, and even the goal of 'ecclesial communion'.[4] The building of *rapport* between churches also reflects the outgoing, giving, gift and gratitude aspect of recognition, as brought out by Ricoeur: recognition is a transaction.[5] But as a transaction in which something is given, there must also be something received; receptivity is an essential element of recognition. When there is a giving and a

3 Honneth, Axel, 2012 (2010), *The I in We: Studies in the Theory of Recognition*, Cambridge: Polity Press.

4 Documented in Lim, Timothy T. M., 2017, *Ecclesial Recognition with Hegelian Philosophy, Social Psychology and Continental Political Theory: An Interdisciplinary Proposal*, Leiden: Brill, ch. 1. Lim surveys and partly synthesizes resources from several disciplines. See also the interdisciplinary approach of Saarinen, Risto, 2016, *Recognition and Religion: A Historical and Systematic Study*, Oxford: Oxford University Press.

5 Ricoeur, *The Course of Recognition*. He concedes that the aspect of gratitude is more prominent in the French *reconnaissance* than in the English 'recognition'.

receiving on both sides, a rich kind of receptive ecumenism is taking place and a new bond is being formed.[6]

The concept of recognition is also freely deployed in personal and social psychology – in developmental psychology of the individual and the psychological dynamics of sociality. In both of these areas it is connected to the concept of *identity*. We recognize someone, something, or some state of affairs as somehow *valid* by identifying its place in reality. Both individual identity (the integrity and social profile of the person) and social identity (the integrity and social profile of groups) are largely constructed in terms of recognition as identification and mutual acceptance, or at least mutual engagement.[7] These two manifestations of identity, individual and social, are inextricably intertwined and mutually constitutive. The concept of identity – its formation, constitution and maintenance, together with its preservation and defence in face of threat – is not the subject of this chapter, though it is bound to creep in here and there. We cannot hope to probe the phenomenon of recognition apart from the making of identity, not least in relation to the traditions, practices and communal consciousness of the churches. But the purpose of this present exercise is more modest than that. In this chapter, I try to get at the experiential, existential texture of 'recognition', what it feels like in life and on our pulses in our interpersonal relations. Then I attempt to apply it to the varying state of *rapport* that pertains not only between the churches but within them, between individual Christians. The central focus of this project is reconciliation, both within churches and between them, and recognition is a vital staging post to that desired end.

6 For receptive ecumenism, see below and footnote 10.

7 Ricoeur, *The Course of Recognition*, ch. 1, explores the connection between recognition and identity.

Recognition and otherness

In contradistinction to the woollier kind of ecumenical theology, I hold that mutual ecclesial recognition is not a synonym for reconciliation, but an essential prerequisite to achieving it. The first concrete step towards the reconciliation of those – whether in different churches or, even more acutely, within the same church – who consciously stand apart from one another on what they believe to be *questions of truth or principle*, is mutual recognition. They believe that others, whom they do not recognize, believe in 'another Jesus ... a different spirit ... a different gospel' (2 Cor. 11.4). To alter this 'othering' attitude, in which we thrust away from us those with whom we disagree profoundly, may well involve a changed perception of the differences between us – in other words, thinking differently about difference. It certainly involves engagement, conversation, dialogue and the willingness to be face to face. But then mutual recognition becomes the starter motor of the process of active *rapprochement* that can lead to reconciliation and thus to fullness of fellowship or communion. Recognition leading to reconciliation must include the recognition of difference and otherness, though otherness and difference are now viewed differently from before. In reconciliation, difference and otherness are not abolished, but affirmed and transcended. What Ricoeur calls 'alterity' reaches its highest point in situations of mutuality because the self-consciousness of each party is enhanced. As Zizioulas perceptively puts it, 'Communion does not threaten otherness; it generates it.'[8] Ricoeur notes 'the irreplaceable character of each of the partners in the exchange'. He expands: 'The one is not the other. We exchange gifts, but not places ... A just distance is maintained at the heart of mutuality, a just distance that integrates respect into intimacy.'[9] This is a wise recipe for family life, friendship and marriage, but it applies

---

8 Zizioulas, John, 2006, *Communion and Otherness*, ed. Paul McPartlan, London and New York: T&T Clark, p. 5.

9 Ricoeur, *The Course of Recognition*, pp. 251, 263.

no less to the drawing together of churches and communions. It suggests that in ecclesial communion the distinctiveness of churches must be respected and preserved.

Without that initial spontaneous surge of recognition, any overtures towards reconciliation on the road to communion will fall flat. There can be no reconciliation without prior recognition. We have no desire to be reconciled to those who mean nothing to us. We long to be reconciled only to those who matter to us existentially, but from whom we find ourselves estranged. To be reconciled is to overcome existential estrangement, however far apart we may find ourselves. To be reconciled means to replace mistrust, alienation and enmity with their opposites: trust, understanding, friendship, fellowship. In fact, these dispositions are all aspects of love, which is the steady intentionality of the whole person directed to the good, the well-being, the flourishing of the other. Relationships of a positive kind with others begin with the first glimmerings of attraction arising from the giving of moral value and respect to the other. When we seek recognition, we are saying to the other: 'Acknowledge me; value me; love me.'

At some point along the road that leads from recognition to reconciliation there takes place an experiential transaction, one of mutual reception as persons and communities.[10] The mutual reception of churches or 'receptive ecumenism' is now an established methodological trope in ecumenical theology.[11]

10 Ricoeur, in *The Course of Recognition*, focuses – following Hegel – on the struggle for recognition on the way to mutual reconciliation.

11 Murray, Paul D. with Luca Badini-Confalonieri (ed.), 2008, *Receptive Ecumenism and the Call to Catholic Learning: Exploring a Way for Contemporary Ecumenism*, Oxford: Oxford University Press; Ryan, Gregory, 2020, *Hermeneutics of Doctrine in a Learning Church: The Dynamics of Receptive Integrity*, Leiden: Brill; Ryan, Gregory, 'The Reception of Receptive Ecumenism', *Ecclesiology* 17 (2021), pp. 7–28; Pizzey, Antonia, 2019, *Receptive Ecumenism and the Renewal of the Ecumenical Movement: The Path of Ecclesial Conversion*, Leiden: Brill; Avis, Paul, 2010, *Reshaping Ecumenical Theology*, London and New York: T&T Clark, ch. 5: 'Towards a Deeper Reception of "Reception"'.

St Paul put a rhetorical question to the Corinthian Christians: 'What do you have that you did not receive?' (1 Cor. 4.7). It was a challenge to the spiritual pride and complacency of the Corinthians. As step by step we draw closer to one another in our churches, we discover that we have already received something from one another, become aware that we are still receiving it, and sense that there is more to receive. We find that that 'something' has worth in our eyes and we covet more of it. The 'worth' that we discern, desire and begin to receive in an act of positive recognition can be construed in terms of the three ultimate values of beauty, truth and goodness that philosophers have identified.

1 Aesthetically speaking, we begin to see something of beauty, of creative energy, of radiance and of attractive form in what we have been separated from hitherto. Many a Protestant or Evangelical Christian, starved of form, colour, drama and tradition in worship, has been drawn to 'the beauty of holiness' in liturgical worship and 'holy order' in ministry. The 'Canterbury trail' is well trodden, especially by young American free-church men and women. In such experiences, we feel the allure, the magnetic pull, of the other. Our apprehension of the other includes the possibility of receiving something akin to healing and completion through the beauty that is embodied in the life of the other.
2 Epistemologically speaking, we also glimpse the possibility of receiving some enrichment of our own understanding from a source that we may have regarded hitherto as 'other' and perhaps as inferior or even unworthy of our participation. Engagement with the other through mutual positive recognition and reception brings some enlightenment of our minds or enlargement of knowledge, a supplement or corrective to our present grasp of the truth. We sense that fellowship with the other will make us wiser and more insightful; it will bring us into closer *rapport* with the whole panoply of revealed truth and informed reflection on it, transcending our present limited perspective.

3 Ethically speaking, the value that we begin to place upon the other, as we perceive the other more clearly and truly, has an ethical character. The other (which may be a person, a community or an institution), with its touch of beauty and its hold on the truth, is also found to be morally admirable; it has higher moral worth in our sight – and thereby draws us into its fellowship. Put another way, we feel morally humbled by – as well as attracted to – the other. Two lovers feel that they do not deserve all that the other gives them. We sense that our fellowship with the other has the potential to make us better and more virtuous persons – thus, in a Christian context, more Christlike.

Recognition as gift

Any significant act of mutual recognition – one that is more than merely casual or incidental – includes a gift-giving. Several benchmark studies, both anthropological and theological, have shown that in formal or ceremonial practices of mutual recognition there is generally an exchange of gifts, the start of an ongoing cycle of exchange.[12] The exchange of gifts signifies mutual reception by the persons who are giving and receiving, receiving and giving. The most precious gift that one can give to a reasonably well-provided person – someone who is not desperate for food, shelter, clothing or medical attention – is the gift of enhanced recognition, the grace of being valued for themselves. As the mention of grace and the gift or exchange of gifts suggests, to positively recognize someone with full intentionality and to express it in words, accompanied by a gift or token or significant action – such as a kiss or an embrace (a hug), or in words alone (or even in a gift or token or kiss or embrace without any words being spoken) – is *performative*. In such a case, the spoken words, whether accompanied by an

12 Mauss, Marcel, 1990 (1925), *The Gift: The Form and Reason for Exchange in Archaic Societies*, London: Routledge; Barclay, John M. G., 2015, *Paul and the Gift*, Grand Rapids, MI: Eerdmans.

overt action or not, are active, creating an interpersonal transaction in which a threshold has been crossed by both parties. Words that award recognition are speech-acts and should be seen as effective practices. They produce what they declare; bringing about a fresh state of affairs.[13]

The dynamics of reception lend a gift-character to mutual recognition, a two-way giving and receiving. We come to see the other party in a different way. The light of recognition and discovery shines from us to them and from them to us. We have each received a treasure and, like any treasure-hunter, our eyes light up with joy and eagerness; we cannot wait to actually get our hands on the treasure trove, the 'pearl of great price' (Matt. 13.45–46). The dawning of enlightenment about one another drives away irrational fears based on false perceptions and morbid imaginations. Those false perceptions and dark imaginings are forms of pathological stereotyping and fantasizing about the 'other', about how different they are to us, how hostile, how threatening, to what we hold dear. Zizioulas points out that, in our culture, protection from the other is regarded as a necessity; we are encouraged to consider the other as our enemy before we can treat him or her as our friend. 'There is a pathology built into the very roots of our existence ... *fear of the other*.'[14] Such paranoid fantasies are psychological constructions without foundation, baseless imaginings fomented in the turbid machinations of the human heart, driven by fear and ignorance. When they are dispelled by the light of reality and vanish into thin air, the stage is set for constructive steps towards reconciliation, the bringing together into unity and harmony of what has hitherto subsisted in estrangement, discord or enmity.

---

13 Austin, J. L., 1975 (1962), *How to Do Things with Words: The William James Lectures delivered at Harvard University in 1955*, Oxford: Clarendon Press; Searle, John R., 1969, *Speech Acts: An Essay in the Philosophy of Language*, Cambridge: Cambridge University Press; Evans, Donald D., 1963, *The Logic of Self-Involvement*, The Library for Philosophy and Theology, London: SCM Press.

14 Zizioulas, *Communion and Otherness*, p. 1, italics original.

Biblical exemplars of recognition

Joseph and his brothers

Martin Luther's massive *Lectures on Genesis* include what must surely be one of the most extended biblical commentaries on the Joseph saga ever undertaken, running to hundreds of pages in the English translation. Luther was enthralled by the story, identifying Joseph with Christ and with the faithful tempted and persecuted Christian, including himself. He engages the Hebrew text, lectures apparently in Latin, but is sometimes so excited that he breaks into colloquial German. Luther revels in the drama created by a situation of unreciprocated recognition, followed by the shattering revelation of Joseph's identity. Joseph recognizes his brothers when they come to Egypt to buy food, but naturally they do not recognize him. As Luther points out, the possibility that the august Egyptian prince before them could be their lost brother Joseph, whom they had sold into slavery many years before, was the last thing on their minds. Luther refers the tribulations and eventual triumphs of Joseph's life to the inscrutable workings of divine providence and to the salutary chastisement that, as the Bible so often reminds us, Christians must undergo. Luther is so moved when Joseph has to stifle his tender emotions, putting on a harsh countenance when he is actually longing to embrace his brothers and later withdrawing to another room to release his feelings in weeping, that he says, in effect, 'Words fail me.' In his profound humanity, although always *coram deo* (before the face of God), Luther brings out the exquisite poignancy of this emotionally fraught situation of unreciprocated recognition, revealed identity, and ultimate reconciliation.[15]

---

15 Luther, Martin, 1965–6, *Luther's Works*, ed. Jaroslav Pelikan and Helmut Lehmann, St Louis, MO: Concordia Publishing House, vol. 7: *Lectures on Genesis Chapters 38–44*, pp. 216–377, and vol. 8: *Lectures on Genesis Chapters 45–50*, pp. 1–117, trans. Paul D. Pahl. Sympathetic analysis of the text and narrative in von Rad, Gerhard, 1972, *Genesis: A Commentary*, rev. edn, Philadelphia, PA: Westminster Press.

Thomas Mann's version of the Genesis saga in his *Joseph and His Brothers* must surely be one of the most powerful evocations of the phenomenology of personal recognition in all European literature. Published in four volumes between 1933 and 1943, while Mann (1875–1955) was living in exile from Nazi Germany, first in Switzerland and then in the United States, *Joseph and His Brothers* runs to 1,492 pages in the superb English translation by John E. Woods, but we do not reach the beginning of the encounters of the brothers with Joseph in Egypt until page 1294.[16] Thomas Mann was a Lutheran and his wife Katia, who came from a wealthy secularized Jewish family, had converted to her husband's Lutheran Christianity. Mann naturally used Martin Luther's translation of the Bible, from the original languages into sixteenth-century German, which was and remains (with revisions) the standard translation for German Lutheranism. Whether Mann consulted Luther's massive *Lectures on Genesis*, perhaps in the Weimar Edition of the complete works, I do not know, though there are certain resonances. Mann knows his Bible, and not only preserves the theological integrity of the biblical Joseph story and deals sympathetically with the providential framework (whereby the sufferings and vindication of Joseph are used by God to preserve Jacob/Israel's family and clan for God's future purposes of bringing blessing to the whole world), but his narrative contains subtle allusions (never named) to the destiny of Jesus, of whom Joseph is widely recognized as a type, and also unadvertised correspondences between the Old and New Testaments.

Mann explores the subconscious intimations, the teasing effect on the imagination of tacit clues and retrieved memories, that may bring about an irresistible demand within us – as it were, on behalf of the other – to be recognized. There is a

16 Mann, Thomas, 2005, *Joseph and His Brothers*, trans. John E. Woods, 4 vols in one, New York: Alfred A. Knopf (Everyman's Library). Page references in my main text.

difference, we are reminded, between recognizing a thing or person, on the one hand, and knowing or acknowledging that you recognize it or them, on the other (pp. 1298, 1321): the brothers are writhing in the space between the two. Mann tantalizingly evokes the suspense felt by Joseph in not knowing how either he himself or his brothers will react when the moment finally comes when he can declare 'It is I' (p. 1302). But Joseph can be quietly confident of the outcome because, he says, 'The whole story has already been written ... in God's book, and we shall read it together amid laughter and tears' (p. 1303). When the ten brothers appear before the majestic figure of Joseph, the great Provider of Egypt, almost a second Pharaoh,

> With a heart full of laughing and weeping and anxiety, he gazed at them and recognized them all under their beards ... But they, gazing at him in return, did not even think of recognizing him, and their eyes, though seeing, were blind to the possibility that it could be he. (p. 1307)

They had no idea why both the image of Joseph and their inveterate guilt at what they had done to him years before 'rose up in their souls' in the wake of, or indeed during, their first audience with him (p. 1321). Mann plaits together their dim, unacknowledged glimmers of recognition of the brother they had sold into slavery and the unbidden upsurge of guilt about what they had done (p. 1347). It is Benjamin, the youngest and dearest son of Jacob and full brother of Joseph (by the mother of both, Rachel), who first comes to know – but not to accept or admit that he knows – who Joseph is: 'his was a dazed and anxious mind, that sought, found, lost, and suddenly, indisputably, found again, setting his heart racing in fierce beats'. Benjamin smelt in his mind the fragrance of their shared childhood; 'something familiar was trying to be recognized, assuming a transparency that from one moment to the next would set his heart pounding' (pp. 1354–5). Benjamin's was a human heart on the verge of belief. A cry of recognition was forcing its way out, bursting open the prison of his heart (p. 1363).[17] Only when Joseph has played them back and forth like an angler to the point of their complete exhaustion and despair, bringing Judah – demonstratively breaking the oath of secrecy that they had sworn to one another to conceal the crime – to confess it before the victim and his brothers and to utter a will to make atonement, can Joseph reveal himself and invite their overt recognition across the gulf of time. Thus they were 'set the task of turning mere association into identification, of recognizing in this man – who, granted, had long had something to do with Joseph in their minds – the brother they had done away with' (p. 1378). Never, in a lifetime of reading, have I found such a delicate and empathetic portrayal of the mystery of mutual recognition. The story comes out as a comedy skirting along the edge of the precipice of tragedy.

Jesus' resurrection appearances

The Gospel narratives of the resurrection appearances of Christ are rich in intriguing cases of non-recognition, misrecognition, and the final, thrilling burst of recognition of the risen Christ. Running like a thread throughout these narratives is the motif of divine revelation breaking through human spiritual blindness. Of course, there are no resurrection appearances in Mark's Gospel, which originally ended with chapter 16, verse 8, where the women flee from the tomb in great distress (though there is a promise of an appearance (v. 7)). The first resurrection appearance narrated by Luke takes place on the Emmaus Road where two disciples, only one of whom is named (Cleopas), are joined by a mysterious stranger who is in fact Jesus, but 'their eyes were kept from recognizing him' (Luke 24.16). The emphasis here appears to be on an

17 In a different context, we may infer something of a similar gradual build-up, suppressed excitement and sudden release of recognition in the accounts of Peter's confession of Jesus as Messiah: Mark 8.29 and parallels.

act of divine withholding, rather than on the difference in the physical appearance of Jesus after the resurrection, as in other narratives. (The physical unrecognizability of the risen Jesus is also repeatedly emphasized in other accounts, with the result that the motif of divinely imposed spiritual blindness begins to seem rather strained, even though it is deliberately employed by the evangelists.[18]) Calvin resists the idea that the risen Christ was not easily recognizable because his 'bodily form' was altered. Rather, recognition was withheld: 'Though Christ stayed like Himself, He was not recognized, as the eyes of the beholders were checked.'[19] On the road to Emmaus, after a rehearsal of the events of the Lord's ministry and Passion, a rumour of resurrection, and some exposition (which unfortunately is not filled out for us) of the prophetic predictions of the suffering Messiah, the disciples reached their destination, but the stranger makes as though to go on. He is not deceiving them with regard to his intentions (Calvin insists on this against those in his own day who apparently employed this incident to discredit the Scriptures morally). He is not presuming on an invitation because, after all that he has explained to them about the fulfilment of the Scriptures, the ball is now in their court. Happily, he is prevailed upon to join them for a meal. The stranger takes bread, blesses it, breaks it and gives it to them – with obvious echoes of the table fellowship of Jesus with 'sinners', the feeding of the multitudes and the Last Supper. At that point 'their eyes were opened and they recognized him ... he had been made known to them in the breaking of the bread' (vv. 30–31, 35). When the risen Christ later appears to the whole group of disciples, they are terrified

18 See the comments in Marshall, I. Howard, 1978, *The Gospel of Luke*, New International Greek Text Commentary, Carlisle: Paternoster Press; Grand Rapids, MI: Eerdmans, p. 893. See also Wright, N. T., 2003, *The Resurrection of the Son of God*, London: SPCK, pp. 604–7.

19 Calvin, John, 1972, *A Harmony of the Gospels Matthew, Mark and Luke, Volume III, and the Epistles of James and Jude*, Calvin's Commentaries, eds David W. Torrance and Thomas F. Torrance, Edinburgh: The Saint Andrew Press, p. 232.

because 'they thought they were seeing a ghost' (v. 37). Still wondering and doubting, Jesus invites them to touch him and to view his wounded hands and feet; then he eats some fish in front of them (vv. 38–43; an early Christian source added honeycomb). The physical reality of the risen Jesus is emphasized, though not at the expense of his physical dissimilarity. Because it is not obvious that the one who appears to the disciples is Jesus, a divine gift of recognition is needed.

Similarly, in Matthew's account of the ascension (Matt. 28.17), full recognition of the risen Jesus, leading to adoration at his feet, is overtly mingled with a failure of recognition ('but some doubted'). Why should doubt be mentioned at this of all moments – the Lord's return to glory – unless because the risen Christ is being intentionally presented yet again as an ambiguous and indeterminate figure, one who did not fully conform to the contours of identity that the disciples held for him? He no longer fits into this world; he is on his way beyond and is in the process of leaving it behind, so his recognizability is compromised.

In John 20.13–15, Mary Magdalene, wandering grief-stricken outside the tomb, mistakes Jesus for the gardener and pleads with him to return Jesus' body. Did Jesus look very different, or was Mary so immersed in grief and morbidity – in thoughts of ghastly executions, mangled bodies, tombs, bones and skulls and the finality of death – as to be blind to who it was present with her in the Easter Garden? Calvin stresses that it would not have been fitting for the appearance of the risen Christ to have been constantly changing, 'Proteus-like'. So the cause of Mary's misrecognition must have lain in her state of mind. Calvin believes that this was God's will in order that the truth of Christ's resurrection might be more fully and firmly revealed to her than otherwise.[20] As Andrew Lincoln suggests, at this point there is a desperate need for the gift of recogni-

20 Calvin, John, 1971, *The Gospel According to St John, 11–21, and The First Epistle of John*, Calvin's Commentaries, ed. David W. Torrance and Thomas F. Torrance, Edinburgh: The Saint Andrew Press, p. 197.

tion. Jesus grants it; he speaks one word: her name, 'Mary'. His word 'breaks her absorption with the realm of the dead, as she hears the voice of the Son of God (cf. 5.24–25).'[21] At once she is awakened, as though from a spell, recognizes him and responds with one word, 'Rabbi'. This is surely the high point of the recognition of Jesus. She seeks to clasp him, but he resists: his state and status are not the same as they were in their previous relationship. A new form of encounter with Christ is about to begin for Mary; it will be one of mutual indwelling, as it will for all the disciples (John 14.19–20; 15.4–10), a state whereby nothing could be higher or more wonderful, except Glory.[22] This case of mis-recognition has been resolved by personal address, by naming, as heart speaks to heart. But, more than that, it has been broken by Christ's revelatory, life-giving word. As Calvin points out, in tune with the Reformation's emphasis on the prevenience of the grace of God, 'the Good Shepherd calls every one of the sheep of his flock by name' (John 10.3–4). So 'the voice of the Shepherd penetrates Mary's mind, opens her eyes, arouses all her senses and so affects her that she forthwith entrusts herself to Christ'.[23]

The revelatory emphasis is paramount also in John 21.1–14, which is introduced by the author or editor of this appendix to the body of the Gospel with the words: 'After these things Jesus showed [*ephanerōsen*, revealed or manifested] himself again to the disciples ... and he showed [or revealed or manifested, *ephanerōsen*] himself in this way' (v. 1). Although the verb *phaneroō* is also used of the resurrection appearances in the additional texts to Mark's Gospel (16.12, 14), it is a signature Johannine word, being used nine times in the fourth Gospel, including in the narrative of the marriage at Cana of Galilee. It was at this marriage that Jesus produced an abundance (indeed, an excess) of wine, so showing forth, revealing

21 Lincoln, Andrew T., 2005, *The Gospel According to St John*, Black's New Testament Commentaries, London and New York: Continuum, pp. 492–3.

22 Lincoln, *The Gospel According to St John*, p. 493.

23 Calvin, *The Gospel According to St John*, p. 198.

or manifesting his glory – his identity, power, authority and mission – and enabling his disciples to believe in him (John 2.1–11). Now, at the lakeside and after all that has happened to him and to them, the risen Christ awaits his fishermen disciples' return from their expedition, though 'the disciples did not know that it was Jesus'. After they have hauled in a miraculous draught of fish, the Beloved Disciple intuits that it is Jesus, but we are not told how he recognized him. Presumably it is by the same divinely inspired discernment that he exercised when he ran to the tomb with Peter, looked in, saw the grave clothes, and 'believed' (John 20.8). The stranger on the shore invites them to a breakfast of bread and fish. 'None of the disciples dared to ask him, "Who are you?" because they knew it was the Lord.' Why are they ashamed to ask the stranger who he is? Probably because, although he had given them the sign of the huge haul of fish and was now inviting them to a meal, there was irrefutable evidence in their minds – especially the searing memories of the sufferings of the Messiah – that at that moment counted decisively against it being Jesus. How then did they come to know now 'that it was the Lord'? Perhaps when 'he took the bread and gave it to them, and did the same with the fish' (v. 13), which was obviously reminiscent of the feeding of the 5,000 (John 6.1–14). Just as in the recognition scene in the Emmaus story of Luke 24.30–31, it is the distinctive way that Jesus presided at the meal that opens his disciples' eyes to his identity. The same verb, but this time in the third person (*ephanerōthē*), concludes this episode: 'This was now the third time that Jesus was revealed to the disciples after being raised from the dead' (v. 14). Inviting sinners to his table (or joining them at theirs), and breaking bread with them and for them, was one of the most characteristic and identifiable actions of Jesus Christ in his earthly ministry, a signature action. It was the signature act whereby Jesus chose to reveal his character and mission. It revealed him as one who accorded recognition to sinners and outcasts unconditionally, as their reconciler to the God of Israel and the community of Israel, and as the bringer and giver of life and strength through the symbolism of 'the staff of life'. This same action continues to be one of his most characteristic and identifiable actions in the church at all times. In the form of Holy Communion, the sharing of bread and wine with his disciples is the present recognizing and reconciling ministry of the glorified Lord Jesus Christ through the Holy Spirit.

It is the almost unanimous testimony of the resurrection narratives that the risen Jesus is not recognized at first. He is cloaked in anonymity and veiled in mystery. True, according to the Gospels they were not expecting to see him. That he would suddenly appear in the midst of them was the last thing that they would have been expecting. But, more than that, he looked different; he was manifestly 'other'. His wounds in his hands and feet were the most indicative signs of continuity, evidence that it was indeed the same 'person' who had come to them again. As Jesus suddenly appears in the midst when the doors are locked or walks alongside them on the road or waits for them on the shore – and then disappears as mysteriously as he came – the disciples are overwhelmed with mingled feelings of fear, awe and wonder. The stories of mis-identification are surely meant to show that, while the risen Christ is unquestionably continuous with the Jesus of Galilee and Jerusalem, there is also significant discontinuity. What we find is a disruption and transformation of identity that produces ambiguity, disorientation and doubt. Perhaps this is only to be expected because, though he is risen, he is 'not yet ascended' (John 20.17) and not yet glorified at the right hand of the Father (John 12.23, 28; 13.31–32; 17.1, 5, 22, 24; cf. Mark 16.19). The work of the promised Holy Spirit is to convey to the disciples the truth of the glorified identity of Christ (John 16.12–15).

What is constant in these narratives is that, just as Joseph, in revealing his identity to his brothers, reconciled them to himself, forgiving them for trading him into slavery, thus effectively wiping out his life, and giving them a new reconciled life of ample provision under his protection – so the risen Christ, in revealing his identity to his disciples, reconciles them to himself, forgiving them for deserting him in his hour of trial and need, and recommissions them to carry forward his work in the world.

Recognition and personhood

To be positively recognized by others, especially those whom we respect, esteem and look up to, is a universal human longing, a basic need, a visceral desire. The event of affirming regard by others helps to construct our consciousness of who we are and where we fit in. It contributes to our fundamental sense of self-worth (esteem) and thus to our flourishing as integrated persons.[24] To live within an ambience of meaningful recognition is a basic necessity; it belongs to our existence as human beings. Zizioulas writes: 'As a person you exist as long as you love and are loved ... Personal identity can emerge only from love ...'[25] An individual who was consistently unrecognized by the significant persons around them would be invisible and would hardly exist as a person. He or she would be devalued and dehumanized, a 'displaced person', excluded from the human and social world. The Psalmists described this experience of abandonment when they cried to God: 'I looked also upon my right hand: and saw there was no man that would know me. I had no place to flee unto: and no man cared for my soul' (Ps. 142.4–5, BCP). Writing on 'the social self', William James imagined such a plight:

> No more fiendish punishment could be devised, were such a thing physically possible, than that one should be turned loose in society and remain absolutely unnoticed by all the members thereof. If no one turned round when we entered, answered when we spoke, or minded what we did, but if every person we met 'cut us dead', and acted as if we were not existing things, a kind of rage and impotent despair

24 Storr, Anthony, 1963, *The Integrity of the Personality*, Harmondsworth: Penguin.

25 Zizioulas, *Communion and Otherness*, p. 167.

> would ere long well up in us, from which the cruellest bodily tortures would be a relief.[26]

A person who means nothing to those around them is hardly a person at all, but the mere shadow, shade or trace of a human being. Primo Levi brings this out unforgettably in *If This is a Man*, his narrative of what it meant to be an inmate of Auschwitz concentration camp where the deliberate programme of 'dehumanization' ('the demolition of a man') was the prerequisite of 'extermination'. There is also perhaps, in Levi's title, an implied reference to the concentration camp guards who, in the process of systematically dehumanizing and degrading the inmates, became radically dehumanized and debased themselves.[27]

We are constituted as persons by the recognition of others, held in our being by their gaze, even if it is sometimes a gaze that questions, challenges or threatens. The cognizance accorded particularly by 'significant others' is constitutive of our identity. These significant others are, first, parents (especially the mother), then siblings and other close relatives, then friends and playmates; then teachers and other mentors, including clergy and pastors. It is sad to have to add that for many young people today 'significant others' include so-called 'celebrities', whom they have probably never met in person or interacted with in meaningful ways. The public images of such celebrities are largely fabrications and their life stories are freely fictionalized. While there is an element of projection on to the other in all our relationships, in the case of celebrities, whom we only know through the mass media, projection becomes the only reality. Nevertheless, it is what they are thought or imagined to be that can be introjected into the developing psyche, contributing to the forming of emerging identity. For good or ill, acts of sustained recognition award us our place in the world and give

26 James, William, 1890, *The Principles of Psychology*, London: Macmillan, vol. 1, pp. 293–4.

27 Levi, Primo, 1987 (1979), *If This is a Man* [and] *The Truce*, trans. Stuart Woolf, intro. Paul Bailey, London: Abacus.

us our social, as well as individual, identity – and when they fail or prove unworthy, they store up problems for the future development and maturation of the individual. Normally, however, reciprocal experiences of emotion-filled recognition form the psychological building blocks of individuation.

Among the voluminous literature on the relational dimension of human psychological and emotional development – which I am construing under the rubric of reciprocal recognition – I could mention the following sources that are known to me. Obviously, the works of Sigmund Freud are foundational, but they tend to be narrowly focused on sexuality and in particular genitality, and the problems of arrested genitally focused psychological development leading to failure to make satisfying relationships. Freud recognized that the newborn baby finds the principal object of its instinctive, voracious, desire in the mother's breast, so that the presence of the mother becomes associated in the baby's mind with the satisfaction of desire (appetite, warmth, touch, the need for comfort). When the breast is withdrawn as the baby is weaned, the baby now lacks an external object for its libido and so transfers it to itself. This is the period that Freud calls auto-eroticism and it follows three phases: oral, anal and genital or 'phallic', in which the baby discovers its sexual organs as an object of sensual pleasure. Each of the three phases is superseded in healthy child development by the next, until a period of quiescence supervenes, which lasts until puberty when the child begins the process leading to mature sexual (for Freud, mainly genital) identity. However, something of the content of each phase is carried over into adult sexuality. Problems of sexual identity (and, therefore, of relationships) occur, according to Freud, when an individual's identity is arrested at one of the earlier, infantile, stages, or when some trauma in adult experience causes a regression to one of the immature stages of infancy. In this syndrome, Freud believes, lies the origin of neuroses.[28]

28 Freud, Sigmund, 1977, *Three Essays on Sexuality* (1905), ed. Angela Richards, trans. James Strachey, The Pelican Freud Library, Harmondsworth: Penguin, pp. 31–169.

Freud's work on the pathological aspects of the process of psychological and emotional maturation of the individual, connected to the infant's perception of the failure of the mother to provide what it demands, especially the breast, was discussed classically, within the Freudian tradition, by *inter alia* Ernest Jones, Karl Abraham, Anna Freud and Melanie Klein and this fed into the 'object-relations' approach.[29]

In the classic *Child Care and the Growth of Love*, John Bowlby, reporting the findings of his post-war research, which was sponsored by the World Health Organization, concluded that 'mother-love in infancy and childhood is as important for mental health as are vitamins and proteins for physical health'.[30] D. W. Winnicott argued that being seen, noticed and accepted in infancy makes us aware of our existence. In 'The Capacity to be Alone' Winnicott shows that the experience of being alone in the presence of the 'good-enough' mother, or of another loving, caring person, is important for the maturing of the child.[31] W. R. D. Fairbairn emphasized the developing child's longing for human relationships (confusingly called 'objects'), rather than being driven by imperious, impersonal, genitally focused desires, as Freud had supposed. In this line of enquiry, Fairbairn was largely followed by Harry Guntrip.[32] Similarly, Erik H. Erikson argued that personal identity was

29 Jones, Ernest, 1918, *Papers on Psychoanalysis*, London: Bailliere Tindall & Cox; Abraham, Karl, 1965, *Selected Papers*, with a memoir by Ernest Jones, London: Hogarth Press; Freud, Anna, 1966, *The Ego and the Mechanisms of Defence*, London: Hogarth Press; Segal, Hanna, 1964, *Introduction to the Work of Melanie Klein*, London: Heinemann.

30 Bowlby, John, 1953, *Child Care and the Growth of Love*, London: Pelican, p. 182.

31 Winnicott, D. W., 1965, 'The Capacity to be Alone', in D. W. Winnicott, *The Maturation Process and the Facilitating Environment*, London: Hogarth Press; Winnicott, D. W., 1971, 'Mirror Rôle of Mother and Family in Child Development', in D. W. Winnicott, *Playing and Reality*, London: Tavistock Clinic.

32 Fairbairn, W. R. D., 1952, *Psychoanalytical Studies of the Personality*, London: Tavistock Clinic and Routledge and Kegan Paul; Guntrip, Harry, 1977, *Personality Structure and Human Interaction*, London: Hogarth Press.

formed by the conjunction of a consciousness of the continuity of one's existence and a perception that 'significant others' recognized one's sameness and continuity. Erikson explored infant development under the rubric of the 'mutuality of recognition' between the infant and the mother.[33]

The very fabric of human society is made up of countless acts of mutual or reciprocal perception – not glancing, casual perceptions, but sustained or intense perceptions – of others and their perceptions of us. Human community, the web of social belonging, is constituted by mutual recognition and the accepted, stereotyped practices – from facial expressions and manual gestures to complex, negotiated interactions, protracted over time – that implement those perceptions, translating them into lived reality; in other words, how we behave and act towards one another. Social interaction is infused with reciprocal recognition. The word 'recognition' covers a world of human experience. But, if everything is recognition, nothing is recognition. Therefore, some analysis and interpretation of what we mean by recognition is needed. The best way to do this is to attempt some conscious reflexivity about what we are experiencing when we make an act of recognition and to look at how we use the word in everyday life.

To recognize, to *re-cognize*, someone or something is literally to 're-think' them, to revisit them in thought, to do a 'double take', in which the meaning or significance of that person or thing becomes more apparent to us, even perhaps in a revelatory way. We have probably been aware of them all along in the background of consciousness and in an inchoate way, by means of some rather nebulous pre-apprehension (*Vorgriff*), or through a kind of 'tacit knowing' of significant elements within the whole that we dimly perceive.[34] But when we are

33 Erikson, Erik H., 1968, *Identity: Youth and Crisis*, London: Faber and Faber, pp. 50, 96; see also Erikson, Erik H., 1977, *Childhood and Society*, London: Paladin, p. 371.

34 Polanyi, Michael, 1958, *Personal Knowledge*, London: Routledge and Kegan Paul; Polanyi, Michael, 1967, *The Tacit Dimension*, London: Routledge and Kegan Paul.

prompted, or perhaps compelled, to take a second look, we see more clearly and deeply into who they are as persons, what they stand for, and their relevance to us, for good or ill. We may find that what we see there basically matches up with the idea that we already have in our mind; there is a basic 'fit'. But what we see there – or, rather, discover – also serves to challenge, educate and correct our thinking about the recognized object, so that we perceive it differently: we 're-think' it. There are resonances here with Wittgenstein's discussion of 'seeing as', when we see an object differently to before and think to ourselves, 'I would never have recognized it like that before now.'[35] Then we may realize that we have 'mis-recognized' it in our first glance. A kind of *anamnesis* takes place: an intentional act of remembering that retrieves the object from the past and brings it into the foreground of the present moment in its presence, integrity and effect (akin to the *anamnesis* of the Eucharist). Classical and patristic uses of 'recognition' from various roots are infused with the Platonic notion of knowledge as recognition. We have given the object of our recognition, whether thing or person, a revised status, a reconstructed identity. In our knowing, we have moved into a new place. When such recognition is mutual, both knowing (that is, recognizing) subjects come to occupy the same personal space, or at least overlapping spaces.

Although the English verb 'to recognize' and the noun 'recognition' literally suggest a cognitive process, recognition is far from being a purely intellectual event. Any act of meaningful – not trivial, casual or glancing – recognition also involves the emotions and the will. As an act of the whole person, it recruits all our faculties. There is an intentionality in such an act of recognition, a going forth, a logic of self-involvement or even entanglement. Recognition also impinges on the ethical dimension because it involves moral value-judgements about the object or person that is recognized and about what the implica-

35 Wittgenstein, Ludwig, 1958, *Philosophical Investigations*, trans. G. E. M. Anscombe, 2nd edn, Oxford: Basil Blackwell, pp. 194–214.

tions might be for us – for good or ill. An event of recognition is shot through with spontaneous moral discernment. This may produce an evaluation of approval, admiration and attraction with respect to what is judged to be good, salutary and beneficial. An ethical judgement is never merely theoretical, a pure statement of what is the case; it entails an imperative to choose to act in a certain way. It calls for a decision and a choice, however tacitly formed. It affects our behaviour, our reaction to what is recognized.[36] As Aristotle said, 'Moral virtue is a state of character [or disposition] concerned with choice, and choice is deliberate desire.'[37]

The act of recognition is often emotionally charged. At the emotional extremes, it may become infused with revulsion or fear, it may also effect a transition to attachment, love and personal union. Some moments of intense mutual recognition carry an erotic charge. Two people falling in love is an example of total mutual recognition infused with total mutual self-involvement. We feel, whether or not we articulate it like this at the time: 'This is the person I have been waiting for all my life; this person completes my existence.' Here the element of 'fit' is particularly pronounced, because – as everyone knows – the person we fall in love with is an idealized person, a projected and constructed *persona*. Falling in love is also probably the clearest example of the way that becoming the donor and recipient of a powerful act of reciprocal recognition changes who we are. It alters our sense of our own identity. Recognition is always identity-constituting, sometimes radically so. And falling in love is the most striking evidence that recognition is an act of our entire being. Obviously, falling in love does not stop with heartfelt emotion or even the meeting and merging of minds ('Let me not to the marriage of true minds / Admit impediments': Shakespeare, Sonnet 116). It demands physical

36 Hare, R. M., 1952, *The Language of Morals*, Oxford: Clarendon Press, pp. 29–31.

37 Aristotle, 2009, *Nichomachean Ethics*, trans. David Ross; rev. with intro. and notes Lesley Brown, Oxford: Oxford University Press, p. 102 (1139a, ll. 22–23).

expression and ultimately bodily union. As John Donne put it, 'To our bodies turne wee then, that so / Weake men on love reveal'd may looke; / Loves [sic] mysteries in soules doe grow, / But yet the body is his booke.'[38] Positive recognition ultimately demands the resources of body, mind and spirit.

In the Christian life there are extended moments of mutual recognition that are both solemn and joyful. Many of these are 'liminal' – in theological language 'sacramental' – events. They include: sacramental initiation and ordination; the exchange of marriage vows; profession within a religious community; and induction into a new role or ministry within the church. Through such liminal events, which are both transitional and transformative experiences, one is given added self-worth, individual purpose and social value. Such awesome rites are provided not merely for the individual's own sake, but in order that they may contribute added value to the community to which the individual has now acquired a new relationship. Such formalized and ritualized acts of mutual recognition are carefully prepared for and have significant consequences. We feel different afterwards; our perspective on life and on the other party or parties who are involved is changed. Our self-awareness is qualitatively enhanced. We begin a fresh page of our life that stretches into the foreseeable future. There is a sense in which we become a new person – born again – as we pass through liminality.[39]

However, discrete acts of recognition – whether of the everyday sort or of sacramental significance – are only the beginning of the new relational life that they open up to us. They do not 'stop right there', but sweep us forward into fresh and deeper encounters. Experiences of meaningful recognition initiate an interpersonal adventure; they launch an ongoing trajectory.

38 John Donne, 'The Extasie', in Helen Gardner (ed.), 1966, *The Metaphysical Poets*, rev. edn, Harmondsworth: Penguin, p. 77.

39 On the concept of liminality, see Van Gennep, A., 1960, *The Rites of Passage*, London: Routledge and Kegan Paul; Turner, Victor, 1969, *The Ritual Process*, London: Routledge and Kegan Paul/Chicago, IL: Aldine Press.

The initial act of recognition, whether of great or little moment, is an epistemic condition of possibility; it makes further steps in fellowship and communion available, including – as we shall see in the next and final chapter – reconciliation.

Recognition and grace

There is a highly nuanced vocabulary around recognition/acknowledgement in various European languages, classical and modern, as we would expect in the case of such an elemental ingredient of human identity and sociality.[40] The rich semantic resources of recognition or acknowledgement have flowed into theological discourse, especially in connection with the themes of justification and church unity. With regard to justification, the longing for acceptance by God that we find in the troubled, anguished soul before it receives assurance of salvation is essentially a thirst for divine recognition, a kind of benign acknowledgement, from above to below. We may say that in the divine act of justification we are being positively recognized – that is to say, accepted, endorsed and welcomed by God. Eberhard Jüngel, drawing on the insights of Martin Luther (especially Luther's pivotal distinction between the human person and their works) and Karl Barth, has used recognition as a key term in his doctrine of justification, adopting the term used by Hegel, *Anerkennen* (translated as 'recognize', 'accept' and 'acknowledge' in the English version).[41] This divine recognition may be the truth enshrined in the Pauline image (one that seems artificial and impersonal to most of us today) of 'forensic' justification – that is, imputed or 'reckoned' righteousness, as in a law court. To me, Jüngel's use of divine

40 See Saarinen, *Recognition and Religion*.

41 Jüngel, Eberhard, 2006, *Justification: The Heart of the Christian Faith*, London and New York: T&T Clark; Webster, J. B., 1986, *Eberhard Jüngel: An Introduction to his Theology*, Cambridge: Cambridge University Press, pp. 98–9.

recognition or acknowledgement to describe justification seems much too cool and impersonal. It seems to make justification merely epistemological. Justification must be an act of divine embrace and transformation.

Karl Barth placed the emphasis on the converse aspect of divine–human recognition: the God-ward, Christ-ward, human act of recognition or acknowledgement that is enabled by the Holy Spirit. The event of Christian faith, for Barth, involves: first, acknowledgement (*Anerkennen*), basic compliance and receptivity with regard to the word of God, the message of the gospel; second, recognition (*Erkennen*), whereby we see the 'form' of Christ in Scripture and in the church's proclamation; and third, confession (*Bekennen*) of faith in the midst of the community and before the world. Thus, for Barth, the act of faith is essentially cognitive, a form of knowledge, and this is indispensable. But it is also, for Barth, a fiduciary act and an act of obedience, certainly not merely the knowledge of biblical texts or of the church's doctrinal propositions. Furthermore, such an event of faith in Christ is not possible without the church; it presupposes, according to Barth, 'the mediatorial ministry of the Christian community which is his body'.[42]

So in Jüngel and Barth respectively we have a continual process of two-way theological recognition: from heaven to earth – that is, from the divine to the human (= justification); and from earth to heaven – that is, from the human to the divine (= penitence and faith). Paul captures both directions of the flow of recognition when he writes to the Galatians: 'You have come to recognize [from *ginōskō*, I come to recognize or know] God, or rather to be recognized by God' (Gal. 4.9). But this divine–human–divine reciprocity of recognition makes possible – it renders essential and imperatively calls for – a recognition from earth to earth, human to human in the experience and practice of fellowship, of communion. 'Welcome one another

42 Barth, Karl, 1975–, *Church Dogmatics*, ed. G. W. Bromiley and Thomas F. Torrance, trans. G. W. Bromiley, Edinburgh/London and New York: T&T Clark, IV/1, pp. 751–79; quotation on p. 760, cf. p. 778.

[from *proslambanō*, I welcome, accept, receive], therefore, just as Christ has welcomed [accepted, received] you, to the glory of God' (Rom. 15.7; cf. 14.1; Philemon 17). Recognition works in the vertical plane or dimension and in the horizontal plane or dimension, but these are not two unconnected transactions, because the divine–human economy of recognition is one and undivided. How God in Christ recognizes and accepts us in justification immediately affects how we regard one another, especially in the church, which is properly the fellowship of mutual recognition; and by the same token, how we, as Christians, recognize, accept, welcome and receive one another reflects on the testimony to Jesus Christ in the world, the public proclamation of the gospel, and thus impinges on God and the glory of God.

Varieties of recognition

In the quest for Christian unity, formal mutual recognition as churches belonging to the one church of Jesus Christ, followed by liturgical acts of reconciliation, is a well-travelled, two-stage pathway to deeper unity, pioneered by the Meissen Agreement between the Evangelical Church of Germany (EKD) and the Church of England in 1991, a truly reconciling achievement in the light of World War Two.[43] Ecclesial recognition is the gateway to ecclesial communion. For example, the Second Vatican Council gives formal recognition to non-Roman Catholic baptized Christians when it says, 'All who have been justified by faith in baptism are members of Christ's body … and so are

43 *The Meissen Agreement* (1991): www.churchofengland.org/sites/default/files/2017-11/The%20Meissen%20Agreement.pdf. See also *An Anglican-Methodist Covenant: Common Statement of the Formal Conversations between the Methodist Church of Great Britain and the Church of England*, 2001, Peterborough: Methodist Publishing House; London: Church House Publishing: www.anglican-methodist.org.uk/full-text-of-the-covenant/.

deservedly recognized (*agnoscuntur*) as sisters and brothers in the Lord.'[44] This kind of formal articulation of ecclesial recognition is the essential prerequisite for steps towards reconciliation between churches. Obviously, no one would want to be reunited sacramentally to those whom they believe not to be Christians and members of the body of Christ. In the endeavour of ecumenical rapprochement, we need to study tangible ways of demonstrating the fact of mutual recognition on the way to mutual reconciliation.

Sometimes in everyday life (and we find this in ecumenical theology too) we use the more objective, less emotionally laden terms 'to acknowledge' or 'acknowledgement', which may be in any case more appropriate to the less personal and relational 'recognition' of a set of truths, an institution or a state of affairs. 'To acknowledge' carries various levels of personal interest or investment. 'To acknowledge' can have the minimal meaning of 'to accept rather grudgingly the existence of' something or someone. A slightly enhanced meaning of 'to acknowledge' approximates to 'to tolerate' and suggests a kind of complacent coexistence rather than a dynamic towards unity in some form. But 'to acknowledge' (in English, obviously) can also have the sense of 'to confess the validity of', 'to accept the reality of', 'to come to terms with', 'to give respect to', 'to give something or someone their due'. 'Acknowledgement' (*Anerkennen*) is a key term in Karl Barth; it seems rather cool, but carries a heavy freight of significance. For, in Barth, what is acknowledged in faith is nothing less than Jesus Christ himself.[45]

Similarly, we may also recognize a person in a dispassionate way, in the sense of acknowledging 'that is who they are', though they mean little to us personally – for example, a newsreader or weatherperson who pops up on the television or computer screen. We recognize them all right, but it usually makes little difference to us if someone else reads the news or gives the weather forecast; it is the message, not

44 *Unitatis redintegratio* 3.

45 Saarinen, *Recognition and Religion*, pp. 161–4.

the messenger, that matters. If, on the other hand, the person we see on a screen or in a book, newspaper or magazine is a historical figure who lived before the advent of photography, but is instantly recognizable (say Queen Elizabeth I, Napoleon Bonaparte, George Washington or the Duke of Wellington) and we are looking at their portrait, we are not particularly existentially involved. But we can also have a strong emotional reaction, favourable or unfavourable, to figures from the past whom we recognize immediately (Martin Luther and John Calvin; J. S. Bach; Samuel Johnson, William Wordsworth; Adolf Hitler and Joseph Stalin; Winston Churchill; John F. Kennedy, Elvis Presley, Martin Luther King, Marilyn Monroe, Margaret Thatcher, to mention but a few household names).

We can never have this recognition-experience with regard to Jesus Christ. What is the theological significance of the fact that we do not know what Jesus of Nazareth looked like, that we do not have a face to recognize and to relate to? Although the would-be-beloved face of Jesus has been represented in art in a thousand different ways, what he actually looked like is withheld from us. I think perhaps this fact, this absence, belongs to the mystery of divine providence and is not accidental.

As Levinas and Ricoeur particularly have brought out, to recognize someone with positive regard in a scenario of lived personal encounter carries a strong existential freight. We give the other our full attention face-to-face and in the process become emotionally vulnerable. The experience is shot through with ethical import and volitional consequences as a sense of mutual responsibility arises between us. We become mutual debtors. The encounter marks us, changes us; it makes a difference to our sense of self and to our awareness of obligation. Such an interpersonal encounter, in which the hearts and lives of two people become intertwined, can alter the direction of our lives for good or ill. The Scriptures knew this truth long before Levinas or Ricoeur articulated it philosophically. The book of Proverbs says, 'Just as water reflects the face, so one human heart reflects another' (Prov. 27.19). And in John's Gospel Jesus tells his disciples that he has held nothing back from them: 'I have called you friends because I have made known to you everything ...' (John 15.15).[46]

Selfhood, Godhood and the inhabited world

In the dynamics of recognition, we can identify three interlinked spheres of operation, three *loci*: oneself, one's God, and the wider social world. Studies of recognition have spoken of self-recognition, akin to growth in self-knowledge; recognition *of* God in conversion and *by* God in justification; and mutual recognition within human social relationships. We are not talking about three self-contained and separate areas of experience, but about three interlinked and overlapping spheres. For Christian theology and spirituality these dynamics of recognition all take place before the face of God, *coram deo*:

1 *Self.* Self-recognition for a religious and devout person, a person of faith, includes a sense of a self that is empty and needy without God. The psalmist longs and thirsts for God like a parched desert, feeling depleted and incomplete until refreshed with God's presence and life (Pss. 42 and 43). In St Augustine's familiar words, 'You have made us for yourself and our souls are restless until they find their rest in you.'[47] Reflexive recognition is strongly present in the writings of Luther and Calvin (as also in the Italian Renaissance

---

46 Levinas, Emmanuel, 1991 (1974), *Otherwise than Being, or, Beyond Essence*, trans. Alphonso Lingis, London: Kluwer. Helpful interpretation: Morgan, Michael L., 2007, *Discovering Levinas*, Cambridge: Cambridge University Press; Ricoeur, Paul, 1992, *Oneself as Another*, trans. Kathleen Blamey, Chicago, IL and London: University of Chicago Press; Ricœur, Paul, *The Course of Recognition*. More advanced interpretation: Hegel, Georg Wilhelm Friedrich, 2018, *The Phenomenology of Spirit*, trans. and ed. Terry Pinkard, Cambridge: Cambridge University Press, ch. 4.

47 Augustine, 1991, *Confessions*, trans. Henry Chadwick, Oxford: Oxford University Press, p. 3 (I, i, 1).

Christian philosopher Marsilio Ficino).[48] In the opening paragraph of his *Institutes of the Christian Religion*, which reached its definitive Latin edition in 1559, John Calvin linked together knowledge of God and knowledge of ourselves as comprising the totality of true wisdom. Calvin commented that the knowledge of God and of ourselves are so intertwined that it is not clear which of them has preceded and given birth to the other. 'For … no man [sic] can survey himself without forthwith turning his thoughts towards the God in whom he lives and moves.' Conversely, 'every person … on coming to the knowledge of himself, is not only urged to seek God, but is also led by the hand to find him'.[49] Calvin is making a remarkable claim, and today an eminently challengeable one: the better we know ourselves, the more we are drawn towards God; the stronger the awareness of self, the stronger the sense of God. I find this to be true in my own experience and awareness of selfhood, but it is not generally accepted in Western culture where the cult of the autonomous self, almost the 'self-created self', has replaced a pervasive sense of God within one's life. Also, within Reformed theology, the early nineteenth-century theologian Friedrich Schleiermacher developed Calvin's insight, claiming that our pre-reflective self-consciousness contains a recognition of a 'sense of absolute dependence' upon God, dependence on an infinite creating, sustaining and guiding benevolent power. I think that a religious person knows this sense of absolute dependence to be the ground of their identity. Schleiermacher made this principle the linchpin of his dogmatics.[50] Selfhood and Godhood should be

48 Saarinen, *Recognition and Religion*, pp. 142–3.

49 Calvin, John, 1962, *Institutes of the Christian Religion*, trans. Henry Beveridge, London: James Clarke, vol. 1, pp. 37–8 (I, i, 1).

50 Schleiermacher, F. D. E., 1958, *On Religion: Speeches to its Cultured Despisers*, trans. John Oman, intro. Rudolf Otto, New York: Harper and Row (Harper Torchbooks), p. 39. A more modern translation is: Schleiermacher, F. D. E., 1969, *On Religion: Addresses in Response to its Cultured Critics*, trans. and ed. Terrence N. Tice,

inseparable, both conceptually and experientially, not only in theory but in practice. God and self belong together in the Christian worldview and in theistic philosophy.[51] So we are already launched into the next point.

2 *God*. The twin spiritual events of conversion and justification can be seen as acts of recognition vis-à-vis God and the self. They are both the work of God within the human self. Conversion is the whole person's active, transformative recognition of the claims of God and the gospel. In Luther's theology the believer's penitent and trustful response to the gospel is frequently construed as an act approximating to recognition towards God, though the language of recognition is not explicit.[52] Conversion is obviously an act of the human will, but it is originated and assisted by the prevenient action of the Holy Spirit (Eph. 2.8–9). Conversion is an event of reorientation: it redirects the self, its sense of identity, its values and priorities, first towards God, then to oneself and then to the world. Conversely, justification by grace through faith is an act of God that restores the believer to fellowship with God and breathes new grace-filled life into all their attitudes and relationships. When God 'recognizes' a person in justification, God causes them to live before God's face, to live in God's presence and favour. Recognition as God's saving act first becomes explicit in Schleiermacher's use of the Pauline theme of adoption as God's children, construed as an act of recognition.[53] However, these acts of conversion and justification ought not to be conceived in an individualistic way; an interpersonal or communal dimension is always involved. Conversion and justification both point to the social implications of recog-

Richmond, VA: John Knox Press. See also Schleiermacher, 1928, *The Christian Faith*, trans. H. R. Macintosh and J. S. Stewart, Edinburgh: T&T Clark.

51 See Campbell, C. A., 1957, *On Selfhood and Godhood: Gifford Lectures*, London: George Allen and Unwin; New York: Macmillan.

52 Saarinen, *Recognition and Religion*, pp. 87–98.

53 Saarinen, *Recognition and Religion*, pp. 147–8.

nition, interactions with others, repercussions within the world. To turn to God in conversion is to turn away from evil and consequently to fight against it. To receive justification is to be the recipient of divine justice and that cannot be bottled up in some inner 'spiritual' sanctum, but must overflow into working for justice in the world.

3 *World*. An infinite number of acts of reciprocal recognition, of varying degrees of spontaneity or reflexivity, informality or formality, casualness or intensity, whether positive or negative, constitute the daily business of human beings and form the fabric of social interaction. They are what make the world go round. The texture of society is woven by countless acts of mutual recognition of various kinds and various degrees. Communities as well as individuals practise self-recognition, forming over time their unique sense of identity. But a community cannot do this without the recognition that comes from other, collateral, communities. Any community that turns entirely in on itself, becoming totally self-contained and self-referential, is doomed to decay and disintegration through entropy. Recognition across social entities is also, and at the same time, a political matter; it entails the distribution of power, wealth and resources.[54] But social acts of mutual recognition, as they are understood in Christian theology, are not purely immanent – 'secular' or 'humanistic' – processes, but are generated and informed by the presence of the image of God in the other. This is one of the most critical traces of the Creator within the creation (Gen. 1.26–27) and is the foundation of theological anthropology. Sociality deserves to be recognized as the most basic stratum of our existence; there is no possibility of human *being* without it. Sociality is ordained by God, sustained

54 Taylor, Charles, 'The Politics of Recognition', in Charles Taylor, 1995, *Philosophical Arguments*, Cambridge, MA: Harvard University Press, ch. 12, where Taylor develops the connection between identity and recognition. Surprisingly, recognition is not deployed as an interpretative category in Taylor, Charles, 1989, *Sources of the Self: The Making of Modern Identity*, Cambridge: Cambridge University Press.

by God and redeemed by God, in all three ways through the operation of the Word of God (*Logos*: John 1.1–18) and the Spirit of God (Gen. 1.2; 2.7; cf. John 20.22).[55] Our understanding of human sociality rests on the conviction that God's will for humankind is to enjoy *fellowship*. The church, the first-fruits of recreated fellowship in Christ, is the paradigm and exemplar of God's loving purpose for all people and societies. We may say that, in Christian fellowship and communion (*koinonia*, *communio*), the Christ in the one is calling to and answering to the Christ in the other, through the unifying power of the Holy Spirit.

From recognition to reconciliation

Through the persevering efforts of their theological dialogues, assisted by the work of the Faith and Order Commission, a number of the historic Anglican and Protestant churches have been able to offer various degrees of formal recognition to each other on the basis of a shared faith and a common baptism (or process of Christian initiation). The method of mutual ecclesial recognition, as the first formal step towards unity, was pioneered by Anglicans and German Protestants, in a movement towards reconciliation after World War Two, in the Meissen Agreement, and this method then served to make possible a raft of further bilateral agreements.[56] The historic churches have jointly acknowledged that the sacrament of baptism incorporates all who undergo it into the one body of

55 Hardy, Daniel W., 'Created and Redeemed Sociality', in Colin E. Gunton and Daniel W. Hardy (eds), 1989, *On Being the Church: Essays on the Christian Community*, Edinburgh: T&T Clark, pp. 21–47; also in Daniel W. Hardy, 1996, *God's Ways with the World: Thinking and Practising Christian Faith*, Edinburgh: T&T Clark, pp. 188–205.

56 Methuen, Charlotte, 'Mission, Reunion and the Anglican Communion: The "Appeal to All Christian People" and Approaches to Ecclesial Unity at the 1920 Lambeth Conference', *Ecclesiology* 16.2 (2020), pp. 175–205.

Christ. They have been able to see one anothers' churches as sharing in the apostolic mission of the one church of Christ. They have looked at one another with fresh eyes, 're-cognized' one another. They have said, in effect: 'Yes, I see that we are alike in many ways; we are all engaged in the Lord's business; we are all part of something much bigger than any of us. We know now that the heart of the matter is in you, just as we believe it is in us. We gladly acknowledge the spiritual authenticity of your faith, your sacramental life and your ministry and mission. We cannot deny the ecclesial reality of your community.'

However, those churches that are fully committed to the endeavour of Christian unity and seek to obey the Lord's will and prayer in John 21 (and this is the test of such commitment and desire) do not and cannot stop there. They feel compelled to take a further step. So they go on to say together: 'But our journey to fuller mutual recognition has also shown us that there are some important areas in which we are not the same. We do not quite match up with regard to what we each regard as important to the life and mission of Christ's church. There is not enough symmetry for us to enter into full sacramental communion straight away. We have further work in committed dialogue to do. The challenge is daunting, but we (both or all) believe that what is humanly impossible is possible with God.' That critical point of positive mutual recognition restores what was lost to us (as in the parables of the lost sheep, the lost coin and the lost son in Luke 15) through past splits, schisms and separations, and left us impoverished. This rescue and recovery brings joy to the angels in heaven – that is, to the heart of the heavenly Father – but it also brings with it the sombre realization that mutual ecclesial recognition does not go far enough, and that we now face the further challenge of working towards actual ecclesial reconciliation. We have taken the first vital step, but we now need to continue our journey together on the path that is paved with gold, the path to reconciliation, through God and to God.

8

Envisioning a Reconciled and Reconciling Community

Some words of the Scottish Congregationalist theologian and preacher P. T. Forsyth (1848–1921), written more than a century ago, sum up the argument of this final chapter and indeed of the whole book. Commenting on the biblical and theological theme of reconciliation, Forsyth pronounces: 'On this interpretation of the work of Christ the whole Church rests.' Then he adds profoundly: 'the grand end of reconciliation is communion'.[1] In the civilized and democratic world today there is, thankfully, much emphasis on conflict resolution and peace-making, and on the role of mediation in this process. Mediation can sometimes bring about reconciliation, provided that the parties are ready and willing for that to happen. My exposition here presents Jesus Christ as the divine–human mediator and reconciler and his church as a community of reconciliation – both reconciled and reconciling. I am aiming to establish as a truth of faith and as the essence of Christianity a threefold thesis: i) The God of the Bible and of Christian theology is above all a reconciling God. The just, loving and merciful purpose of God for the world is to overcome its alienation from its Creator and the estrangement through sin of God's human creatures from their Creator and from one another. ii) God's work of reconciliation runs throughout all human history, has its historical focal point in the prophetic witness of ancient Israel, and finds its definitive expression and

1 Forsyth, Peter Taylor, 1938 (1910), *The Work of Christ*, London: Independent Press, pp. 53, 57.

completion in the person and work of Jesus Christ to which the Scriptures testify. iii) The reconciling mission of God-in-Christ is worked out in a special and privileged way through the church's worship, witness and proclamation, and above all in the ministry of word and sacrament, with the result that iv) every aspect of church activity should flow from, reflect, and lead back to the reconciliation accomplished by God-in-Christ that is continued in the church; and that this truth has massive implications for the unreconciled state of the church.

When, in the Garden of Gethsemane, Jesus greets Judas, his betrayer, with the words, 'Friend, why have you come?' (Matt. 26.50), he seems to be offering Judas a last chance to reconsider what he is doing, to think again. Jesus is, it seems, inviting Judas to renounce his intention to betray him, and to be reconciled to him in friendship renewed. This friendship was never withdrawn on Jesus' side and never would be, come what may; it remains open to be received again, even by such a one as Judas.[2] From first to last, Jesus reaches out to those who are alienated and estranged, as Judas certainly is, and seeks to reconcile them to the community and to their God. As the little-sung – but for me close-to-home – 'Dorset Carol' says: 'From Heav'n the Son of God descends, / And takes the form of Man. / *To reconcile His foes as friends* / Was all His gracious plan.'

---

2 Translation following KJV and RSV among others. Most versions take the words of Jesus not as a question, but as an instruction to Judas: 'Do what you have come to do.' But to achieve this sense, the verb and the object have to be supplied; the sentiment seems superfluous; and, in any case, Jesus still addresses Judas as 'Friend'. Davies, W. D. and D. C. Allison, *The Gospel According to Saint Matthew*, International Critical Commentary, London and New York: Continuum/T&T Clark, 1997, vol. 3, *Commentary on Matthew XIX–XXVIII*, pp. 509–10. Davies and Allison favour the interpretation that I have used above.

Biblical theology of reconciliation

The biblical concept of reconciliation (*katallagē*) naturally centres on St Paul's theology of salvation or atonement. I am not attempting to expound a doctrine of the atonement here (I have briefly written on the subject previously),[3] but I am focusing on the reconciling aspect of the saving work of God and its connection to the church. Paul's soteriology can be encapsulated in four interlinked affirmations regarding: i) the loving purpose of God to 'reconcile' the world, through Christ, to Godself (2 Cor. 5.18–19; Rom. 5.8); ii) the sacrificial death of Jesus Christ to 'reconcile' humanity to God (Rom. 5.6–10); iii) the gospel as 'the word [*logos*; NRSV, 'message'] of reconciliation' (2 Cor. 5.19); and iv) the ensuing task of the apostles as 'the ministry of reconciliation' – that is, God making an appeal through them: 'Be reconciled to God' (2 Cor. 5.20).

Romans 5.9–11 is a key Pauline text because justification and reconciliation are placed in parallel as two complementary metaphors for the salvation that God has accomplished for us and in us: 'justified ... saved ... / reconciled ... saved'. The consensus of interpreters is that the content of the two terms is the same.[4] Justification is a metaphor drawn from the law courts, while reconciliation reflects the end of hostilities between enemies. It is invidious to ask which of the two is the dominant metaphor or whether one is primary and the other secondary. Each has a secure and determinate position in New Testament soteriology. However, there is something to be said for Fitzmyer's proposal that Paul sees justification as a step towards reconciliation, an event on the way to a final state, as it were, though I doubt Paul had worked that out explicitly; I also note Dunn's warning that 'the temptation to press for a

3 Avis, Paul, 1989, 'The Atonement', in Geoffrey Wainwright (ed.), *Keeping the Faith: Essays to Mark the Centenary of* Lux Mundi, Philadelphia, PA: Fortress Press/Allison Park, PA: Pickwick Publications, ch. 6.

4 Käsemann, Ernst, 1980, *Commentary on Romans*, trans. and ed. Geoffrey W. Bromiley, Grand Rapids, MI: Eerdmans, p. 138.

clear distinction between "justification" and "reconciliation" should be avoided'.[5] Fitzmyer also thinks that Käsemann is barking up the wrong tree in his suspicion of reconciliation for its supposed cultic, liturgical and sacerdotal undertones: reconciliation is a social concept, not a cultic or sacrificial one.[6]

In verses 10–11 Paul places reconciliation within a threefold perspective: past event, present state and future expectation. God has accomplished the great act of reconciliation once for all in Christ and in his death: 'we were reconciled' (5.10a). Now we are in the state of 'having been reconciled'. So we may be confident ('surely') that we will be saved eschatologically (namely, delivered or vindicated at the judgement) 'by his life' – that is, his resurrection (5.10b; cf. 4.25). At this point Käsemann comments: 'The Christ who died for us also lives for us, and destroys the threats of the future as he destroyed the evil power of the past.'[7] 'But more than that', says Paul (and we think, 'What could possibly be "more than that"?'), 'we even exult [NRSV, 'boast'] in God through our Lord Jesus Christ, through whom we have now received the reconciliation' (5.11). At this moment in his train of thought Paul's vision seems to be stretching forward to the eschatological cosmic consummation, as when in 11.15 he refers to 'the reconciliation of the world (*katallagē kosmou*)' and in 2 Corinthians 5.19 proclaims that God in Christ was 'reconciling the world (*kosmon katallassōn*) to himself'.

The Lutheran theologian Ernst Käsemann plays down the significance of the concept of reconciliation in the New Testament and even in Paul.[8] Käsemann claims to find no normative

---

5 Dunn, James D. G., 1988, *Romans 1–8*, Word Biblical Commentary 38A, Waco, TX: Word, p. 259.

6 Fitzmyer, Joseph A., 1992, *Romans: A New Translation with Introduction and Commentary*, Anchor Bible 33, New York: Doubleday/ London: Geoffrey Chapman, p. 401.

7 Käsemann, *Commentary on Romans*, p. 139.

8 Käsemann, Ernst, 1971 (1964), 'Some Thoughts on the Theme "The Doctrine of Reconciliation in the New Testament"', in James M. Robinson (ed.), trans. Charles E. Carlson and Robert P. Scharleman,

doctrine of reconciliation in the New Testament and maintains that the New Testament does not provide the material for elaborating the notion of 'Christ the Reconciler' or of his work as primarily one of reconciliation. Käsemann claims that the theme of reconciliation is marginal to the soteriology of the New Testament taken as a whole. It is simply one among a number of metaphors, including the metaphor of justification that Käsemann, as a Lutheran, upholds as normative. The idea of reconciliation, he points out, is confined to the Pauline literature (except for a few non-theological references), but even so is not significant for Pauline theology as a whole. Paul is merely using the liturgical, cultic material that he found in the tradition. Käsemann identifies the background of the concept as juridical and cultic (associated with ritual expiation [*hilaskesthai*]), which for him, as a Lutheran, is redolent of the pre-Vatican II Roman Catholic mass (Käsemann's essay was published in German in 1964) and on that account is deeply suspect. Dunn, however, points out that the term *katallagē*, reconciliation, 'is hardly attested in cultic contexts within the wider Hellenistic usage'.[9]

Against Käsemann's marginalizing of reconciliation in Paul, we could point to its probable firm anchorage in Saul's/Paul's biography. George Caird suggests that it was probably Paul's experience as a persecutor of the church that led him to use the expression 'enemies' (*echthroi*) in parallel to 'sinners' in the context of reconciliation (Rom. 5.8, 10–11).[10] Paul knew himself to be the chief of sinners (1 Tim. 1.15) because he had persecuted the church of God (Gal. 1.13, 23; 1 Cor. 15.9). Caird points out that because 'justified' and 'reconciled' are brought together in a parallelism in vv. 10–11, it will not do to play off one against the other (as Käsemann does). We also note that the expression 'the enmity' or 'the hostility' (*tēn*

The Future of Our Religious Past: Essays in Honour of Rudolf Bultmann, London: SCM Press, ch. 3.

9 Dunn, *Romans 1–8*, p. 259.

10 Caird, G. B., 1994, *New Testament Theology*, completed and ed. L. D. Hurst, Oxford: Clarendon Press, pp. 156–7.

echthran) is used twice in Ephesians 2.14–16 to describe the state of alienation between Jews and Gentiles and the need for their reconciliation. The whole passage, Ephesians 2.15–18, links God's gift of peace with God's work of reconciliation, as does Colossians 1.20 when it says, 'Through him God was pleased to reconcile to himself all things, whether on earth or in heaven, by making peace through the blood of his cross.' The verb a*pokatallasso* is unique, not only in the New Testament, but also in the LXX and in Classical Greek, to these two texts. The fruit of God's act of reconciliation is named as peace (*eirēnē*) – peace between Jew and Gentile and between heaven and earth. Ephesians and Colossians are widely regarded among New Testament scholars as pseudo-Pauline, but the idea of 'peace' as the goal that is achieved through God's act of reconciliation in Christ is quintessentially Pauline, with Romans 5.1 being the key text: 'Since we are justified by faith, we have peace with God through our Lord Jesus Christ.'

If some interpreters, such as Käsemann, are afraid that the reconciliation theme allows human effort and human merit to be smuggled in by the back door, it is important to be reminded that, while in the Old Testament humans are said to make reconciliation in relation to Yahweh, albeit by the cultic means that Yahweh has prescribed and provided, in the New Testament God is always the agent of reconciliation; it is always the work of God and human beings are the recipients.[11] The point is made forcefully by Bultmann: reconciliation is synonymous with 'righteousness' or 'justification'; the metaphors are mutually corroborative. Reconciliation is a prevenient act of God, evincing the 'absolute priority of God' and creating 'an objective factual situation brought about by God'. All that humans need to do or can do is to 'receive' it. Bultmann insists that, for Paul, reconciliation is effected both 'without us' and 'before us'. The idea that God needs to be reconciled, or that human

11 Richardson, Alan, 1958, *An Introduction to the Theology of the New Testament*, London: SCM Press, pp. 215–17.

effort should play a part in this, never enters Paul's head.[12] In Paul it is 'we' who have been reconciled to God (Rom. 5.10–11), not God who has been reconciled to us. That truth deserves to be taken as the foundation of all Christian thinking about reconciliation.

Propitiation or expiation?

In the face of Paul's clear statements that God is the one who reconciles, it seems perverse of John Calvin (who on this point can represent many others, both before and since), in his commentary on this passage in Romans and in the *Institutes of the Christian Religion*, to insist that God needed to be 'propitiated' and that Christ suffered to bring this about, dying on the cross in order that we might be reconciled to God. Typical of Calvin's language on this score is: 'Christ procured the favour of God for us', 'appeased the wrath of God', and 'rendered the Father favourable and propitious towards us'. Influenced here by Roman law and the tradition of Augustine and Anselm, Calvin asserts that our sins and their 'just vengeance' were 'transferred' to Christ 'by imputation', so that by his death 'the justice of God was satisfied'. To give him his due, Calvin has no doubt that it was God's love that motivated God's acts for our salvation: when we gaze upon the crucified Christ, we behold 'in him the heart of God poured out in love'.[13] But his version of penal substitution runs into the intolerable paradox that God's love and justice are seen to conflict and can be reconciled only at the price of Christ's death on the cross. 'How could he have given us in his only begotten Son a singular pledge of his love, if he had not previously embraced us with free favour?' Calvin falls back on Augustine's defeated

12 Bultmann, Rudolf, 1952, *Theology of the New Testament*, 2 vols, trans. Kendrick Grobel, London: SCM Press, vol. 1, pp. 285–7.

13 Calvin, John, 1959, *The Gospel According to St John*, ed. David W. Torrance and Thomas F. Torrance, trans. T. H. L. Parker, Edinburgh: Oliver and Boyd, vol. 1, p. 74 (on John 3.16).

confession that 'In a manner wondrous and divine he loved us even when he hated us.'[14]

Let us be perfectly clear: it is blasphemy to suggest, even rhetorically, that the loving Creator 'hates' any person, indeed any creature. The book of Wisdom in the Apocrypha teaches differently: 'For you love all things that exist, and detest none of the things that you have made, for you would not have made anything if you had hated it ... You spare all things, for they are yours, O Lord, you who love the living' (11.24, 26). The Collect for Ash Wednesday in the *Book of Common Prayer* (1662) echoes Wisdom, with the words 'Almighty and everlasting God, who hatest nothing that thou hast made, and dost forgive the sins of all them that are penitent'. The prayer is addressed to the 'God of all mercy'. The Scottish Presbyterian scholar James Denney (1856–1917), who perforce knew all about strong forms of Calvinism, protested against any postulating of a conflict of justice and mercy in God. In his final book, *The Christian Doctrine of Reconciliation*, Denney points out that 'Mercy and justice do not need to be reconciled, for they are never at war. The true opposite of justice is not mercy, but injustice, with which God can have nothing to do ...'[15] C. F. D. Moule writes of the popular preached version of the atonement that it presents 'a positively immoral story – an angry God needing to be propitiated, and accepting by way of propitiation the sacrifice of an innocent victim in lieu of the guilty'. Moule dubs this 'a pernicious travesty of the gospel' and points us instead to the heart of the New Testament teach-

14 Calvin, John, 1961, *The Epistles of Paul the Apostle to the Romans and Thessalonians*, trans. Ross MacKenzie, Calvin's Commentaries, ed. David W. Torrance and Thomas F. Torrance, Edinburgh: The Saint Andrew Press, p. 110; Calvin, John, 1962, *Institutes of the Christian Religion*, 2 vols, trans. Henry Beveridge, London: James Clarke, vol. 1, pp. 433–40 (II, xvi, 1–7).

15 Denney, James, 1917, *The Christian Doctrine of Reconciliation*, London: Hodder and Stoughton, p. 22. See also Denney, James, 1911 (1902), *The Death of Christ* (including *The Atonement and the Modern Mind*), 2nd edn, London: Hodder and Stoughton.

ing that 'God and Christ are one in being, so that the sacrifice of Christ is a sacrifice made by God', not one made to God.[16]

The truth is that God does not need to be propitiated but our sins need to be 'expiated' (*hilaskesthai*) at the mercy seat (Hebrew *kapporeth*, 'covering'; LXX and NT *hilasterion*, 'expiation') which God in love and mercy has provided. The King James Bible, in translating *hilasterion* as 'propitiation', followed the Vulgate *propitiatorium*, instead of looking to the background of the term in the Hebrew Bible's concept of the mercy seat of the Ark of the Covenant. God has provided the mercy seat because God looks upon humankind with unwavering mercy and love and wills to effect reconciliation. 'God so loved the world that he gave his only Son ...' (John 3.16). The all-too-familiar notion, stated so crisply by Calvin and further debased in the global slew of primitive evangelical preaching – that God required to be propitiated by the death of his Son – involves the intolerable corollary that God's 'attitude' towards God's human creatures could be altered or changed. It implies that the divine disposition needed to be changed, and was actually changed, from one of aversion and anger to one of mercy and compassion, and from one of rejection to one of acceptance. In biblical theology, God is always the initiating, acting subject of the atoning, reconciling action, not an object to be acted upon. To slightly paraphrase Paul: 'God put forth Christ Jesus as a *hilasterion* – a sacrifice of atonement – through the shedding of his blood' (Rom. 3.25). The object of 'propitiation', if that is what we want to say, can only be God; but the object of expiation can only be human sin. To propitiate means to assuage wrath or stern displeasure; but to expiate means to remove ('cover', 'wipe away') the sin that is the cause of separation. The intention behind the offering of an atoning sacrifice is to effect the reconciliation of two parties who have become estranged. To speak as though God needed to be reconciled to us, rather than we to God, is to turn the gospel on its head and to cancel its meaning as 'good news'.

16 Moule, C. F. D., 1998, *Forgiveness and Reconciliation: Biblical and Theological Essays*, London: SPCK, p. 19.

The heart of Paul's gospel

James D. G. Dunn points out that Paul's use of the verb *katallassō* with God as subject and sinners as object was a new, unprecedented idea, not attested before Paul.[17] God is seen by Paul as the injured or offended partner who will not 'walk away', but seeks at all costs to restore the broken relationship. Dunn believes that the essence of the Christian message is reconciliation and that it is the heart of Paul's gospel. Paul's many appeals for individuals to be reconciled to one another (e.g., 1 Cor. 1.10–12; Phil. 4.2), and even for a whole church (Corinth) to be reconciled to him and to his apostleship, show that in Paul's theology the church itself, the very body of Christ, is seen as the *locus* or site of reconciliation.

Ralph Martin – contra Käsemann – also takes reconciliation as the overarching concept for Paul's articulation of the gospel.[18] Martin sets out to locate a comprehensive model for Paul's theology, one that starts from the sovereign, gracious initiative of God, and that has the cross at its centre and is thus a *theologia crucis*. But he also seeks a model that has ethical and social implications for how we should live and behave as Christians in the church and in society today. Martin cites Peter Stuhlmacher who had already proposed that 'the proclamation of Jesus Christ as Messianic Reconciler' is the 'genuinely theological and critical center' of the New Testament *kerygma*.[19] Martin also cites his own teacher T. W. Manson: 'Reconciliation is thus the keyword of Paul's Gospel so far as its working out is concerned. The driving force behind the Gospel is the love of God. The *modus operandi* is reconciliation.'[20] Ridderbos also

17 Dunn, James D. G., 2003 (1998), *The Theology of Paul the Apostle*, London: T&T Clark/Grand Rapids, MI: Eerdmans, pp. 228–30.

18 Martin, R. P., 1981, *Reconciliation: A Study of Paul's Theology*, London: Marshall, Morgan and Scott/Atlanta, GA: John Knox Press.

19 Cited in Martin, R. P., *Reconciliation*, p. 3, from Stuhlmacher, Peter, 1977, *Historical Criticism and Theological Interpretation of Scripture*, Philadelphia, PA: Fortress Press, pp. 90–1.

20 Cited in Martin, R. P., *Reconciliation*, pp. 3–4, from Manson, T.

puts reconciliation in prime position within Paul's theology, albeit alongside and complementary to justification. It forms the 'foundation and summation' of the Christian life, according to Paul.[21]

It is a perversion of New Testament atonement theology – albeit one that pervades the pre-modern theological traditions, occurring in Irenaeus, Augustine, Anselm and Calvin, for example – that God needs to be reconciled to us, rather than we to God; and also that God's wrath against sinners needs to be propitiated by the death of Christ – quenched in his blood – before that reconciliation can happen.

Friedrich Schleiermacher[22]

Schleiermacher (1768–1834) reversed the persistent distortion within the tradition of atonement theology by emphasizing the subjective dimension of reconciliation, locating theologically God's act of reconciliation within the category of collective human religious experience, but without losing sight of the objectivity of the divine initiative. Schleiermacher was able to achieve this for two reasons. First, for him, as created beings we are absolutely dependent on God in every aspect of our lives, and the sense or awareness of this dependence is the core of our religious experience and a lens through which all aspects of Christian doctrine should be viewed. Second, Schleiermacher refused to separate reconciliation from redemption, as though redemption had first to take place in

W., 1963, *On Paul and John: Some Selected Theological Themes*, ed. Matthew Black, London: SCM Press, p. 50.

21 Ridderbos, Herman, 1977 (1975), *Paul: An Outline of His Theology*, trans. John Richard de Witt, Grand Rapids, MI/London: SPCK, pp. 182–6, quote at p. 186; cf. Ridderbos, Herman, 1978, *Studies in Scripture and Its Authority*, Grand Rapids, MI, pp. 72–90: 'The Biblical Message of Reconciliation'.

22 For a concise exposition of reconciliation in modern Protestant theology, see Saarinen, Risto, 2021, 'Reconciliation' in *St Andrews Encyclopedia of Theology*, www.saet.ac.uk/.

order to make it possible for reconciliation to follow. Redemption and reconciliation were two sides of the coin of God's saving action for Schleiermacher. God redeems by reconciling and reconciles by redeeming. The subjective and objective aspects are brought together and integrated. Christ assumes believers into vital fellowship with himself through the Holy Spirit and communicates to them the unclouded blessedness of his filial relationship to God, all within the community of the church. Thus, the fruits of reconciliation are manifested not only within the individual believer, but also within the fellowship of the church. Schleiermacher condemns as 'magical' any external doctrine of God's act of reconciliation that makes the impartation of Christ's blessedness to the believer independent of vital fellowship with him. 'In his suffering unto death', writes Schleiermacher, alluding to 2 Corinthians 5.19, 'there is manifested to us with perfect vividness the way in which God was in him to reconcile the world to himself'.[23]

Albrecht Ritschl

Ritschl (1822–89) further developed the two connected biblical insights that are determinative for Schleiermacher's atonement doctrine: i) It is not God who needs to be reconciled to us, but we to God (with the concomitant rejection of the penal satisfaction (Anselm) or penal substitution (Calvin) theory of the atonement). ii) The church is the sphere of the human practical and experiential reception of God's work of reconciliation and is therefore a fully integral factor in the accomplishment of God's act of reconciliation. Pannenberg claims that Ritschl radically subjectivized the reconciling act of God, reducing it to a function of human spiritual sensibility.[24] Be that as it may,

23 Schleiermacher, F. D. E., 1928, *The Christian Faith*, trans. H. R. Mackintosh and J. S. Stewart, Edinburgh: T&T Clark, pp. 361, 431, 435, 453, 456.

24 Pannenberg, Wolfhart, 1991–7, *Systematic Theology*, 3 vols,

one strength of Ritschl's doctrine is that, like Schleiermacher, he makes the church fully integral to God's act of reconciliation. Ritschl claims the authority of Luther for speaking of the justification of the community and of the priority of the community over the justification of the individual (Ritschl seems to equate 'reconciliation', 'justification' and 'forgiveness of sins', often using these terms interchangeably). For Ritschl, our assurance of forgiveness of sins and our membership of the Christian community are 'identical'. He believes that it is only by making these two concepts 'equivalent' that we can make the theological connection between the forgiveness of sins and 'the personal life of Christ, particularly the completion of his life in his sacrificial death'. Ritschl is able to effect this vital connection because (like Pannenberg a century later) he expounds an inclusive, not exclusive, representation by Jesus Christ of the community in his life of obedience, culminating in his sacrifice on the cross. Jesus Christ, standing himself in the closest conceivable relationship to God, is able to draw us into the same relationship in such a way that our sins present no obstacle to communion between ourselves and God. No transactional, forensic or propitiatory theory of the atonement is needed to effect reconciliation with God; Jesus brings his community back to God through the perfect fulfilment of his personal life culminating in his death.[25]

Karl Barth

The biblical theme of reconciliation was placed fairly and squarely at the centre of modern Christian theology by Karl Barth (1886–1968). He gave it a dominant and strategic position in his *Church Dogmatics*, signalling the theme briefly in

trans. Geoffrey W. Bromiley, Grand Rapids, MI: Eerdmans/Edinburgh: T&T Clark, vol. 2, pp. 403–16.

25 Ritschl, Albrecht, 1900, *The Christian Doctrine of Justification and Reconciliation*, trans. H. R. Mackintosh and A. B. Macaulay, Edinburgh: T&T Clark, pp. 542–56.

the first volume (CD I/1)[26] and extending his exposition in Volume IV, *The Doctrine of Reconciliation*, over two massive parts and two further substantial parts (the third Part being divided into two). For Barth, the German *Versöhnung* stands for the whole span of God's saving work in Jesus Christ, specifically both 'atonement' and 'reconciliation' (IV/1/2/3: 1–2).[27] *Versöhnung* is, for Barth, an umbrella term standing for the entire content of Christian belief. He does not limit his treatment of 'reconciliation' to the cross, as popular evangelical preaching tends to do, or even to the whole saving work of Christ, but he draws together several broad tracts of Christian doctrine under this heading, including Christology, aspects of ecclesiology, and the Christian life (theological ethics).[28]

In this quest for an integrated, holistic systematic theology, Barth regards the themes of reconciliation and revelation as interchangeable in reality, though distinguishable in thought. He equates the two terms, treating them as interchangeable, though allowance should be made for the rhetorical and homiletical register of Barth's exposition throughout. 'Reconciliation' is 'another word for' revelation, and vice versa. On the one hand, God's revelatory acts within salvation history have a reconciling effect; on the other, God's reconciling acts within salvation history are themselves revelatory (I/1, p. 409). Barth's insistence on the inseparability of these two themes is a salutary antidote and corrective to any sequential or piecemeal presentation of soteriology, whereby we might assume that we need first to get the content of the doctrine of revelation clear

26 Barth, Karl, 1975–, *Church Dogmatics*. ed. G. W. Bromiley and Thomas F. Torrance, trans. G. W. Bromiley, Edinburgh: T&T Clark, I/1, pp. 319–414. References are embedded in my main text.

27 See, further, Webster, John, 1995, *Barth's Ethics of Reconciliation*, Cambridge: Cambridge University Press.

28 The Editors' Preface to CD IV/1 notes that Barth gives *Versöhnung* 'a rich content that includes both "atonement" and "reconciliation"'. While 'reconciliation' is used to translate the title (*Die Lehre von der Versöhnung*), both terms are employed in the body of the English text according to context (p. vii).

and on that basis proceed to set out the content of the doctrine of reconciliation. No, the doctrines of revelation and reconciliation are intertwined, inseparable and thus mutually informing and interpreting.

For Barth, following a tradition inaugurated by Ferdinand Christian Baur (1792–1860), reconciliation is of the essence of Christianity. However, Barth favours not 'essence' language but the metaphors of 'heart' and 'centre' (also 'basis' and 'core') as applied to the Christian faith. These metaphors are repeatedly applied by Barth to the content of the doctrine of reconciliation in the first 50 pages of CD IV/1. Barth introduces his treatment of this theme by stating that here: '[w]e enter that sphere of Christian knowledge in which we have to do with the heart of the message received by and laid upon the Christian community and therefore with the heart of the Church's dogmatics: that is to say, with the heart of its subject-matter, origin and content'. He adds that the doctrine of reconciliation 'has a circumference, the doctrine of creation and the doctrine of the last things ... But the covenant fulfilled in the atonement is its centre' (CD IV/1/, p. 3). This means that Jesus Christ is the centre because, as Barth starkly puts it, 'Jesus Christ is the atonement' (IV/1, p. 34). There is no aspect of the divine act of reconciliation that is outside of Jesus Christ or that can be added to his person and work.

As we read Barth on reconciliation, in the context of modern Protestant theology, we watch with some bemusement how he reacts against Schleiermacher, Ritschl and Liberal Protestantism generally – and how much he still has in common with them and it. We also become aware of how much he 'anticipates' and 'points to' – viewed retrospectively, of course – the thought of Wolfhart Pannenberg. And as we read Pannenberg, we take note of the points at which he builds on Schleiermacher, Ritschl and Barth or diverges from them.

Barth strikes the right and proper note by affirming that the message of reconciliation is first and foremost a message about God, and only secondarily – though necessarily – a message about us, the unworthy human recipients of reconciliation. It is God's initiative and God's work; in reconciliation we have to do with an event and an act undertaken by God for the sake of humankind (IV/1, pp. 6–7). So pivotal is God's act of reconciliation that we must say that the whole history of God and humankind, of God and God's creation, becomes a redemptive history, bringing about our participation in God and the life of God, which is the completion and fulfilment of our created being (pp. 8–10). The name 'Jesus Christ' contains and embodies the work of God in reconciliation (pp. 18–22). Barth then affirms (including by means of a long exegetical excursus) that God's covenant with Israel forms 'the presupposition' of the divine act of reconciliation and therefore of the essential Christian message, the gospel. Barth affirms that God's covenanted 'faithfulness' extends beyond Israel to all nations and to the whole creation. In the coming of Jesus Christ into the world we have the fulfilment of the covenant promise – the very heart of the covenant – 'I will be your God and you will be my people.' This prophetic hope and promise is fulfilled in the one who is Emmanuel, 'God with us.' All that Israel heard and received became 'an event' in Jesus Christ (p. 38). The historical event of the atonement 'stands at the heart' of the Christian message and the Christian faith precisely because in this event in time 'God maintains and fulfils his Word as it was spoken at the very first' (p. 47).

God's covenantal action in Jesus Christ is an act of free grace. Humankind is not able to atone for sin. If reconciliation is to take place, it must come from God (p. 39) as a sovereign act of God (p. 81). The human response and acceptance of God's covenant grace should be infused with thankfulness. 'The only answer to *χάρις* [grace] is εὐχαριστία [thanksgiving]' (pp. 42–4). If Barth had not been so deficient in his sacramental theology, he would immediately have made a connection at this point with the central liturgical event of Christian worship, the Eucharist. He does not, but we certainly can.

How does God effect the reconciliation of the world, according to Barth? We must go back, he says, to the basic meaning of *katallassein*. 'The conversion of the world to himself took place in the form of an exchange, a substitution', an acceptance of complete solidarity with humankind, first in the incarnation, the enfleshment of the Word of God, and then in his suffering unto death. As Paul writes in 2 Corinthians 5.21: 'For our sake [God] made [Christ] to be sin who knew no sin, so that in him we might become the righteousness of God' (p. 75). Jesus Christ is the Mediator between God and humankind because he constitutes 'the middle point in which the sovereign act of the reconciling God and the being of reconciled man are one' (p. 123). For Barth, reconciliation rests upon Christology (p. 125). It is in the union of his true deity and true humanity, carried through life and death, that the reconciliation exists. It is a fact and a reality in him and all who are 'in him' – that is, the Christian community, the church – are brought into a reconciled relationship with God. This must be the basis of the reconciliation of the church with itself, so to speak. How can Christians and churches remain separated and alienated from one another when their very existence is one of having been reconciled to God in the body of his Son which has passed through life, death and resurrection? This is the great ecclesiological question that we are wrestling with in this book.

However, Barth himself does not follow through the 'ecclesiological logic' of his argument. He sets up a 'No Through Road' sign on our would-be ecclesiological trajectory. Barth insists that we cannot assimilate Paul's affirmation of the divine act of reconciliation (2 Cor. 5.21) to Paul's previous statements in verses 18–20, that God has entrusted to us (apostles) the ministry of reconciliation so that we beseech you, 'Be reconciled to God.' The two statements are not commensurate or continuous for Barth; he inserts a break between them. Paul's appeal is not 'an extension of the atonement' but a result of it. Reconciliation is not 'a process' that needs to be kept in motion until it reaches a distant goal. 'It does not need to be repeated or extended or perfected ... [I]t is present in all its fullness in every age' (p. 76). Perhaps this is because Barth insists that the cross and the resurrection must be affirmed as two distinct events (p. 299). He does not have Edwyn Hoskyn's grasp of the unity of 'Crucifixion-Resurrection'.[29] Barth does not quite achieve a unified sense of the Paschal Mystery, the total reconciling work of Christ from incarnation, through ministry, the Passion, Last Supper, death and resurrection to the descent of the Spirit, the church, the Eucharist and his heavenly intercession. In this royal road of reconciliation Christ is never without his people, his *ecclesia*, whatever Barth may say.[30]

So it is striking that Barth makes no mention of the church or the sacraments at this point. We have to look to Pannenberg for the way through to the ecclesiological consequences. As mentioned already, in 2 Corinthians 5.18–21 Paul depicts a continuum between God's reconciling act in Christ and the apostolic ministry. God continues to appeal to human beings to be reconciled and does this through the proclamation of the apostles. Barth would not approve, but it is not too much to say that the Christ event and the kerygmatic event of the church's proclamation in word and sacrament form one single articulated, ongoing event within salvation history, as we shall now see expounded – up to a point – by Pannenberg.

Wolfhart Pannenberg

Second only to Karl Barth in the sustained purpose and power of his exposition of our theme, Wolfhart Pannenberg (1928–2014) structures his whole exposition of the economy of salvation by means of the concept of reconciliation. I find Pannenberg's treatment particularly attractive and satisfying, more so even than Barth's, for reasons that will shortly become clear; however, I am not uncritical of some secondary aspects

---

29 Hoskyns, Edwyn Clement, and Francis Noel Davey, 1981, *Crucifixion-Resurrection: The Pattern of the Theology and Ethics of the New Testament*, ed. and intro. Gordon Wakefield, London: SPCK.

30 See, further, on this last point, Avis, Paul, 2020, *Jesus and the Church: The Foundation of the Church in the New Testament and Modern Theology*, London and New York: T&T Clark, especially ch. 9: 'The Paschal Mystery the Foundation of the Church'.

of Pannenberg's exposition. Here I will engage in a dialogue with Pannenberg's theology – or perhaps more of a reflection stimulated by it – with a particular focus on the ongoing momentum, through the worship, witness and proclamation of the church, of God's act of reconciliation, which I find located in the incarnation, ministry, character, Passion, death, resurrection and ascension of Jesus Christ.

Pannenberg's theology achieves a world of discourse that finds its principle of integration in the theme of reconciliation centred on the Christ-event and radiating out from it. In Pannenberg's mature dogmatics the idea of reconciliation serves as the interpretative and explanatory key not only to the work of Christ, but to the whole unfolding of the salvific economy of the triune God. As the Pannenberg expositor Kent Eilers puts it, 'Because Pannenberg's doctrine of reconciliation takes the form of an account of God's reconciling acts, [it] is thereby woven throughout the doctrines of God, creation, Christology, soteriology, ecclesiology, and consummation', with the biblical affirmation of God's covenant faithfulness providing the unifying thread.[31] Faithfulness, by its nature, requires time to reveal itself and to do its work, both of which it performs by the making of promises and the keeping or fulfilling of promises. Faithfulness by definition always has a history. Pannenberg shows how God's faithfulness unfolds through the reconciling acts in history that reveal to faith the holiness, goodness, graciousness, patience and wisdom of the triune God. Since the Christ-event is the most critical, most intense and most definitive of these reconciling acts of God that flow in a continual sequence through human history, it too must be construed as the united action of the undivided Trinity. The one God, Father, Son and Holy Spirit, carry out the ultimate reconciling event in the person and work of Jesus Christ and all that flows from it to bring to completion the salvation of the world.

31 Eilers, Kent, 2011, *Faithful to Save: Pannenberg on God's Reconciling Action*, London: T&T Clark, p. 7.

However, I would not, as Pannenberg does, call the Christ-event the 'anticipation' of reconciliation, to be followed, in his terms, first by the 'actualization' or 'realization' of it through the church and in the individual human heart, and finally by its future 'completion' at the *eschaton*. The language of 'anticipation' sounds as though the Christ-event were merely looking forward and preparatory to something – the main event – that would follow (*Systematic Theology* 2, pp. 412–13). The Christ-event itself – what I have called above the triune God's ultimate reconciling event in the person and work of Jesus Christ – is *proleptically* the actual accomplishment and completion of God's act of reconciliation. It is an eschatological event, stretched between history and eternity, whose momentum continues in time in its outworking, application and reception. So, I can endorse Eilers's formula, summarizing Pannenberg, that the Christ-event achieved reconciliation as a 'completed reality', but not as a 'completed process'.[32] The process nevertheless accomplishes its purpose over time, as the objects of God's reconciliation – namely, God's human creatures – accept, receive and enter into it within the reconciled and reconciling community of the church.

On the one hand, in Pannenberg's theology, there is the loving, gracious, sovereign initiative of the triune God, acting in history – in time and space – continually and consistently, to reconcile, restore and return the estranged creation to Godself. On the other hand, there is the responsibility and freedom of human creatures to respond to God's reconciling acts and to allow themselves to become reconciled to God, their Creator and Redeemer. '[B]y his reconciling action God holds fast to his creation, and does so indeed in a way that respects his creatures' independence.'[33] This balance and integration

32 Eilers, *Faithful to Save*, p. 77. For a comparable approach, see Fiddes, Paul, 1989, *Past Event and Present Salvation: The Christian Idea of Atonement*, London: Darton, Longman and Todd.

33 Pannenberg, *Systematic Theology*, vol. 3, p. 643 (*Systematic Theology* is cited hereinafter in the text as *ST*, by volume and page). See

between the divine and human aspects of reconciliation is possible for Pannenberg because he holds that the process of divine reconciling action gathers up the human response to it within its embrace. And this inclusion of the human element is possible – and is in fact required – in Pannenberg's theology because he construes the human response to, and reception of, divine reconciliation as one of *participation*. As such the human response is not mere consent to a doctrine or truth, whether regarding a forensic kind of justification or any other formulation, but a real entering into and enjoyment of the love, grace and power of God in our hearts and lives within the community.

The unity, integrity and consistency of God's reconciling work is the guiding theme in Pannenberg's theology. The faithfulness of God is God's 'constancy in the actual process of time and history, and especially his holding fast to his saving will [*Festhalten an seinem Heilswillen*], to his covenant, to his promises, and also to the orders of creation' (*ST* 1, p. 437). There can be no playing off of Father against Son in the atonement. The death of Jesus was at once the 'giving up' of him by the Father and his own act of obedience and self-oblation. And equally there can be no separation of Christ and the Spirit in the church and in Christians. Pannenberg writes: 'As the self-offering of the Son for the reconciliation of the world and his being offered up by the Father are one and the same event and form a single process, so we are to see the work of the exalted Christ and that of the Spirit in us as different aspects of one and the same divine action for the reconciliation of the world' (*ST* 2, p. 450). Thus through its participation by grace in the work of reconciliation, the church is drawn into the unity, integrity and consistency (faithfulness) of the saving work of the triune God.

For Pannenberg, a key element in the participation of the creature in the divine process of reconciliation is the apostolic

---

also Eilers, *Faithful to Save*, pp. 2, 63–70 (I follow Eilers's translation here).

kerygma or proclamation of that reconciliation: 'Be reconciled to God!' That means: 'Be reconciled to God through participating faith in Christ's reconciling death on the cross and his resurrection.' So the apostolic message of reconciliation is itself an expression of that reconciliation. Pannenberg's statement that 'the apostolic ministry of reconciliation is itself reconciliation' (*ST* 2, p. 413) is rhetorically powerful and I fully endorse the point he is making, but his language needs nuancing. The apostolic ministry is primarily one of proclamation; however, proclamation is not itself reconciliation, but the offer of reconciliation, the invitation to become reconciled. The proclamation effects reconciliation with God when it is accepted in penitence, faith, confession and participation (which are all comprised in sacramental initiation).

When so accepted, the church's proclamation of reconciliation is held within God's act of reconciliation in Christ and belongs inseparably to it. On those terms, the message or proclamation of the church, in word and sacrament, belong integrally to God's act of reconciliation in Christ. Just as, in the proclamation of Jesus, the reign of God was drawing near and in fact was already present for the salvation of those who received it (Mark 1.14–15), so too the reign of God draws near and is already present in the proclamation, worship and fellowship of the church (Luke 10.9; Acts 20.25; 28.23, 31; Rom. 14.17). The loving, gracious and sovereign continual action of God for the reconciliation of the world, that was definitively proclaimed by the apostles to the known world, is continued and perpetuated in the worship, mission and ministry of the church.

The church is confessed to be 'apostolic' in the Nicene-Constantinopolitan Creed because it continues and carries forward the mission and proclamation of the apostles. Through the mission of the apostles, as it is continued in the church, 'the event of reconciliation that has its origin and centre in the death of Jesus Christ still goes forward', as Pannenberg puts it (*ST* 2, pp. 412–13). For Pannenberg, it is not adequate to defend God's act of reconciliation as only a 'past event', as

Barth tends to do (*ST* 2, p. 437). The work of reconciliation, grounded in the Christ-event, truly includes the whole process of the restoration of our fellowship and communion with God, broken by human sin, which is carried forward, as far as this life is concerned, through the means of grace in the church, principally word and sacrament. In fact, I can push the argument further: what empirical evidence is there, if any, that a divine work of reconciliation – that is, the reconciliation of humankind to God and consequently of humankind among themselves – has actually taken place? The evidence that such a wonderful, unimaginable event has occurred can only be the existence in the world, as an empirical fact, of a patently reconciled community, one that shines as a beacon of reconciliation in the midst of the world's prejudices, hatreds and violence. A visibly reconciled and actively reconciling community is the sole possible and plausible witness to all that God has given and all that Jesus has suffered and all that the Spirit makes present – purely out of absolute and unconditional love for the world.

The living process of reconciliation in salvation history, culminating in – but not confined to – the death and resurrection of Christ, should be understood as the work of the undivided Trinity (*ST* 2, pp. 437–54). So it is essential at this point to name the Holy Spirit of God as the source of the energy and vitality of the ongoing effectiveness and fruitfulness of the once-for-all-time reconciling work of Christ. Just as the Spirit of God is the instrument of creation (Gen. 1.2; Ps. 33.6; Isa. 42.5), so too the Spirit is the instrument – or, better, the personal agent – of reconciliation. Because of the created affinity between the Spirit of God and the human spirit, grounded in the image of God in humankind (Gen. 1.26–27), the Holy Spirit works not *upon* us, as it were from the outside, but *within* us, in a way that is at once supernatural and natural (1 Cor. 2.9–13; Rom. 8.26–27). The simultaneous immanence and transcendence of the human spirit, dwelling within to hold together our personal identity and yet reaching out and beyond the bounded self to the external world of people and things and to the future, mirrors the immanence and transcendence of the Spirit of God in the Spirit's relation and connection to creation.[34]

Jesus tells his disciples in John's Gospel that the Paraclete 'will teach you everything, and remind you of all that I have said to you' and that the Spirit 'will testify on my behalf' and 'will glorify me, because he will take what is mine and declare it to you'; and also that the Spirit 'will take of what is mine and declare them to you' (John 14.26; 15.26; 16.14). Because 'the Spirit will testify', says the Jesus of John's Gospel, 'you also are to testify'; and because the Spirit will 'declare to you', you also are to declare (cf. 1 John 1.2, 3, 5); and because 'the Spirit will teach you', you also are to teach (cf. Acts 2.42).

The Holy Spirit is the constant factor, active presence and operative power in the work of reconciliation. The Spirit was the author of the conception of Jesus in Mary's womb and the same Spirit came upon him at his baptism in the Jordan. The Spirit led him into the wilderness to be tested by temptations and the Spirit empowered his wonderful words and mighty works (Luke 1.35; 3.21–22; 4.1 and parallels; Matt. 12.28). The very same Holy Spirit enabled him to offer himself as a sacrifice to God and raised him from death on the third day (Heb. 9.14; Rom. 1.4). The risen Lord in the New Testament is inseparably connected to the presence and power of the Holy Spirit and – especially in the light of the Easter event – his pre-Easter life, history and ministry can also be seen to have been empowered by the Spirit. Like us, Jesus received the Spirit and the Spirit's gifts – he was a *recipient* of the Spirit – though it is said of him that he received the Spirit 'without measure' (John 3.34; cf. *ST* 3, pp. 5–6).

The Holy Spirit was not withdrawn when Jesus had completed his earthly ministry – far from it; the Spirit was poured out in greater abundance, now having been poured out on 'all flesh' as the Spirit of the victorious Jesus Christ (John 7.39;

34 See also Pannenberg, Wolfhart, 1970, *What Is Man?*, Philadelphia, PA: Fortress Press.

20.22; Acts 1.4–5; 2.1–4, 16–17, 33, 38). The momentum in history of the Christ-event is pneumatological. Both the ministry of the word and the celebration of the sacraments receive their vitality and effectiveness from the infused power of the Holy Spirit. The momentum of the Christ-event – its effect, the difference it makes – continues uninterruptedly in the mission of the church because of Christ's promises, which are now fulfilled through the presence and power of the Holy Spirit: 'I will not leave you orphaned; I am coming to you' and 'I am with you always, to the end of the age' (John 14.18; Matt. 28.20). Thus far my exposition of Pannenberg and gloss on him.

Pannenberg versus Barth

Against this integrated Christological-pneumatological-ecclesiological background, Pannenberg rejects as perverse Karl Barth's deliberate separation between the reconciliation effected by Christ, supremely on the cross, on the one hand, and the apostolic ministry of reconciliation and its continuation in the church, on the other. Barth will not allow any human appropriation of God's sovereign, transcendent work of reconciliation to impinge on the once-for-all, 'self-contained' act of God in the cross of Christ (Pannenberg, *ST* 2, p. 413; cf. Barth, CD IV/1, p. 76.). Barth is surely right to insist that the apostolic preaching of the gospel of reconciliation is not an 'extension' of God's reconciling act in Christ, nor a second instalment of it. But Barth presses his point too far when he seems to say that the apostolic proclamation belongs to a separate order of the divine economy. Pannenberg, by contrast, stresses the openness and dynamism of God's reconciling act in Christ. The divine reconciling work 'opens up' to an ongoing process and 'goes forward' through the preaching of the apostles and the church. Barth's denial of this substantive, concrete continuity between Christ and his apostles, cross and church, seems inconsistent because, after all, it belongs to

Barth's own doctrine of the threefold form of the word of God that the preached word (the third form) *is* the word of God.[35] As the Second Helvetic Confession (1566) affirms, 'When the word of God is now proclaimed in the church by preachers legitimately called [*legitime vocatus*], we believe that the proclaiming of the word of God is the word of God [*ipsum dei verbum annunciari*] and is received [as such] by the faithful [*et a fidelibus recipi*].'[36]

Above all, Barth's exclusion clause seems to overlook the truth that, as John's Gospel makes abundantly clear, it is the Holy Spirit's proper mission to make present and to render effective and fruitful the work of Christ in the world. The Holy Spirit is the enabler of our appropriation of God's reconciling act in Christ and of our participation in it. Though wrought by the Spirit, it is still the work of Christ, running through the life of the church in history. It is first mediated through the apostolic and early post-apostolic community in its canonical and other writings and in its formative practices of worship, sacraments, proclamation and confession of faith, and is then transmitted and perpetuated through the testimony in word and deed that is given by the church over time. It is not, of course, that the reconciling act of God in Christ is transcended in its ongoing application in history, as though it had been superseded by something else. Rather, there is one great, continuous process of the reconciliation of the world, initiated and carried out by the triune God in history, having its focal, definitive and determinate point in Christ, but with its momentum and trajectory continuing into the future, especially in the church's proclamation in word and sacrament of the gospel of reconciliation, beginning with the apostolic community

35 Barth, CDI/1, pp. 88–124; Currie, Thomas Christian, 2016, *The Only Sacrament Left to Us: The Threefold Word of God in the Theology and Ecclesiology of Karl Barth*, Cambridge: James Clarke/Eugene, OR: Pickwick.

36 *Confessio Helvetica Posterior*, AD *1566*, I.4, in Philip Schaff (ed.), 1877, *The Creeds of the Evangelical Protestant Churches*, London: Hodder and Stoughton, p. 237.

and never ceasing until the *eschaton*. To have integrity, our theology of reconciliation – our soteriology – needs to hold together in unity – even if inevitably in tension – the *originating* reconciling act of God in Christ and the *continuing* reconciling act of God in Christ, as one great reconciling process, or – *sub specie aeternitatis* – one great cosmic reconciling action from beginning to end.

I would qualify Pannenberg's schema in two ways and I mention these two points to further elucidate my understanding of the relation or connection of reconciliation to the church. First, I would not say that the Christ-event, including the death and resurrection, comprise the 'originating' act of reconciliation, because to use that term seems more suited to the long preparatory phase of *Heilsgeschichte*, in the chequered history of Israel, the prophetic testimony to the just and loving purposes of God in the world, the sacrificial cultus, the three archetypes of prophet, priest and king (with the conflicts and tensions attendant upon it all in the development of ancient Israel's religion), and the attestation that the Hebrew Scriptures give to all of that. But I would call this 'Old Testament' dimension not the stage of 'origination', but of 'preparation', because reconciliation originates in the heart of God, in the salvific purposes of God for the world. The phase that Pannenberg calls 'originating' I would rename 'defining', because the whole Christ-event is the defining, unsurpassable presentation and expression of God's reconciling action.

So, second, in this way I would be adding a third element to Pannenberg's twofold schema ('originating' and 'continuing' reconciliation): namely, the prophetic preparation – together with the law, the worship cultus and the Wisdom tradition of Israel – for the Christ-event, as they are all embodied in the Hebrew Scriptures, because these also and equally belong to the great unfolding reconciling action of God in our midst. So now we have not two but three phases of God's reconciling action: *preparing, defining and continuing* reconciliation.

With the notion of 'continuing' reconciliation, Pannenberg makes an important contribution to our understanding of the connection of the Christ-event with the church and, more broadly, with the *missio Dei*. Pannenberg is pointing us to the vital role of the impact and the reception of reconciliation in human life, individual and social. As Pannenberg puts it: 'The more decidedly we think of the reconciliation of the world as an act of God himself [sic], the more urgently the question arises as to the role of the human recipients. Reconciliation cannot take place unless it happens to them.' Pannenberg follows this agenda-setting statement with the question: 'Do we not have to regard not merely God's reconciling act [in the cross of Christ] but also its human acceptance as constitutive of the event?' (*ST* 2, p. 415). The need to recognize an ongoing 'outworking' of reconciliation points us to the role of the church in the purposes of God. But a church that has a role in God's work of reconciliation must itself be reconciled.

Reflection on reconciliation in modern theology

The progress made in modern theology in the era between Schleiermacher and Ritschl, on the one hand, and Barth and Pannenberg, on the other, in the doctrine of atonement or reconciliation, brings out its highly paradoxical character. First, while God does not need to be reconciled, only God can reconcile. Second, God has no need to be reconciled, but in absolute love God 'longs' to effect reconciliation. Third, humankind needs to be reconciled to God and is utterly incapable of achieving this in its own strength, but somehow human nature, the human race, humanity as such, needs to be caught up in the reconciling act. Hence the biblical statement that the one mediator between God and humankind, the man Christ Jesus, acts on behalf of God, but from the side of humankind, to effect the reconciliation of humankind to God in a way that includes all who are made one with him through faith and the grace of the sacraments (cf. 1 Tim. 2.5). In gathering his people to himself and offering or presenting them to the Father in a representative or corporate way, Jesus as the Christ does this through his whole life, character, ministry and destiny, culminating in, but not confined to, his cross and resurrection, and 'ever lives' to offer and present his people before the face of God 'in the heavenly places', an intercession that is reflected in the liturgical action of the Eucharist.[37]

The one great divine reconciling process finds its focal, definitive and determinate point in the Christ-event. I deliberately do not say, '... in the death of Christ' or '... in the cross of Christ'. That is indeed the dominant language of Paul and consequently of Barth and Pannenberg, but I believe it to be flawed, or at least unduly restricted. In this connection, Hoskyns and Davey pose 'the problem of the Pauline Epistles' as the question 'why the death of Christ was of such importance to St Paul that he never escapes from it'.[38] In his missionary efforts among the Galatians Paul had 'publicly exhibited [or set forth] Jesus Christ as crucified' (Gal. 3.1). Among the Corinthians he was determined to know nothing except Christ crucified (1 Cor. 2.2). Pannenberg can therefore write: 'The starting point for the apostle's message of reconciliation lies in the atoning death of Christ' (*ST* 2, p. 428). That statement is true of Paul, but I suggest that as atonement theology it is incomplete. Nothing should or can ever take away from the decisive significance of the cross, but I think 'the starting point' (to use Pannenberg's phrase) of the message of reconciliation in fact lies much further back, before the death of Christ in time, in the trajectory of salvation history. We need to remember who it was who hung there, why he made his journey to the cross, how he saw himself fulfilling the destiny of Israel and the calling of Second Isaiah's Servant of the Lord, articulated by the prophets as well as foreshadowed by priests and kings. In other words, we should not appear to separate – even by a passionate insistence on its overwhelming significance – the death of Christ from the broad historical sweep of revelation

37 Avis, Paul, 2020, *Jesus and the Church*, ch. 9: 'The Paschal Mystery the Foundation of the Church'.

38 Hoskyns and Davey, 1981, *Crucifixion-Resurrection*, p. 118.

and salvation. The divine–human destiny of Jesus Christ as a whole embraces the incarnation, his life of consecrated obedience to the will of God, his identification with sinful humanity from his baptism onwards (including, significantly, his table fellowship with 'sinners' and outcasts), his ministry of proclaiming the coming of the reign of God in his person, words and deeds, his Passion from Holy Thursday to Holy Saturday, and his resurrection and ascension. There is all that to factor in, besides the cross itself, though the cross remains the climax and pivotal point. The cross would not have the meaning for Christian faith that it does have without the whole salvation history context, both before and after that event. Through faith and the sacraments – or, rather, the sacraments received in faith – we are united with Christ and identified with him in every stage of the salvation history that he accomplished for us from his birth of Mary, through his baptism and anointing, his obedience and consecration, his Passion, death and burial, to his resurrection, ascension and heavenly intercession (Rom. 6.1–14; Heb. 7.25).

Paul and the Gospels

This whole sequence of Christological salvation history is certainly not entirely absent in the letters of Paul. His starting point, with regard to the gospel of Christ, is the promise that God gave of the gospel 'beforehand', long before the coming of Christ, 'through his prophets in the holy scriptures', a gospel 'concerning God's Son, who was descended from David according to the flesh' (Rom. 1.1–4). In that preamble to the epistle to the Romans we already find mention of the prophets and kings of Israel within the divinely appointed *praeparatio evangelica*. It is also vital for Paul and his message that there was, so to speak, a pre-history of the cross: it was the preexistent Son of God who 'emptied himself, taking the form of a slave, being born in human likeness and being found in human form' (Phil. 2.7).

But at this point there is a remarkable – and I would say disturbing – divergence between the evangelists and St Paul. The four Gospels are full of Jesus' words and actions, his signs, travels and interaction with others, whether reaching out in healing, responding to questions with a question of his own in a Socratic manner, or taking on the Pharisees in theological controversy. The Gospels also occasionally tell of his emotions, that he was angry, troubled or sorrowful. All the varied experiences of Jesus must be included in his reconciling work. As Hoskyns and Davey insist, 'It is impossible to exaggerate the emphasis which, in every fragment of the gospel material, is laid upon the audible and visible fact of what Jesus said and did, that is to say, upon his life.' This picture cannot be simply attributed to the design of the evangelists: 'Unless the records are altogether untrustworthy, for Jesus himself the importance of what he said and did lay in the event.'[39] Thus, for the Gospels, the actual life of Jesus is 'of final importance, and the record of it carries conviction in a manner different from all other known biography'.[40] It is the life of the person of Jesus Christ that is the critical factor in the theology of reconciliation. The narrative of the Gospels tells us of the moral and spiritual character of Christ, which is seen as an integral part of his reconciling or redeeming work.

What is it that is most compelling, that we are seized with, when we read the Gospels or hear them read? I venture to suggest – to start with a few extreme examples – that it is not the virginal conception of Mary, the turning of water into wine at Cana, or even the walking on the surface of the Sea of Galilee, that grips us. It is not the parables considered apart from the one who told them, or the Beatitudes considered apart from

39 Hoskyns and Davey, *Crucifixion-Resurrection*, p. 104.

40 Hoskyns and Davey, *Crucifixion-Resurrection*, p. 105. The designation of the Gospels as 'biography', though used slightly rhetorically by Hoskyns and Davey here, raises questions that I cannot enter into at this point, both for lack of scholarly expertise on the subject and because it would take us away from the main trajectory of the argument.

the one who exemplified them to perfection. Neither is it the crucifixion itself or the resurrection itself, as *phenomena*. But surely what enflames our hearts is the moral and spiritual character and personhood of the one who spoke as no one had ever spoken before (John 7.46), and for that was put to death and who yet rose again. The pre-Passion story, with all that it portrays of the person, nature, words and actions and even emotions of Jesus, should not be skimmed over in a hurry to arrive at the cross as the only – even if unquestionably the most critical – place of reconciliation. It is true that the life of Christ can be understood only in the light of his death, but it is also true that the death of Christ can be understood only in the light of his life. The path that Jesus took on his way to the cross, the moral landscape that he so painfully and selflessly traversed, was indispensable to his reconciling task – as indispensable as the cross itself.

But, astonishingly, the apostle Paul shows almost no interest in any of these biographical, narrative particulars, though he knew at least some elements of the oral tradition (and possibly some pre-canonical writings that in the main have not survived in any recognizable form) which would have preserved memories of the words and deeds of Jesus – and perhaps some fascinating biographical details. I think we are justified in assuming that Paul's stance was deliberately adopted, and all the more so if we are correct in interpreting 2 Corinthians 5.16b in this light, where Paul proclaims rather proudly that he no longer wishes to know Christ 'according to the flesh [*kata sarka*]'. The meaning of Paul's statement is obscure and contested among interpreters, but there can be no question that Paul shows little interest in what we would call the 'historical Jesus'.[41] Theologically, his whole attention is held and his imagination captivated by God's stupendous cosmic act of reconciliation in the cross of Christ. In stark contrast to the method of the Gospels, Paul tends to speak in a rather

41 See the discussion in Thrall, M. E., 1994, *2 Corinthians 1–7*, International Critical Commentary, London and New York, pp. 412–20.

grandiloquent and 'global' way about the person and work of Christ: 'born of a woman, born under the law' (Gal. 4.4), 'the Son of God loved me and gave himself for me' (Gal. 2.20). And his phrase in the liturgical hymn in Philippians 2, 'obedient unto death, even death on a cross' (Phil. 2.8), powerfully encapsulates the earthly destiny of Christ Jesus, but it hardly does justice to the incarnate history of Jesus of Nazareth and does not intend to do so. In terms of the empirical factuality of Jesus, Paul is outstripped among the Epistles even by the Platonizing Epistle to the Hebrews, which dwells on the temptations, struggles and sufferings of the Son of God. This is a deficiency in Paul's perspective on the Christ-event.

It is also a feature of the creeds that they pass straight from the incarnation to the crucifixion. So the Apostles' Creed moves from 'was conceived of the Holy Spirit, born of the Virgin Mary' to 'was crucified under Pontius Pilate, dead and buried', and the Nicene-Constantinopolitan Creed passes immediately from 'and was made man' to 'and was crucified also for us under Pontius Pilate'. Such credal compression could give the impression that Jesus' ministry of gospel-proclamation, teaching and healing, exorcism and denouncing hypocrisy and injustice – as well as his manifest moral and spiritual character – were either not relevant to his saving, reconciling work or are being merely presupposed, 'taken as read'. Some modern eucharistic prayers, such as those of the Church of England's *Common Worship*, partly, though half-heartedly, compensate for this absence in the creeds by mentioning 'all that Jesus did' or recalling that 'he lived on earth and went about among us'. These summary liturgical gestures are even more vague than those embedded in the apostolic kerygma as it is presented in the Acts of the Apostles. The Acts refers to the tradition that Jesus of Nazareth was 'a man attested to you by God with deeds of power, wonders, and signs that God did through him among you' (Acts 2.22) and that he 'went about doing good and healing all who were oppressed by the devil' (10.38). On the whole, though, the preaching described in Acts of the Apostles focuses almost entirely on the crucifixion and resurrection of Jesus and to that extent it is true to the message of Paul himself.

At the other end of the journey that took Jesus to – and through – the cross, it is clear that the resurrection, exaltation and glorification of Christ are vital to Paul's soteriology (Phil. 2.9–11). In this area, he does provide some detail – not of what actually 'happened' in the resurrection or of what the risen Christ was like, but he enumerates those who encountered him, including himself (1 Cor. 15.4–8). It is Luke who provides the circumstantial detail in the Acts of the Apostles (9.1–9; 22.6–11; 26.12–18), while Paul himself tends to be somewhat opaque about what he experienced (Gal. 1.15–16). While Paul certainly affirms that the death of Christ justifies (Rom. 5.9–10), he also says in one place that Christ's resurrection justifies ('was raised for our justification', Rom. 4.25). Paul also recognizes that, after the crucifixion itself, a vindication of Jesus as the Messiah was needed, so he affirms that he 'was declared to be the Son of God with power, according to the Spirit of holiness by the resurrection from the dead' (Rom. 1.4). The true identity of Jesus and his power to save are revealed, not only in his suffering and dying, which is what seems to fill Paul's consciousness, but (and this is a major theme in the non-Pauline Epistle to the Hebrews) in Jesus as the one who has *passed through* suffering, death and resurrection and yet continues the same 'yesterday, today and forever' in his divine–human identity (Heb. 2.17; 4.14–15; 5.7–10; 7.16, 24–25; 13.8).

Edwyn Hoskyns (1884–1937) very emphatically linked the cross and the resurrection 'as closely as two words can be linked', as signified in the title of his posthumously edited and published exposition of New Testament theology, *Crucifixion-Resurrection*, holding it up as 'the theme of the Church'.[42] An alternative formulation, 'Crucifixion *and* Resurrection', would not meet the case, Hoskyns insists, because it might suggest that the resurrection was 'merely an additional occurrence ...

42 Hoskyns and Davey, *Crucifixion-Resurrection*, p. 89. See also Hoskyns, Edwyn, 1938, *Cambridge Sermons*, ed. Charles Smyth, London: SPCK, pp. 91–3.

or series of occurrences', whereas 'the resurrection of Jesus ... is much more than an occurrence. It controls the whole material of the New Testament and could be said to make of it the gospel of God.'[43] 'Crucifixion-Resurrection', he affirms, occupies 'a central and all-embracing position' in the minds of the New Testament writers.[44] It defines reality for them. They are inseparable, not only in theology, but also in reality, because it is at 'the point of absolute negation', in the crucifixion, that resurrection life bursts through.[45]

It is important to remember that Paul's is not the only New Testament perspective on reconciliation. Each of the Gospels, as it articulates its distinctive theology of the Christ-event, has a particular slant on the life, ministry, death and resurrection of Jesus. The community that originated 'Q', the sayings source used by Matthew and Luke alongside Mark and their own unique material, was particularly interested in Christ's teachings, rather than in his miraculous deeds or his death and resurrection, perhaps seeing Jesus as a prophet and 'more than a prophet', perhaps an embodiment of divine wisdom. It is also widely held that the Passion narrative – not only the death of Jesus, though obviously culminating in his death and burial, but as a discrete whole – was at the heart of the early Christian memory and transmission, oral and written, of the Christ-event. Again, the fragmentary, diverse, contradictory and sometimes bizarre character of the resurrection narratives in all four Gospels suggests that, as narratives, they were not the core element in the earliest kerygma (though the vindication of Jesus after death by God was). And the fact that only Matthew and Luke include nativity stories, and that the two accounts cannot be easily harmonized, removes birth narratives from the earliest forms of the kerygma also.

Nevertheless, each of the Gospels is eloquent in its own way on the theme of reconciliation. All four Gospels agree that

43 Hoskyns and Davey, *Crucifixion-Resurrection*, p. 92. I have substituted italics for Hoskyns's capitals in the copula.

44 Hoskyns and Davey, *Crucifixion-Resurrection*, p. 101.

45 Hoskyns and Davey, *Crucifixion-Resurrection*, pp. 96–7.

Jesus' proclamation was a call to Israel, as God's erring and backsliding people, to return in penitence to the Lord in view of the impending arrival of the reign of God, bringing judgement upon the nation and the vindication of God's righteous purposes. They show Jesus seeking to gather God's scattered flock once again, especially the poor, the afflicted and the excluded. They all present Jesus as living a life totally consecrated to God and God's will – 'a living sacrifice', to use Paul's later phrase (Rom. 12.1) – and as moving towards a sacrificial death. What else do the Synoptic Gospels actually present but a gospel of reconciliation?

In St John's Gospel the Word (*Logos*) that was with God and was God in the beginning (*en archē*) and was made flesh (*sarx egeneto*) performs a reconciling work. The Logos has been at work far and wide in the world since the creation, bringing life and light to all of humankind. But the now incarnate Logos is also the Messiah of Israel who calls Israel to himself and to his God and their God; and he is the sacrificial Lamb of God who effects the expiation of their sins (1.1–14, 20, 34, 29, 36; 20.17). In John's Gospel Jesus invites his disciples into a new relationship of friendship with himself and with the Father (15.1–17). He enables them to abide in or indwell himself and to be indwelt by him, just as he indwells the Father and the Father indwells him (15.1–17; 17.20–26). For John, the very flesh of the incarnate Logos proves to be salvific when we are united to it by the Holy Spirit in the Eucharist. The flesh of Jesus is the place where God's salvation ('eternal life') is to be found and it is by feeding on it that the believer 'abides' in him and he in them (6.51–59). A communion between God, Father, Son and Holy Spirit is created through the flesh and blood – that is to say the total sacrifice – of Jesus.

In St John's Gospel Jesus acts, as both Revealer and Reconciler, in complete accord with the Father's nature and will.[46] What Jesus does, the Father is doing (5.17–30). What Jesus

46 Hoskyns and Davey, *Crucifixion-Resurrection*, ch. 5, 'The Humanism of the Fourth Gospel', is suggestive for the theme of this section.

says, the Father is saying (7.26; 12.49–50; 14.24; 17.8, 14, 17). What Jesus is like, the Father is like (12.45; 14.9). The authority that Jesus possesses has been bestowed on him by the Father (17.2) and the judgement that Jesus exercises is exercised on behalf of the Father (5.30; 8.16; 9.39; 12.47–49). The glory of Jesus is the Father's glory (8.54; 13.31–32; 17.1, 5, 22, 24). But the rapport between Jesus and the Father in John's Gospel, though intimate and unclouded, is not symmetrical. The relationship of Jesus to the Father is one of complete dependence, total obedience and indestructible filial love (6.38; 8.29; 17.26; 14.31). The reconciling life, death and resurrection of Jesus in the Fourth Gospel are depicted as the reconciling work of the Father accomplished through the power of the Holy Spirit. The life and work of Jesus are presented as a continual self-abnegation and self-oblation to the Father and they lead up to the absolute self-abnegation and self-oblation of a willing, intentional embrace of death. But, in this Gospel, death is not spoken of without a promise of life beyond death in the same breath. This must necessarily be so, for the Word is the source of life whose words 'are spirit and are life' (6.63); the Son of God brings life to the world and gives life to whom he wills (1.1–9; 5.21, 24; 6.63; 7.38; 11.25–26). The Good Shepherd lays down his life that he may take it again (10.17–18). A grain of wheat falls into the ground and dies in order that it may bear fruit (12.24). The 'lifting up' of Jesus signifies simultaneously both his crucifixion and his exaltation (3.14; 8.27; 12.32–34). He is presented as glorified both on the cross and in eternal fellowship with the Father, but his glory is one and undivided (12.27–28; 17.1, 4–5, 21, 24). What else is 'John' describing throughout his Gospel but a theology of reconciliation, a reconciliation that is located and grounded in the humanity of the incarnate Word, but which points to and reveals the reconciling, redeeming purpose of the Father and its carrying out within earthly time and space in the power of the Holy Spirit?

What do all the Gospels give us but a biblical theology of reconciliation by any other name? The message of reconciliation is evident throughout, even though the technical term *kattalegē* may not be used. It is the thing, rather than the word, that matters. The Scriptures in both Testaments are infused with and pervaded by the theme of reconciliation between God and the estranged children of God, and *therefore* between humans and those from whom they are estranged – in biblical terms, their 'neighbour'. Salvation history (*Heilsgeschichte*) is the historical unfolding of the reconciling purpose of the triune God. The process or programme of reconciling action begins with the call of the patriarchs of Israel: Abraham, Isaac and Jacob. It continues through the witness and oracles of the prophets and the foreshadowing or typology of priests and kings in Israel. The Christ-event itself is framed by the mission of John the Baptist, at one end, and the proclamation of the apostles and the building of the first Christian communities, at the other. I would argue that all that contextualizes the Christ-event and prepares for it, up to and including the mission of John the Baptist, should not be seen as merely preparatory or ancillary to it. Neither should all that follows from it in the mission of the apostles, early missionaries and martyrs, and in the mission of the church through subsequent ages, be regarded as merely consequent and resultant to the reconciling act of God in the Christ-event. Both the 'lead-in' and the 'follow-up' to the central, pivotal and generative Christ-event are integral to the reconciling process that stems from God's salvific will. God's loving purposes and gracious acts for the redemption of the world are devoted to reconciliation from beginning to end, from *Alpha* to *Omega*.

Three spheres of reconciliation

I am gripped by an insight of the poet Percy Bysshe Shelley (1792–1822): '... reconcile thyself with thine own heart / And with thy God, and with the offended world'.[47] This quote from

47 Shelley, Percy Bysshe, 1968 (1943), *The Cenci*, I,1, ll.35–37,

Shelley's tragedy *The Cenci* (1819) argues that reconciliation is required in three all-embracing spheres of reality: that there are three areas of life where reconciliation has its perfect work. As Shelley puts it: '... reconcile thyself with thine own heart / And with thy God, and with the offended world'. Though reconciliation begins within ourselves, reconciliation with God is pivotal, and must then extend to the rest of the world that is offended and wounded by what in us and in our relation to God needs to be put right. These three *foci* of reconciliation (self, God and the world) correspond to the three spheres where recognition can take place – self, God and the world – as we discussed in the previous chapter, on recognition as a stepping stone to reconciliation. So both recognition and reconciliation take place (when they do) in relation to the self, God, and the world.

- *Self*: The first arena of reconciliation is an interior matter: to be reconciled to one's own heart (as Shelley puts it), one's inner life, the deep springs of thought and action and the turbulent conflicts of conscience therein. An unreconciled heart is a source of pain and grief, literally of heartache. This thought puts me in mind of the words of Psalm 42, which in Miles Coverdale's translation in the Anglican *Book of Common Prayer* (1662) reads: 'Why art thou so full of heaviness, O my soul: and why art thou so disquieted within me?' (v. 6). Inner turbulence cries out to be plumbed to the depths, understood and resolved. The Scottish theologian James Denney (1856–1917) wrote, in his work on the theology of reconciliation, that what we humans 'crave to be reconciled to is life, the conditions of existence in their sternness and transiency'.[48]

  The healing of alienation from our deeper selves is the first challenge on the journey of reconciliation. It is the moral

in *Shelley Poetical Works*, ed. Thomas Hutchinson, Oxford: Oxford University Press, p. 280.

48 Denney, James, 1917, *The Christian Doctrine of Reconciliation*, London: Hodder and Stoughton, p. 1.

and spiritual character of Christ, as portrayed in the New Testament; it is its formation within us – through prayer and worship, word and sacrament, by the power of the Holy Spirit – that brings such reconciling healing of the inner person over a lifetime, through whatever human means the Holy Spirit chooses to make use of, which may include the insights of psychotherapy. The Psalm quoted above continues (Ps. 42.15): 'O put thy trust in God: for I will yet thank him, which is the help of my countenance and my God.' And this brings us to the next point.

- *God*: The second arena of reconciliation (which is, of course, intimately related to the first) is for us to be reconciled to God, our Creator and Redeemer, our beginning and our end. Even the Christian believer knows the sense of estrangement from God, the feeling of distance, that has typically been described by guides to the spiritual life as a season of dryness or darkness. St Paul writes: 'All this is from God, who has reconciled us to himself through Christ and has given us the ministry of reconciliation; that is, in Christ God was reconciling the world to himself ... and entrusting the ministry of reconciliation to us. So we are ambassadors for Christ, since God is making his appeal through us; we entreat you on behalf of Christ, be reconciled to God' (2 Cor. 5.18–20). How thought-provoking that Paul writes to converts, to Christian believers, urging them to be reconciled to God! An alternative interpretation to the one put forward here – namely, that Paul is calling upon the Corinthian Christians to be reconciled afresh to God – is that Paul is quoting from the message with which he (and the other apostles) have been entrusted to proclaim to non-Christians. The aorist tense *katallagēte* indicates a once-for-all moment of decision and conversion, rather than a continual process of becoming reconciled.

However, it seems rather implausible to me that Paul could so far forget his Corinthian audience as to revert to missionary mode, as though addressing the unconverted. I suspect that he is simply revealing that the heart of his proclamation at all times and to all persons was the imperative of being reconciled to God.[49] Paul's exhortation is an antidote to all spiritual complacency and pride. It suggests that we all have further to go in the process of allowing God to reconcile us to Godself. We can all, by grace, learn to live more closely to God in heart, mind and life. In the poem that became a favourite hymn, especially for Lent, William Cowper (1731–1800) wrote: 'Oh! for a closer walk with God, A calm and heav'nly frame; A light to shine upon the road that leads me to the Lamb!'[50]

- Shelley's third arena of reconciliation is 'the offended world'. The 'world' is the *oecumene*, the entire human community, the social world, which we are told 'God so loved … that he gave his only Son' (John 3.16). The term 'the world' must embrace all humankind and all the societies, communities and institutions within it, including the church or churches. So the expression 'the world' includes the 'already church' (those who think they are the church) and the 'not yet church' (who may become the church, if the 'already church' does not put them off), the existent church and the potential church. Together, the existent church and the potential church make the 'becoming church'. So the world is not something entirely 'other' than the church.

The dialogue, which I place firmly within the world, between the 'already church' and the 'not yet church', is not merely one-way. The church, which is inevitably part of the world, proclaims the gospel of reconciliation to the rest of the world. The world desperately needs the ministry of reconciliation. As Roger Haight puts it, 'Human existence itself calls out for reconciliation.'[51] But does it find it in the

49 See the discussion in Thrall, 2 *Corinthians 1—7*, pp. 437–8.

50 Cowper, William, 1931, *Cowper's Poems*, ed. Hugh l'Anson Fausset, London: Dent/New York: Dutton, p. 178.

51 Haight, Roger, SJ, 2021, 'The World Mission of the Christian Church', in Mark D. Chapman and Vladimir Latinovic (eds), *Changing the Church: Transformations of Christian Belief, Practice, and Life*, Cham, Switzerland: Palgrave Macmillan, ch. 14, at p. 128.

church? Sometimes the boot is on the other foot. The world sees an unreconciled church and takes offence at it or uses it as an excuse to ignore the claims of the gospel. The world too has something to say to the church. The world, in the sense of the 'not yet church' or 'potential church', has indeed often taken offence at the church in the sense of the 'already church'. And the world has good cause to be offended by the church, especially at the present time when sexual abuse scandals and the culpable failure of some of those responsible for the care of the church to deal with them with integrity and transparency have added to the mountain of sins and crimes committed by the church, sapped the foundations of the institutional church today and undermined its position and standing within the commonwealth of institutions that make up civil society.

The moral authority of the church has been compromised and its leaders, as a caste, stand discredited. As an institution it has undermined itself from within. The church, which purports to be the teacher of truth and the arbiter of morals, has fallen appallingly behind the rest of the world's own best standards of integrity. 'Physician, heal thyself!' (Luke 4.23). The catalogue of the church's failings, sins and crimes is crushing. The progressive dechristianization of the Western world in recent times must be laid, at least in part, at the door of the church itself. We know what must be done to be reconciled to the offended world: repentance, reparation, reform – in other words, transformation.

Last word

My final word and summing up is this. Divine revelation in Scripture teaches us that Christians and their churches cannot be reconciled to God in separation from other Christians and their churches. We cannot simply leave sisters and brothers, with our community and theirs, behind us in some kind of personal reconciling dash back to God, a Neoplatonic 'flight of the alone to the Alone'. Jesus teaches in Matthew 5.23–24: 'When you are offering your gift at the altar, if you remember that your brother or sister has something against you, leave your gift there before the altar and go; first be reconciled to your brother or sister, and then come and offer your gift.' Reconciliation with brother and sister is a prior condition for fellowship with God at the altar – that is to say, at the Eucharist and Holy Communion. The two forms of reconciliation stand or fall together because God's act of reconciliation is inherently unitive; it unites as it reconciles. Thus, Ephesians says with regard to the coming together 'in Christ' of Jewish and Gentile Christians:

> For he is our peace; in his flesh he has made both groups into one and has broken down the dividing wall, that is, the hostility between us ... that he might create in himself one new humanity in place of the two, thus making peace, and might reconcile both groups to God in one body through the cross, thus putting to death that hostility through it ... for through him both of us have access in one Spirit to the Father. (Eph. 2.15–16)

The practical implication of this biblical teaching would seem to be that, once we have actively recognized our fellow Christians and their churches as standing where we stand, we cannot rest until, by the grace of God and the power of the Holy Spirit, we have effected full sacramental reconciliation between us, knowing that our own state of reconciliation is troublingly compromised and called into question by the unreconciled state of the churches to which we belong. So we find ourselves committed to an unended quest, one with its goal in God.

Bibliography

Abbott, Walter M., SJ (ed.), 1966, *The Documents of Vatican II*, London and Dublin: Geoffrey Chapman.

Abraham, Karl, 1965, *Selected Papers*, with a memoir by Ernest Jones, London: Hogarth Press.

Alberigo, Giuseppe (ed.), 1995–2006, *History of Vatican II*, ET ed. Joseph Komonchak, 5 vols, Maryknoll, NY: Orbis/ Leuven: Peeters.

Anglicans and Catholics in Communion: Patrimony, Unity, Mission, in *The Messenger of the Catholic League*, 2010, 292, April–August.

Aristotle, 2009, *Nichomachean Ethics*, trans. David Ross; rev. with intro. and notes Lesley Brown, Oxford: Oxford University Press.

Atherstone, Andrew, and Andrew Goddard (eds), 2015, *Good Disagreement: Grace and Truth in a Divided Church*, Oxford: Lion.

Augustine, 1991, *Confessions*, trans. Henry Chadwick, Oxford: Oxford University Press.

Austin, J. L., 1975 (1962), *How to do Things with Words: The William James Lectures Delivered at Harvard University in 1955*, Oxford: Clarendon Press.

Avis, Paul, 1988, *Gore: Construction and Conflict*, Worthing: Churchman Publishing.

Avis, Paul, 1989, 'The Atonement', in Geoffrey Wainwright (ed.), *Keeping the Faith: Essays to Mark the Centenary of* Lux Mundi, Philadelphia, PA: Fortress Press/Allison Park, PA: Pickwick Publications, ch. 6.

Avis, Paul, 2001, *Church, State and Establishment*, London: SPCK.

Avis, Paul, 2002, *Anglicanism and the Christian Church: Theological Resources in Historical Perspective*, 2nd edn, London and New York: T&T Clark.

Avis, Paul, 2003, *A Church Drawing Near: Spirituality and Mission in a Post-Christian Culture*, London and New York: T&T Clark.

Avis, Paul (ed.), 2003, *Public Faith: The State of Religious Belief and Practice in Britain*, London: SPCK.

Avis, Paul, 2005, *A Ministry Shaped by Mission*, London and New York: T&T Clark.

Avis, Paul, 2006, *Beyond the Reformation? Authority, Primacy and Unity in the Conciliar Tradition*, London and New York: T&T Clark.

Avis, Paul, 2007, *The Identity of Anglicanism: Essentials of Anglican Ecclesiology*, London and New York: T&T Clark.

Avis, Paul, 2010, *Reshaping Ecumenical Theology*, London and New York: T&T Clark.

Avis, Paul (ed.), 2011, *The Journey of Christian Initiation: Theological and Pastoral Perspectives*, London: Church House Publishing.

Avis, Paul, 2012, 'The Book of Common Prayer and Anglicanism: Worship and Belief', in Stephen Platten and Christopher Woods (eds), *Comfortable Words: Polity, Piety and the Book of Common Prayer*, Norwich: Canterbury Press, ch. 9.

Avis, Paul, 2012, 'Are we Receiving Receptive Ecumenism?', *Ecclesiology* 8.2, pp. 223–34.

Avis, Paul, 2013, *The Anglican Understanding of the Church*, 2nd edn, London: SPCK.

Avis, Paul, 2015, 'Anglican Conciliarism: The Lambeth Conference as an Instrument of Communion', in Mark D. Chapman, Sathianathan Clarke and Martyn Percy (eds), 2015, *The Oxford Handbook of Anglican Studies*, Oxford: Oxford University Press, ch. 46.

Avis, Paul, 2020, *Jesus and the Church: The Foundation of the Church in the New Testament and Modern Theology*, London and New York: T&T Clark.

Avis, Paul, 2022, *The Enlightenment – A Theological Assessment*, London and New York: T&T Clark.

Bar-Siman-Tov, Yaacov (ed.), 2004, *From Conflict Resolution to Reconciliation*, Oxford: Oxford University Press.

Barclay, John M. G., 2015, *Paul and the Gift*, Grand Rapids, MI: Eerdmans.

Barrett, D. B., G. T. Kurian and T. M. Johnson, 2001, *World Christian Encyclopedia*, 2nd edn, New York: Oxford University Press.

Barth, Karl, 1968, *Ad Limina Apostolorum: An Appraisal of Vatican II*, Richmond, VA: John Knox Press.

Barth, Karl, 1975–, *Church Dogmatics*, ed. Geoffrey Bromiley and Thomas F. Torrance, trans. Geoffrey Bromiley, Edinburgh/London and New York: T&T Clark.

Barton, Stephen (ed.), 1996, *The Family in Theological Perspective*, Edinburgh: T&T Clark.

Bash, Anthony, 2007, *Forgiveness and Christian Ethics*, Cambridge: Cambridge University Press.

Bergen, Jeremy, 2011, *Ecclesial Repentance: The Churches Confront their Sinful Pasts*, London and New York: T&T Clark.

Berger, Peter L., 1980, *The Heretical Imperative*, London: Collins.

Boersma, Hans, 2009, *Nouvelle Théologie and Sacramental Ontology: A Return to Mystery*, New York: Oxford University Press.

Bowlby, John, 1953, *Child Care and the Growth of Love*, London: Pelican.

Brigham, Erin M., 2012, *Sustaining the Hope for Unity: Ecumenical Dialogue in a Postmodern World*, Collegeville, MN: Liturgical Press.

Bultmann, Rudolf, 1952, *Theology of the New Testament*, trans. Kendrick Grobel, 2 vols, London: SCM Press.

Bunyan, John, 1935 (1678, 1684), *The Pilgrim's Progress from this World to that which is to come, Delivered under the Similitude of a Dream*, London: Oxford University Press.

Burke, Edmund, 1834, *On the Sublime and the Beautiful*, *The Works of the Right Hon. Edmund Burke with a Biographical and Critical Introduction and Portrait after Sir Joshua Reynolds*, London: Holdsworth and Ball, vol. 1.

Burridge, Richard A., and Jonathan Sacks (eds), 2018, *Confronting Religious Violence: A Counternarrative*, London: SCM Press; Waco, TX: Baylor University Press.

Caird, Edward, 1904, *The Evolution of Theology in the Greek Philosophers*, vol. 1, Glasgow: Maclehose.

Caird, G. B., 1994, *New Testament Theology*, completed and ed. L. D. Hurst, Oxford: Clarendon Press.

Calvin, John, 1960, *The First Epistle of Paul to the Corinthians*, trans. John W. Fraser, *Calvin's Commentaries*, ed. David W. Torrance and Thomas F. Torrance, Edinburgh: The Saint Andrew Press.

Calvin, John, 1961, *The Epistles of Paul the Apostle to the Romans and Thessalonians*, trans. Ross MacKenzie, Calvin's Commentaries, ed. David W. Torrance and Thomas F. Torrance, Edinburgh: The Saint Andrew Press.

Calvin, John, 1962, *Institutes of the Christian Religion*, trans. H. Beveridge, 2 vols, London: James Clarke.

Calvin, John, 1971, *The Gospel According to St John, 11–21, and The First Epistle of John*, Calvin's Commentaries, ed. David W. Torrance and Thomas F. Torrance, Edinburgh: The Saint Andrew Press.

Calvin, John, 1972, *A Harmony of the Gospels Matthew, Mark and Luke, Volume III, and the Epistles of James and Jude*, Calvin's Commentaries, ed. David W. Torrance and Thomas F. Torrance, Edinburgh: The Saint Andrew Press.

Campbell, C. A., 1957, *On Selfhood and Godhood: Gifford Lectures*, London: George Allen and Unwin; New York: Macmillan.

Cargill Thompson, W. D. J., 1972, 'The Philosopher of the "Politic Society": Richard Hooker as a Political Thinker', in W. Speed Hill (ed.), *Studies on Richard Hooker: Essays Preliminary to an Edition of his Works*, Cleveland and London: Case Western Reserve University Press.

Cavanaugh, William, 2009, *The Myth of Religious Violence*, Oxford: Oxford University Press.

Chadwick, Owen, 1975, *The Secularization of the European Mind in the Nineteenth Century*, Cambridge: Cambridge University Press.

Chapman, Mark D., Sathianathan Clarke and Martyn Percy (eds), 2015, *The Oxford Handbook of Anglican Studies*, Oxford: Oxford University Press.

Chapman, Mark D., and Vladimir Latinovic (eds), 2021, *Changing the Church: Transformations of Christian Belief, Practice, and Life*, Cham, Switzerland: Palgrave Macmillan.

Chesterton, G. K., 1958, *Essays and Poems*, ed. Wilfred Sheed, Harmondsworth: Penguin.

Clements, Keith, 2013, *Ecumenical Dynamic: Living in More Than One Place at Once*, Geneva: World Council of Churches.

Coleman, Roger (ed.), 1992, *Resolutions of the Twelve Lambeth Conferences 1967–1988*, Toronto: Anglican Book Centre.

Collins, Paul M., and Barry Ensign-George (eds), 2011, *Denomination: Assessing an Ecclesiological Category*, London and New York: T&T Clark.

Confalonieri, Luca Badini, 2012, *Democracy in the Christian Church: An Historical, Theological and Political Case*, London and New York: T&T Clark.

Conversations Around the World 2000–2005: The Report of the International Conversations between The Anglican Communion and The Baptist World Alliance, 2005, London: Anglican Communion Office.

Cowper, William, 1931, *Cowper's Poems*, ed. Hugh l'Anson Fausset, London: Dent; New York: Dutton.

Cox, Noel, 2010, 'Legal Aspects of Church-State Relations in New Zealand', *Journal of Anglican Studies* 8.1, pp. 9–33.

Crewdson, Joan, 1994, *Christian Doctrine in the Light of Michael Polanyi's Theory of Personal Knowledge: A Personalist Theology*, Toronto Studies in Theology, vol. 66, Lewiston/Queenston/Lampeter: The Edwin Mellen Press.

Currie, Thomas Christian, 2016, *The Only Sacrament Left to Us: The Threefold Word of God in the Theology and Ecclesiology of Karl Barth*, Cambridge: James Clarke/Eugene, OR: Pickwick.

Davies, W. D., and D. C. Allison, 1991, *The Gospel According to St Matthew*, 3 vols, International Critical Commentary, London and New York: Continuum/T&T Clark.

Davis, Charles, 1980, *Theology and Political Society: The Hulsean Lec-*

tures in the University of Cambridge 1978, Cambridge: Cambridge University Press.

De Lubac, Henri, 1950, *Catholicism: A Study of Dogma in Relation to the Corporate Destiny of Mankind*, trans. L. C. Sheppard, London: Burns, Oates and Washbourne.

De Lubac, Henri, 1954, *Méditation sur l'Église*, 3rd edn, Paris: Aubier.

Denney, James, 1911 (1902), *The Death of Christ* (including *The Atonement and the Modern Mind*), 2nd edn, London: Hodder and Stoughton.

Denney, James, 1917, *The Christian Doctrine of Reconciliation*, London: Hodder and Stoughton.

Doe, Norman, 1998, *Canon Law in the Anglican Communion*, Oxford: Clarendon Press.

Doe, Norman, 2013, *Christian Law: Contemporary Principles*, Cambridge: Cambridge University Press.

Doe, Norman, 2015, 'The Ecumenical Value of Comparative Church Law: Towards the Category of Christian Law', *Ecclesiastical Law Journal* 17.2, pp. 135–69.

Dunn, James D. G., 1988, *Romans 1–8*, Word Biblical Commentary 38A, Waco, TX: Word.

Dunn, James D. G., 2003 (1998), *The Theology of Paul the Apostle*, London: T&T Clark/Grand Rapids, MI: Eerdmans.

Dunn, James D. G., 2003, *Jesus Remembered, Christianity in the Making, Volume 1*, Grand Rapids, MI: Eerdmans.

Eilers, Kent, 2011, *Faithful to Save: Pannenberg on God's Reconciling Action*, London: T&T Clark.

Elert, Werner, 1962, *The Structure of Lutheranism*, St Louis, MO: Concordia Publishing House.

Eliot, T. S., 1974 (1963), *Collected Poems 1909–1962*, London: Faber and Faber.

Erikson, Erik H., 1968, *Identity: Youth and Crisis*, London: Faber and Faber.

Erikson, Erik H., 1977, *Childhood and Society*, London: Paladin.

Evans, Donald D., 1963, *The Logic of Self-Involvement*, The Library for Philosophy and Theology, London: SCM Press.

Faggioli, Massimo, 2012, *Vatican II: The Battle for Meaning*, Mahwah, NJ: Paulist Press.

Faggioli, Massimo, 2014, *John XXIII: The Medicine of Mercy*, Collegeville, MN: Liturgical Press.

Faggioli, Massimo, 2015, *A Council for the Global Church: Receiving Vatican II in History*, Minneapolis, MN: Fortress Press.

Faggioli, Massimo, and Andrea Vicini, SJ (eds), 2015, *The Legacy of Vatican II*, Mahwah, NJ: Paulist Press.

Fairbairn, W. R. D., 1952, *Psychoanalytical Studies of the Personality*, London: Tavistock Clinic and Routledge and Kegan Paul.

Fiddes, Paul, 1989, *Past Event and Present Salvation: The Christian Idea of Atonement*, London: Darton, Longman and Todd.

Fitzmyer, Joseph A., 1992, *Romans: A New Translation with Introduction and Commentary*, Anchor Bible 33, New York: Doubleday/London: Geoffrey Chapman.

Flanagan, Brian P., 2018, *Stumbling in Holiness: Sin and Sanctity in the Church*, Collegeville, MN: Liturgical Press Academic.

Flannery, Austin, OP (ed.), 1975, *Vatican Council II: Vol. 1: The Conciliar and Post-Conciliar Documents*, Northport NY: Costello/Dublin: Dominican Publications.

Flynn, Gabriel, and Paul Murray (eds), 2011, *Ressourcement: A Movement for Renewal in Twentieth-Century Catholic Theology*, Oxford: Oxford University Press.

Forsyth, Peter Taylor, 1938 (1910), *The Work of Christ*, London: Independent Press.

Fresh Expressions in the Mission of the Church: Report of an Anglican-Methodist Working Party, 2013, London: Church House Publishing.

Freud, Anna, 1966, *The Ego and the Mechanisms of Defence*, London: Hogarth Press.

Freud, Sigmund, 1977, *Three Essays on Sexuality* (1905), ed. Angela Richards, trans. James Strachey, The Pelican Freud Library, Harmondsworth: Penguin.

Gaillardetz, Richard R., 2015, *An Unfinished Council: Vatican II, Pope Francis, and the Renewal of Catholicism*, Collegeville, MN: Liturgical Press.

Gaillardetz, Richard R. (ed.), 2020, *The Cambridge Companion to Vatican II*, Cambridge: Cambridge University Press.

Gaillardetz, Richard R. and Catherine E. Clifford (eds), 2012, *Keys to the Council: Unlocking the Teaching of Vatican II*, Collegeville, MN: Liturgical Press.

Gardner, Helen (ed.), 1966, *The Metaphysical Poets*, rev. edn, Harmondsworth: Penguin.

Granfield, Patrick, 1979, 'The Church as Societas Perfecta in the Schemata of Vatican I', *Church History* 48.4, pp. 431–46.

Guarino, Thomas G., 2018, *The Disputed Teachings of Vatican II: Continuity and Reversal in Catholic Doctrine*, Grand Rapids, MI: Eerdmans.

Guntrip, Harry, 1977, *Personality Structure and Human Interaction*, London: Hogarth Press.

Haight, Roger, SJ, 2021, 'The World Mission of the Christian Church', in Mark D. Chapman and Vladimir Latinovic (eds), *Changing the*

Church: Transformations of Christian Belief, Practice, and Life, Cham, Switzerland: Palgrave Macmillan, ch. 14.

Hardy, Daniel W., 1989, 'Created and Redeemed Sociality', in Colin E. Gunton and Daniel W. Hardy (eds), *On Being the Church: Essays on the Christian Community*, Edinburgh: T&T Clark, pp. 21–47.

Hardy, Daniel W., 1996, *God's Ways with the World: Thinking and Practising Christian Faith*, Edinburgh: T&T Clark.

Hardy, Daniel W., 2001, *Finding the Church*, London: SCM Press.

Hare, R. M., 1952, *The Language of Morals*, Oxford: Clarendon Press.

Hastings, Adrian (ed.), 1991, *Modern Catholicism: Vatican II and After*, London: SPCK; New York: Oxford University Press.

Hauerwas, Stanley, 2011, *Learning to Speak Christian*, Eugene, OR: Cascade Books.

Hays, Richard B., 1996, *The Moral Vision of the New Testament*, New York: HarperCollins.

Healy, Nicholas M., 2000, *Church, World and the Christian Life: Practical-Prophetic Ecclesiology*, Cambridge: Cambridge University Press.

Hebert, A. G., 1946, *The Form of the Church*, London: Faber and Faber.

Heft, James L., with John W. O'Malley (eds), 2012, *After Vatican II: Trajectories and Hermeneutics*, Grand Rapids, MI: Eerdmans.

Hegel, Georg Wilhelm Friedrich, 2018, *The Phenomenology of Spirit*, trans. and ed. Terry Pinkard, Cambridge: Cambridge University Press.

Heidegger, Martin, 2002 (1969), *Identity and Difference*, trans. and intro. Joan Stambaugh, Chicago and London: Chicago University Press.

Henson, Herbert Hensley, 1943, *Retrospect of an Unimportant Life* [3 vols], *Volume 2, 1920–1939*, London: Oxford University Press.

Hillerbrand, H. J. (ed.), 2004, *The Encyclopedia of Protestantism*, 4 vols, New York and London: Routledge.

Honneth, Axel, 2012 (2010), *The I in We: Studies in the Theory of Recognition*, Cambridge: Polity Press.

Hooker, Richard, 1977–, *The Folger Library Edition of the Works of Richard Hooker*, ed. W Speed Hill, Cambridge, MA: Belknap Press of Harvard University Press, vols 1 and 4.

Hoskyns, Edwyn Clement, 1938, *Cambridge Sermons*, ed. Charles Smyth, London: SPCK.

Hoskyns, Edwyn Clement, and Francis Noel Davey, 1981, *Crucifixion-Resurrection: The Pattern of the Theology and Ethics of the New Testament*, ed. and intro. Gordon Wakefield, London: SPCK.

House of Bishops of the Church of England, 1997, *May They All Be One*, London: Church House Publishing.

Housley, Norman, 2002, *Religious Warfare in Europe, 1400–1536*, Oxford: Oxford University Press.

Hudock, Barry, 2015, *Struggle, Condemnation, Vindication: John Courtney Murray's Journey toward Vatican II*, Collegeville, MN: Liturgical Press.

Hudson, Winthrop S., 1955, 'Denominationalism as a Basis for Ecumenicity: A Seventeenth-Century Conception', *Church History* 24.1, pp. 32–50.

Ingle-Gillis, W. C., 2007, *The Trinity and Ecumenical Church Thought*, Aldershot and Burlington, VT: Ashgate.

Inter-Anglican Standing Commission on Unity, Faith and Order, 2021, *God So Loved the World: Papers on Theological Anthropology and Salvation*, London: Anglican Consultative Council.

James, William, 1890, *The Principles of Psychology*, 2 vols, London: Macmillan, vol. 1.

Jeremias, Joachim, 1971, *New Testament Theology* [2 vols; vol. 1], *Part One: The Proclamation of Jesus*, trans. John Bowden, London: SCM Press.

John Paul II, 1995, *Ut Unum Sint*, Vatican City.

Joint International Commission for Theological Dialogue between the Roman Catholic Church and the Orthodox Church, *The Mystery of the Church and of the Eucharist in the Light of the Mystery of the Holy Trinity* (Munich, 1982), II, 1: www.ecupatria.org/documents/the-mystery-of-the-church-and-of-the-eucharist-in-the-light-of-the-mystery-of-the-holy-trinity/.

Jones, David, 1959 (1955), 'Art and Sacrament', in David Jones, *Epoch and Artist*, London: Faber and Faber.

Jones, Ernest, 1918, *Papers on Psychoanalysis*, London: Bailliere Tindall & Cox.

Jordan, W. K., 1932, *The Development of Religious Toleration in England*, 2 vols, London: Allen and Unwin.

Juergensmeyer, Mark, Margo Kitts and Michael Jerryson (eds), 2015, *The Oxford Handbook of Religion and Violence*, Oxford: Oxford University Press.

Jüngel, Eberhard, 2006, *Justification: The Heart of the Christian Faith*, intro. John Webster, trans. Jeffrey F. Cayzer, London and New York: T&T Clark.

Käsemann, Ernst, 1971 (1964), 'Some Thoughts on the Theme "The Doctrine of Reconciliation in the New Testament"', in *The Future of Our Religious Past: Essays in Honour of Rudolf Bultmann*, James M.

Robinson (ed.), trans. Charles E. Carlson and Robert P. Scharleman, London: SCM Press, ch. 3.

Käsemann, Ernst, 1980, *Commentary on Romans*, trans. and ed. Geoffrey W. Bromiley, Grand Rapids, MI: Eerdmans.

Kasper, Walter, 1989, *Theology and Church*, trans. Margaret Kohl, London: SCM Press.

Kasper, Walter, 2004, *That They May All Be One: The Call to Unity Today*, London and New York: Continuum.

Kasper, Walter, 2009, *Harvesting the Fruits: Basic Aspects of Christian Faith in Ecumenical Dialogue*, London and New York: Continuum.

Kasper, Walter, 2015, *The Catholic Church: Nature, Reality and Mission*, ed. R. David Nelson, trans. Thomas Hoebel, London and New York: Bloomsbury.

Kates, Frederick W., 1948, *Charles Henry Brent: Ambassador of Christ*, London: SCM Press.

Kaye, Bruce, 2018, *The Rise and Fall of the English Christendom: Theocracy, Christology, Order and Power*, London and New York: Routledge.

King, Benjamin J., 2014, '"The Consent of the Faithful" from Clement to the Anglican Covenant', *Journal of Anglican Studies* 12.1, pp. 7–36.

Kinnamon, Michael, 2012, 'What Can the Churches Say Together about the Church?', *Ecclesiology* 8.3, pp. 289–301.

Kinnamon, Michael, and Brian E. Cope (eds), 1997, *The Ecumenical Movement: An Anthology of Key Texts and Voices*, Geneva: World Council of Churches/Grand Rapids, MI: Eerdmans.

Koffeman, Leo J., 2014, *In Order to Serve: An Ecumenical Introduction to Church Polity*, Zurich and Berlin: LIT.

Koffeman, Leo, 2015, 'The Ecumenical Potential of Church Polity', *Ecclesiastical Law Journal* 17.2, pp. 182–93.

La Taille, Maurice de, SJ, 1941, *The Mystery of Faith: Regarding the Most August Sacrament and Sacrifice of the Body and Blood of Christ, Book I: The Sacrifice of Our Lord*, London: Sheed and Ward.

Lakeland, Paul, 2015, *A Council That Will Never End:* Lumen Gentium *and the Church Today*, Collegeville, MN: Liturgical Press.

Lamb, Christopher L., and Matthew Levering (eds), 2008, *Vatican II: Renewal Within Tradition*, Oxford: Oxford University Press.

Lamb, Matthew L., and Matthew Levering (eds), 2017, *The Reception of Vatican II*, New York: Oxford University Press.

Landau, Christopher, 2021, *A Theology of Disagreement: New Testament Ethics for Ecclesial Conflicts*, London: SCM Press.

Lanzetta, Serafino M., 2016, *Vatican II: A Pastoral Council*, Leominster: Gracewing.

Lecler, Joseph, 1960, *Toleration and the Reformation*, 2 vols, London: Longmans.

Levi, Primo, 1987 (1979), *If This is a Man* [and] *The Truce*, trans. Stuart Woolf, intro. Paul Bailey, London: Abacus.

Levinas, Emmanuel, 1991 (1974), *Otherwise than Being, or, Beyond Essence*, trans. Alphonso Lingis, London: Kluwer.

Leys, Adrianus C. N. P., 1995, *Ecclesiological Impacts of the Principle of Subsidiarity*, Kampen: Kok; KTC no. 28, pp. 120–34.

Lim, Timothy T. M., 2017, *Ecclesial Recognition with Hegelian Philosophy, Social Psychology and Continental Political Theory: An Interdisciplinary Proposal*, Leiden: Brill.

Lincoln, Andrew T., 2005, *The Gospel According to St John*, Black's New Testament Commentaries, London and New York: Continuum.

Loane, Edward, 2016, *William Temple and Church Unity: The Politics and Practice of Ecumenical Theology*, Cham, Switzerland: Palgrave Macmillan.

Lonergan, Bernard J. F., SJ, 1973 (1971), *Method in Theology*, London: Darton, Longman and Todd.

Lonergan, Bernard J. F., SJ, 1983 (1957), *Insight: A Study of Human Understanding*, London: Darton, Longman and Todd.

Long, Edward LeRoy, JR, 2001, *Patterns of Polity: Varieties of Church Governance*, Cleveland, OH: Pilgrim Press.

Longman, Timothy Paul, 2010, *Christianity and Genocide in Rwanda*, Cambridge: Cambridge University Press.

Lossky, Nicholas, et al. (eds), 1991, *Dictionary of the Ecumenical Movement*, Geneva: World Council of Churches/London: Churches Together in Britain and Ireland/Grand Rapids, MI: Eerdmans.

Luckmann, Thomas, 1983, *Life-World and Social Realities*, London: Heinemann Educational.

Luhmann, Niklaus, 1982, *The Differentiation of Society*, New York: Columbia University Press.

Luther, Martin, 1883–, *D. Martin Luthers Werke*, Weimar: Weimarer Ausgabe.

Luther, Martin, 1955–, *Luther's Works*, ed. Jaroslav Pelikan and Helmut Lehman, St Louis, MO: Concordia/ Philadelphia, PA: Fortress Press.

Mann, Thomas, 2005, *Joseph and His Brothers*, trans. John E. Woods, 4 vols in one, New York: Alfred A. Knopf (Everyman's Library).

Mannion, Gerard, 2013, 'A (Strange) Sort of Homecoming?', in Martyn Percy and Robert Boak Slocum (eds), 2013, *A Point of Balance: The Weight and Measure of Anglicanism*, New York: Morehouse/Norwich: Canterbury Press, ch. 10.

Mannion, Gerard (ed.), 2016, *Where We Dwell in Common: The Quest for Dialogue in the Twenty-first Century*, Basingstoke: Palgrave Macmillan.

Manson, T. W., 1963, *On Paul and John: Some Selected Theological Themes*, ed. Matthew Black, London: SCM Press.

Markham, Ian S. et al. (eds), 2013, *The Wiley-Blackwell Companion to the Anglican Communion*, Malden, MA and Oxford: Wiley-Blackwell.

Marshall, I. Howard, 1978, *The Gospel of Luke*, New International Greek Text Commentary, Carlisle: Paternoster Press; Grand Rapids, MI: Eerdmans.

Martin, R. P., 1981, *Reconciliation: A Study of Paul's Theology*, London: Marshall, Morgan and Scott/Atlanta, GA: John Knox Press.

Mauss, Marcel, 1990 (1925), *The Gift: The Form and Reason for Exchange in Archaic Societies*, London: Routledge.

McPartlan, Paul, 1993, *The Eucharist Makes the Church: Henri de Lubac and John Zizioulas in Dialogue*, Edinburgh: T&T Clark; new edn, Fairfax, VA: Eastern Christian Publications, 2006.

Merkle, Judith A., 2016, *Beyond Our Lights and Shadows: Charism and Institution in the Church*, London and New York: Bloomsbury/T&T Clark.

Methuen, Charlotte, 2020, 'Mission, Reunion and the Anglican Communion: The "Appeal to All Christian People" and Approaches to Ecclesial Unity at the 1920 Lambeth Conference', *Ecclesiology* 16.2, pp. 175–205.

Milbank, John, 2003, *Being Reconciled: Ontology and Pardon*, London and New York: Routledge.

Miller, Virginia, 2021, *Child Sexual Abuse Inquiries and the Catholic Church: Reassessing the Evidence*, Florence: Firenze University Press.

Milton, John, 1913, *The English Poems of John Milton*, London: Oxford University Press.

Montesquieu, 1973, *Persian Letters*, trans. C. J. Berrs, Harmondsworth: Penguin.

Morgan, Michael L., 2007, *Discovering Levinas*, Cambridge: Cambridge University Press.

Morgan, Teresa, 2015, *Roman Faith and Christian Faith:* Pistis *and* Fides *in the Early Roman Empire and Early Churches*, Oxford: Oxford University Press.

Moule, C. F. D., 1998, *Forgiveness and Reconciliation: Biblical and Theological Essays*, London: SPCK.

Mullin, Robert Bruce, and Russell E. Richey (eds), 1994, *Reimagining Denominationalism: Interpretive Essays*, New York: Oxford University Press.

Murray, Paul D. (ed.), 2008, *Receptive Ecumenism and the Call to Catholic Learning*, Oxford: Oxford University Press.

Neuner, J., SJ, and J. Dupuis, SJ (eds), 1983, *The Christian Faith in the Doctrinal Documents of the Catholic Church*, rev. edn, London: Collins.

Newman, J. H., 1908 (1865), *The Dream of Gerontius*, London: Bagster.

Newman, J. H., 1948 (1841), 'The Tamworth Reading Room', in J. H. Newman, *Essays and Sketches*, ed. C. F. Harrold, 2 vols, New York: Longmans, vol. 1.

Newman, J. H., 1974, *An Essay on the Development of Christian Doctrine: The Edition of 1845*, ed. and intro. J. M. Cameron, Harmondsworth: Penguin.

Niebuhr, H. Richard, 1954 (1929), *The Social Sources of Denominationalism*, Hamden, CT: The Shoestring Press.

Niles, D. T., 1966, *The Message and Its Messengers*, Nashville, TN: Abingdon Press.

Norwood, Donald, 2015, *Reforming Rome: Karl Barth and Vatican II*, Grand Rapids, MI: Eerdmans.

O'Collins, Gerald, SJ, 2014, 'Towards a truly global Church', *The Tablet*, 15 March, pp. 6–7.

O'Malley, John W., 2008, *What Happened at Vatican II*, Cambridge, MA: The Belknap Press of Harvard University Press.

O'Malley, John W. et al., 2007, *Vatican II: Did Anything Happen?*, ed. David G. Schultover, New York and London: Bloomsbury.

Oakley, Francis, 2003, *The Conciliarist Tradition: Constitutionalism in the Catholic Church 1300–1870*, Oxford: Oxford University Press.

Ormerod, Neil, 2014, *Re-Visioning the Church: An Experiment in Systematic-Historical Theology*, Minneapolis, MN: Fortress Press.

Örsy, Ladislas, 1992, *Theology and Canon Law: New Horizons for Legislation and Interpretation*, Collegeville, MN: Liturgical Press.

Pannenberg, Wolfhart, 1970, *What is Man?*, Philadelphia, PA: Fortress Press.

Pannenberg, Wolfhart, 1989, *Christianity in a Secularized World*, New York: Crossroad.

Pannenberg, Wolfhart, 1997, *Systematic Theology, Volume 3*, trans. Geoffrey W. Bromiley, Edinburgh: T&T Clark.

Pascal, Blaise, 1966, *Pensées*, trans. A. J. Krailsheimer, Harmondsworth: Penguin.

Pawley, Bernard C. (ed.), 1967, *The Second Vatican Council: Studies by Eight Anglican Observers*, London: Oxford University Press.

Pelikan, Jaroslav, 1964, *Obedient Rebels: Catholic Substance and Protestant Principle in Luther's Reformation*, London: SCM Press.

Pelikan, Jaroslav, 1968, *Spirit Versus Structure: Luther and the Institutions of the Church*, London: Collins.

Percy, Martyn, 2017, *The Future Shapes of Anglicanism: Currents, Contours, Charts*, London and New York: Routledge.

Pickard, Stephen, 2012, *Seeking the Church: An Introduction to Ecclesiology*, London: SCM Press.

Pizzey, Antonia, 2019, *Receptive Ecumenism and the Renewal of the Ecumenical Movement: The Path of Ecclesial Conversion*, Leiden: Brill.

Polanyi, Michael, 1958, *Personal Knowledge*, London: Routledge and Kegan Paul.

Polanyi, Michael, 1967, *The Tacit Dimension*, London: Routledge and Kegan Paul.

Powell, Anthony, 1975, *Hearing Secret Harmonies*, London: Heinemann (vol. 12 of *A Dance to the Music of Time*).

Pushing at the Boundaries of Unity: Anglicans and Baptists in Conversation, 2005, London: Church House Publishing.

Radner, Ephraim, 1998, *The End of the Church: A Pneumatology of Christian Division in the West*, Grand Rapids, MI: Eerdmans.

Radner, Ephraim, 2012, *A Brutal Unity: The Spiritual Politics of the Christian Church*, Waco, TX: Baylor University Press.

Rahner, Karl, SJ, 1969, *Theological Investigations*, vol. 6, Baltimore, MD: Helicon Press/London: Darton, Longman and Todd.

Rahner, Karl, SJ, 1981, *Theological Investigations XX: Concern for the Church*, trans. Edward Quinn, London: Darton, Longman and Todd.

Ramsey, Arthur Michael, 1936, *The Gospel and the Catholic Church*, London: Longmans, Green & Co.

Raven, Charles (ed.), 2014, *The Truth Shall Set You Free: Global Anglicans in the 21st Century*, London: The Latimer Trust.

Reuver, Marc, 2000, *Faith and Law: Juridical Perspectives for the Ecumenical Movement*, Geneva: World Council of Churches.

Richardson, Alan, 1958, *An Introduction to the Theology of the New Testament*, London: SCM Press.

Richey, Russell E. (ed.), 2010 (1977), *Denominationalism*, Eugene, OR: Wipf & Stock.

Richey, Russell E., 2013, *Denominationalism Illustrated and Explained*, Eugene, OR: Cascade Books.

Ricoeur, Paul, 1992, *Oneself as Another*, trans. Kathleen Blamey, Chicago and London: University of Chicago Press.

Ricoeur, Paul, 2005 (2004), *The Course of Recognition*, trans. David Pellauer, Cambridge, MA: Harvard University Press.

Ridderbos, Herman, 1977 (1975), *Paul: An Outline of His Theology*, trans. John Richard de Witt, Grand Rapids, MI/London: SPCK.

Ridderbos, Herman, 1978, *Studies in Scripture and Its Authority*, Grand Rapids, MI: Eerdmans.

Ritschl, Albrecht, 1900, *The Christian Doctrine of Justification and Reconciliation*, trans. H. R. Mackintosh and A. B. Macaulay, Edinburgh: T&T Clark.

Root, Michael, and James Buckley (eds), 2012, *The Morally Divided Body: Ethical Disagreement and the Disunity of the Body*, Eugene, OR: Cascade Books.

Roozen, David A., and James R. Nieman (eds), 2005, *Church, Identity and Change: Theology and Denominational Structures in Unsettled Times*, Grand Rapids, MI: Eerdmans.

Ross, Alexander, 2020, *A Still More Excellent Way: Authority and Polity in the Anglican Communion*, London: SCM Press.

Rush, Ormond, 2004, *Still Interpreting Vatican II: Some Hermeneutical Principles*, New York/Mahwah, NJ: Paulist Press.

Rush, Ormond, 2019, *The Vision of Vatican II: Its Fundamental Principles*, Collegeville, MN: Liturgical Press.

Ryan, Gregory, 2020, *Hermeneutics of Doctrine in a Learning Church: The Dynamics of Receptive Integrity*, Leiden: Brill.

Ryan, Gregory, 2021, 'The Reception of Receptive Ecumenism', *Ecclesiology* 17, pp. 7–28.

Saarinen, Risto, 2016, *Recognition and Religion: A Historical and Systematic Study*, Oxford: Oxford University Press.

Saarinen, Risto, 2021, art. 'Reconciliation', in *St Andrews Encyclopedia of Theology*, www.saet.ac.uk/.

Santer, Mark, 2007, 'Communion, Unity and Primacy: An Anglican Response to *Ut Unum Sint*', *Ecclesiology* 3.3, pp. 283–95.

Schaff, Philip (ed.), 1877, *The Creeds of the Evangelical Protestant Churches*, London: Hodder and Stoughton.

Schimmel, Solomon, 2002, *Wounds Not Healed by Time: The Power of Repentance and Forgiveness*, Oxford: Oxford University Press.

Schleiermacher, F. D. E., 1928, *The Christian Faith*, trans. H. R. Macintosh and J. S. Stewart, Edinburgh: T&T Clark.

Schleiermacher, F. D. E., 1958, *On Religion: Speeches to its Cultured Despisers*, trans. John Oman, intro. Rudolf Otto, New York: Harper and Row (Harper Torchbooks).

Schleiermacher, F. D. E., 1969, *On Religion: Addresses in Response to its Cultured Critics*, trans. and ed. Terrence N. Tice, Richmond, VA: John Knox Press.

Searle, John R., 1969, *Speech Acts: An Essay in the Philosophy of Language*, Cambridge: Cambridge University Press.

Searle, John R., 1995, *The Social Construction of Reality*, London: Allen Lane.

Sedgwick, Timothy F., 2014, *Sex, Moral Teaching, and the Unity of the Church: A Study of the Episcopal Church*, New York: Morehouse.

Segal, Hanna, 1964, *Introduction to the Work of Melanie Klein*, London: Heinemann.

Shelley, Percy Bysshe, 1968 (1943), *Shelley Poetical Works*, ed. Thomas Hutchinson, Oxford: Oxford University Press.

Storr, Anthony, 1963, *The Integrity of the Personality*, Harmondsworth: Penguin.

Stuhlmacher, Peter, 1977, *Historical Criticism and Theological Interpretation of Scripture*, Philadelphia, PA: Fortress Press.

Sullivan, Maureen, 2002, *101 Questions and Answers on Vatican II*, New York/Mahwah, NJ: Paulist Press.

Tanner, Norman, SJ (ed.), 1990, *Decrees of the Ecumenical Councils*, 2 vols, London: Sheed and Ward/Washington, DC: Georgetown University Press.

Tanner, Norman, SJ (ed.), 2012, *Vatican II: The Essential Texts*, Pref. Edward P. Hahnenberg, Intros Benedict XVI and James Carroll, New York: Image Books.

Tanner, Norman, SJ, 2013, 'How Novel Was Vatican II?', *Ecclesiastical Law Journal* 15, pp. 175–82.

Taylor, Charles, 1989, *Sources of the Self: The Making of Modern Identity*, Cambridge: Cambridge University Press.

Taylor, Charles, 1995, 'The Politics of Recognition', in Charles Taylor, 1995, *Philosophical Arguments*, Cambridge, MA: Harvard University Press, ch. 12.

Temple, William, 1934, *Nature, Man and God: Gifford Lectures*, London: Macmillan.

Temple, William, 1958, *Religious Experience and Other Essays and Addresses*, ed. A. E. Baker, London: James Clarke.

The Lambeth Conferences (1867–1930), 1948, London: SPCK.

The Principles of Canon Law Common to the Churches of the Anglican Communion, 2008, London: Anglican Consultative Council.

The Windsor Report, 2004, London: Anglican Consultative Council.

Thrall, M. E., 1994, 2 *Corinthians 1–7*, International Critical Commentary, London and New York.

Torrance, Thomas F., 1958, 1960, *Conflict and Agreement in the Church*, 2 vols, London: Lutterworth Press: vol. 1, 'Order and Disorder', vol. 2, 'The Ministry and the Sacraments of the Gospel'.

Torrance, Thomas F., 1965, *Theology in Reconstruction*, London: SCM Press.

Torrance, Thomas F., 1975, *Theology in Reconciliation: Essays Towards Evangelical and Catholic Unity in East and West*, London: Geoffrey Chapman.

Towards a Symphony of Instruments: A Historical and Theological Consideration of the Instruments of Communion of the Anglican Communion; Working Paper prepared by the Inter-Anglican Standing Commission on Unity, Faith and Order, 2015, London: Anglican Consultative Council.

Trevelyan, G. M., 1930, *Clio, A Muse, and Other Essays*, London, New York, Toronto: Longmans, Green and Co.

Turner, Victor, 1969, *The Ritual Process*, London: Routledge and Kegan Paul/Chicago, IL: Aldine Press.

Vainio, Olli-Pekka, 2017, *Disagreeing Virtuously: Religious Conflict in Interdisciplinary Perspective*, Grand Rapids, MI: Eerdmans.

Van Gennep, A., 1960, *The Rites of Passage*, London: Routledge and Kegan Paul.

Verkamp, Bernard J., 1977, *The Indifferent Mean: Adiaphorism in the English Reformation to 1554*, Athens, OH: Ohio University Press/ Detroit, MI: Wayne State University Press.

Vischer, Lukas, Ulrich Luz and Christian Link, 2010, *Unity of the Church in the New Testament and Today*, Grand Rapids, MI: Eerdmans.

Volf, Miroslav, 1998, *After Our Likeness: The Church as the Image of the Trinity*, Grand Rapids, MI: Eerdmans.

Von Hügel, Friedrich, 1927 (1908), *The Mystical Element of Religion*, 2nd edn, 2 vols, London: Dent.

Von Rad, Gerhard, 1972, *Genesis: A Commentary*, rev. edn, Philadelphia, PA: Westminster Press.

Webster, J. B., 1986, *Eberhard Jüngel: An Introduction to his Theology*, Cambridge: Cambridge University Press.

Wijlens, Myriam, 1991, 'Theology and the Science of Canon Law: A Historical and Systematic Overview', *Louvain Studies* 16.4, pp. 292–311.

Williams, Rowan, 2016, *The Tragic Imagination*, Oxford: Oxford University Press.

Winnicott, D. W., 1965, 'The Capacity to be Alone', in D. W. Winnicott, *The Maturation Process and the Facilitating Environment*, London: Hogarth Press.

Winnicott, D. W., 1971, 'Mirror Rôle of Mother and Family in Child Development', in D. W. Winnicott, *Playing and Reality*, London: Tavistock Clinic.

Witte, Henk, 2012, '"Ecclesia, quid dicis de teipsa?" Can Ecclesiology be of any help to the Church to deal with advanced modernity?', in

Staf Hellemans and Josef Wissink (eds), *Towards a New Catholic Church in Advanced Modernity*, Zurich and Berlin: LIT, pp. 121–45.

Wittgenstein, Ludwig, 1958, *Philosophical Investigations*, 2nd edn, trans. G. E. M. Anscombe, Oxford: Basil Blackwell.

Wordsworth, William, 1972, *The Prelude: A Parallel Text*, ed. J. C. Maxwell, Harmondsworth: Penguin.

Wright, N. T., 2003, *The Resurrection of the Son of God*, London: SPCK.

Young, Frances (ed.), 1995, *Dare We Speak of God in Public?*, London: Mowbray.

Zaehner, R. C., trans., 1938, *Hindu Scriptures*, London: Dent.

Zizioulas, John, 1985, *Being as Communion*, New York: St Vladimir's Seminary Press.

Zizioulas, John, 2001, *Eucharist, Bishop, Church: The Unity of the Church in the Divine Eucharist and the Bishop during the First Three Centuries*, 2nd edn, trans. E. Theokritoff, Brookline, MA: Holy Cross Orthodox Press.

Zizioulas, John, 2006, *Communion and Otherness*, ed. Paul McPartlan, London and New York: T&T Clark.

Index of Names